Pensions in the Middle East and North Africa

Time for Change

David A. Robalino

with

Edward Whitehouse
Anca N. Mataoanu
Alberto R. Musalem
Elisabeth Sherwood
Oleksiy Sluchynsky

THE WORLD BANK
Washington, D.C.

1818 H Street, NW
Washington DC 20433
Telephone: 202-473-1000
Internet: www.worldbank.org
E-mail: feedback@worldbank.org

1 2 3 4 08 07 06 05

ISBN-10: 0-8213-6185-6

eISBN: 0-8213-6186-4/978-0-8213-6186-3

DOI: 10.1596/978-0-8213-6185-6

Cover design by Naylor Design, Inc.

Cover photo of a door in Morocco: World Bank/Curt Carnemark.

TABLE 1

Main Economic Indicators in Middle East and North African Countries, 2003

Country	GDP (US$ millions)	GDP per capita (US$)	GDP purchasing power parity per capita (US$)	Exchange rate	Population (thousands)	Labor force (thousands)
Algeria	65,993	2,073	6,248	77.4	31,833	11,336
Bahrain	9,606	13,934	16,900	0.38	689	329
Djibouti	625	1,373	2,144	177.7	455	116
Egypt, Arab Rep. of	70,000	1,036	3,950	5.85	67,559	20,359
Iran, Islamic Rep. of	136,830	2,061	7,145	8,194	66,392	18,700
Iraq	13,500	547	1,500	2,000	24,700	6,100
Jordan	9,860	1,858	4,320	0.71	5,308	1,628
Lebanon	19,000	4,224	5,073	1,508	4,498	1,646
Libya	23,600	4,245	6,300	1.29	5,559	1,604
Morocco	44,491	1,477	4,012	9.57	30,113	12,413
Tunisia	24,282	2,454	7,083	1.29	9,895	4,050
West Bank and Gaza	3,455	1,026	727	4.54	3,367	600
Yemen, Republic of	10,831	565	889	183.5	19,173	6,120

Sources: All data, except as indicated, are from the World Bank World Development Indicators database (2003f, 2004f). Bahrain gross domestic product (GDP) and population data are from the Bahrain Monetary Agency. Djibouti population and labor data are from the recent population survey (National Statistical Office). GDP estimates for the Arab Republic of Egypt are based on National Statistical Office data; for Iraq and Libya, IMF data was used. GDP purchasing power parity (PPP) per capita for Bahrain, Iraq, Libya, and the West Bank and Gaza refer to U.S. government estimates (the West Bank and Gaza for 2002). Labor force data for the Islamic Republic of Iran are based on official historic labor force participation rates; for Iraq, the most recent data were used and provided by the government.
Note: Labor force data on the West Bank and Gaza assumes 450,000 employed and a 25 percent unemployment rate.

Contents

Boxes

Figures

Tables

Preface

This is the first comprehensive assessment of pension systems in the Middle East and North Africa. While other regions—Central and Eastern Europe, Central Asia, and Latin America, in particular—have been actively introducing reforms to their pension systems, Middle East and North African countries have lagged behind. This is explained, in part, by the common belief that, because demographics remain favorable—the countries are young and the labor force is expanding rapidly—financial problems are still far in the future and therefore pension reform does not have to be a priority within the broad policy agenda.

The authors show, however, that pension systems in the Middle East and North Africa are facing important structural problems. Their current design imposes unnecessary distortions on the economy and, contrary to general perceptions, can be a source of adverse distributional transfers. Basically, pension funds today favor middle- and high-income workers at the expense of low-income workers. Indeed, the systems cover a relatively modest share of the labor force (33 percent), mostly workers in the public sector and the formal private sector. Moreover, in the majority of systems, the returns that individuals receive on their savings depend on career and wage histories and on enrollment and on retirement strategies. Hence, although redistribution takes place—some individuals receive higher returns than others—it is nontransparent and can be regressive.

But financial problems are starting to develop as well. Even if favorable demographic conditions persisted, pension systems in the Middle East and North Africa would run into trouble eventually. The reason is simple: the benefit promises are not in line with the contribution rates and the retirement ages. The fact is, however, that as in other regions, the populations in Middle East and North African countries will grow older and aggravate the financial problem. Today, most schemes have accumulated large implicit pension debts, ranging between 30 and more than 100 percent of GDP. This debt is related to the promises made to current retirees and contributors and is often larger than the explicit government debt. Unfortunately, this implicit pension debt is seldom taken into account when setting macroeconomic and monetary policies, thus biasing policy choices and affecting the credibility of the fiscal framework. In the absence of rapid interventions, this debt will continue to grow, threatening the welfare of future generations. Indeed, governments will have to default on this debt by abruptly reducing benefits for future generations, increasing revenues (imposing higher taxes on future generations), or reducing expenditures on other items (such as education and health). Thus waiting to intervene can be costly and unfair.

The authors put forward a comprehensive framework to guide discussion about pension reform. They emphasize the need to differentiate between two types of policy choices: (a) those related to the objectives and the mandate of the pension system and (b) those related to the mechanisms to implement this mandate. Regarding the mandate, countries need to make explicit choices about the level of benefits that the pension system will provide, in particular, which share of preretirement income should be replaced by the public system and which share should be the responsibility of individuals. Various factors that influence these choices are discussed. Ultimately, these reflect social and cultural preferences but, at the same time, face economic and biological constraints. Pension benefits that need to be financed by a 50 percent contribution rate or by working 60 years or more are not affordable. When it comes to the design of the system, the authors emphasize that there are many options that could be considered. There is no universal model that should be adopted by all countries: on the contrary, the structure of the pension system needs to respond to local conditions. What is important is that basic principles of design are respected in all cases, so that whichever system is chosen is able to work properly and deliver on its promises.

My hope is that this book will raise awareness about the need to rapidly address the problems facing pension systems in the region in order to minimize negative fiscal, macroeconomic, and welfare impacts. Readers—policy makers, academics, and all of those interested in pension reform—will find an objective analysis of the current situation and useful principles for designing and implementing a sustainable, efficient, and equitable pension system.

CHRISTIAAN J. POORTMAN
VICE PRESIDENT
MIDDLE EAST AND NORTH AFRICA REGION

Acknowledgments

This report was written by David A. Robalino (senior economist, MNSHD) on the basis of inputs and analytical work prepared by Edward Whitehouse (consultant, Axia Economics), Anca N. Mataoanu (consultant, MNSHD), Alberto R. Musalem (lead economist, MNSHD), Elisabeth Sherwood (MNSIF), Oleksiy Sluchynsky (pension economist, MNSHD), Tatyana Bogomolova (social protection specialist, HDNSP), Montserrat Pallarès (social protection specialist, HDNSP), Massimo Sabbatini (consultant), Anne-Marie Vilamovska (consultant), and Rawan Abdel Razek (consultant). Darcy Gallucio edited the first draft of the document, and Rougiata Bah-Sanchez provided excellent administrative support. Peer reviewers were Robert Holzmann (director, HDNSP), Hermann Von Gersdorff (sector manager, Social Protection, ECAHD), and Robert Palacios (senior economist, SASHD). The team would like to thank Michal Rutkowski, Setareh Razmara, Mustapha Nabli, George Schieber, Jacques Baudouy, Yasser El-Gammal, Richard Hinz, Gustavo Demarco, Josephine Bassinette, Warren McGillivray, Ibrahim Muhanna, David Lindeman, Christopher Bender, and Claire Dosner for providing comments, guidance, and valuable insights at various stages of the production process.

The preparation of this report would have not been possible without the support of policy makers, managers, and technical staff in the various countries, who shared their institutional knowledge and responded to innumerable requests for information. The team is particularly indebted to Mr. Hacene Boubedra in Algeria, Mr. Rashid Ismail, and Mr. Shaikh Essa Al Khalifa in Bahrain; Mr. Arbahim All Hamad in Djibouti; Mrs. Amina Ghanem, Mr. Hisham Pawfik, Mr. Ahmed Darar, and Mr. Mahmoud Maged Khattab in the Arab Republic of Egypt; Mr. Majid Yarmand, Mr. Vaez Mahdavi, Mr. Hossein Raghfar, Mrs. Monirosadat Kordestanchi, Mr. Saber Sheibani, Mrs. Fariba Keshavars, Mrs. Zahra Niksirat, Mr. Kamran Gorbanali, Mr. Mohammadi Torbati, and Mr. Mehdi Karbasian in the Islamic Republic of Iran; Mr. Noury Al Hilfi and Mr. Mowafaq Attisha in Iraq;

Mr. Khalid Al-Wazani, Mr. Basem Awadaccah, Mr. Taisfer Al Smadi, Mr. Mohamed Sartawi, Mr. Basel Hindawi, and Mrs. Dana Jamboulat in Jordan; Mr. Mohammad Karaki, Mr. Joseph L. Khalife, Mr. Nabil Semaan, Mr. Samer Sinno, Mr. Said Kaakour, Mr. Izzat El Dada, Mr. Rami Sukkar, Mr. Fouad Sinora, Mr. Jihad Azour, and Mr. Nahas in Lebanon; Mr. Mohamed Bendris, Mr. Mounir Chraibi, Mr. Omar Aroussi, Mr. Thami El Barki, Mr. Thami Yahyaoui, Mr. Khalid Cheddadi, Mr. Mimoun Zbayar, Mr. Mohamed Sabah, Mr. Lotfi Boujendar, Mr. Salah-Eddine Benjelloun, and Mr. Abder Janani in Morocco; Mr. Mohamed Chaabane in Tunisia; and Mr. Mohammed Almourtda in the Republic of Yemen.

About the Authors

David A. Robalino is a senior economist at the World Bank in the Middle East and North Africa Region. Since joining the Bank, he has been providing policy advice to several countries, including Algeria, Bahrain, Djibouti, Egypt, the Islamic Republic of Iran, Iraq, Jordan, Kenya, Libya, Lebanon, Morocco, and Thailand. Prior to joining the Bank, he was a researcher at the RAND Corporation, where he was involved in the development of quantitative methods for economic analysis under conditions of deep uncertainty. He also served on the Presidential Committee for Social Security Reform in Ecuador. Mr. Robalino has published on issues related to macroeconomics and labor markets, social insurance and pensions, health financing, the economics of HIV/AIDS, and the economics of climate change. Mr. Robalino holds a PhD in economic analysis from the RAND Graduate School in Santa Monica, California, a DEA in macroeconomics and econometrics from the Sorbonne University in Paris, France, and a BA in economics, mathematics, and computer science from the Central University in Quito, Ecuador.

Edward Whitehouse is the director of Axia Economics, a consultancy firm based in London that specializes in the microeconomic analysis of public policy. Axia Economics has been involved in numerous projects with the Organisation for Economic Co-operation and Development (OECD) and the World Bank. Analysis provided by Axia Economics covers more than 60 countries. Mr. Whitehouse is also the joint editor of the World Bank's pension reform primer series. He was previously with the *Financial Times* as lead writer and social affairs correspondent. Before that, he worked in the Fiscal Affairs Division of the OECD in Paris and at the Institute for Fiscal Studies in London. He has taught at University College, London, and Oxford University. Mr. Whitehouse has published extensively on topics related to pensions, financial sectors, and labor markets.

Anca N. Mataoanu is an economist with expertise in social insurance and finance. She works for the World Bank as a consultant in social protection policies for the Human Development Department of the Middle East and North Africa Region. Prior to joining the Bank, she conducted research on pension supervision and regulation as a visiting scholar at the Wharton School, University of Pennsylvania. She also worked as an adviser to the deputy minister of labor in Romania, providing support on various policy, financial, and legal aspects of pension reform. Ms. Mataoanu holds an MA in public administration and finance from the University of Pennsylvania and a BA in economics from the Academy of Economic Studies in Bucharest.

Alberto R. Musalem is the chief economist of the Financial Stability Center in Argentina. From 1985 to 2004, he was a staff member of the World Bank. At the Bank, he was an adviser on contractual savings (pension and life insurance) and the tax treatment of financial instruments in the Financial Sector Development Department. He has advised many countries including Argentina, Bahrain, Bulgaria, Costa Rica, Egypt, India, Republic of Korea, Lebanon, Morocco, Philippines, Russia, Saudi Arabia, Sri Lanka, Thailand, and Uruguay. Mr. Musalem also contributed to the research and analysis of the effects of contractual savings on national saving and financial markets, and he led the dialogue on economic, trade, and financial sector policies in several countries of Latin America, the Middle East, and Eastern Europe. Prior to joining the World Bank, he worked for The Rockefeller Foundation and the Ford Foundation as a visiting professor in graduate economics programs in South America and the United States (1971–84) and for the Harvard Institute for International Development as an adviser to the Economic Planning Department of the Government of Colombia on macroeconomics, trade, and financial sector policies (1968–70). He is the author of numerous publications and working papers in Argentina, Brazil, Colombia, Chile, Germany, and the United States. Mr. Musalem holds a PhD in economics from the University of Chicago.

Elisabeth Sherwood is a financial sector specialist in the Middle East and North Africa Region of the World Bank, where she has worked since 1996, focusing on general financial sector development issues and on housing and corporate finance. Ms. Sherwood holds a BA from Princeton University and an MA from Columbia University. She is a CFA charter holder.

Oleksiy Sluchynsky is an economist with expertise in pension policy and reform. He works for the World Bank Group as a specialist in social protection policies for the Middle East and North Africa Region. Most recently, in the capacity of a resident pension reform adviser, he provided support to the pension reform process in Kosovo, developing and advocating the concept for reform, implementing the new pension legislation, and advising the Ministry of Economy and Finance and the

Kosovo Pension Savings Trust on various policy, financial, legal, and administrative matters of the reform. Mr. Sluchynsky has worked as a consultant with the World Bank's Social Protection Team for the Europe and Central Asia Region, researching legal and administrative aspects of pension reform policies in Central and Eastern European countries. He has extensive expertise in administrative and information technology issues in funded pension systems, having researched and written on international best practices, costs, and efficiency of various administrative models for the collection and management of pension contributions. He also worked for the Harvard Institute for International Development's Macroeconomic Reform Project in Ukraine. Mr. Sluchynsky holds an MA in public administration and international development from Harvard University's Kennedy School of Government and an MA in economics and an MSc in computer sciences from the Economics Education and Research Consortium in Kiev, Ukraine.

Executive Summary

Most countries of the Middle East and North Africa set up their current national pension schemes in the 1970s, and no major changes or reforms have been introduced since then. This report shows why pension reform is needed and why it is urgent. It sets out the options and the arguments for different ways forward.

The report highlights six general problems with pension systems in the region: the pension promise is large and unaffordable; schemes are financially unsustainable; badly designed rules introduce unnecessary distortions in labor supply and savings decisions; the schemes are fragmented and administration is weak and costly; coverage rates are modest, with important gaps among the self-employed and in rural areas; and governance structures are not designed to ensure that the funds are managed in the best interests of plan members.

This is a stark prognosis, but there is some room for optimism. Middle East and North African countries do have time to act before the financial problems bite, but the window for action will not last long. It is, indeed, "time for change."

The Prognosis

Pension promises in Middle East and North Africa are large and unaffordable. Pension systems in the Middle East and North Africa target, on average, a pension for full-career workers of nearly 80 percent of earnings before retirement. This is much higher than the pension promise in 24 high-income Organisation for Economic Co-operation and Development (OECD) countries, in 10 countries in Eastern Europe and Central Asia, and 9 countries in Latin America and the Caribbean, where pension replacement rates average 57 percent.

Middle East and North African countries rarely impose a cap on the level of earnings eligible for pensions (or these ceilings are very high). For higher-income workers, earning double the average, the target replacement rate averages more than 75 percent in the Middle East and

North Africa region, compared with less than 50 percent in 43 countries in other regions.

The size and scope of the pension mandate mean that few people will want to provide for retirement outside the mandatory pension system, including middle and high earners. This means that retirement savings are not diversified, making them more risky for individuals than they need be and hampering the development of capital markets through long-term savings institutions. Finally, high mandates are simply unlikely to be affordable.

Pension systems are financially unsustainable as a result not of future aging of the population but of poor system design. Because pension schemes in the Middle East and North African countries are "young," they are still running cash flow surpluses, meaning that contribution revenues exceed benefit expenditures. But this happy position cannot and will not last for long. The financial projections in this report show that the future flow of pensions already promised (that is, the implicit pension debt) adds up to, on average, 80–90 percent of gross domestic product (GDP). This is often larger than conventional government debt. Even where there are pension reserves, these probably will be depleted in 10 years or so.

The financial problem is basically explained by the fact that promised benefits are not in line with retirement rules and contribution rates. Adjusting these parameters—for instance, by increasing the contribution rate—could improve financial sustainability, but the necessary adjustments are unlikely to be feasible.

As an illustration, to pay for pensions of the size that is promised without changing the retirement rules, the pension contribution rate will need to rise to 30 percent or more, just to cover old-age pensions: adding in survivors' and disability benefits, the contribution rate will need to be higher still. A rise in contribution rates of this degree will have substantial effects on labor costs and so on competitiveness. Even without demographic change, pension systems will soon encounter financial problems.

Pension schemes have badly designed rules that damage incentives and arbitrarily redistribute income between members. Basing pension entitlements on final salary, rather than the average of pay over the lifetime, is unfair and open to abuse. The history of earnings recorded by the pension scheme can be manipulated so that the final salary, which determines the pension, is high, while pay in earlier years, on which contributions are levied, is lower. Moreover, individuals whose earnings rise rapidly over their career, who tend to be relatively well paid, receive relatively more from the pension system than those whose earnings rise slowly (that is, they receive larger benefits relative to their contributions).

Pension schemes in the Middle East and North Africa also favor and thus encourage early retirement. While the normal age for pension eligibility is typically 60, people often can draw the pension at age 50 or earlier. Early retirees see no adjustments of their benefits or pay a penalty that does not reflect the cost of paying the pension for a longer period. Again, this implies that workers retiring earlier get a better return on their contributions than those who retire at the normal age or earlier.

Because the implicit returns on the contributions that members pay depend on their wage history and strategies regarding enrollment and retirement, the redistribution that takes place within the pension system is not transparent. Basically, middle- and high-income individuals can receive better treatment than low-income individuals.

Administration of pensions is fragmented, often with two or more schemes for different groups of workers. This is unnecessarily costly and limits the mobility of the labor force across sectors. There are economies of scale in managing pension plans, so running multiple programs means that administrative costs are higher than they need be. An integrated approach, with a single program for all workers, is more efficient.

It is often impossible to transfer pension rights between different pension schemes, or the procedures are cumbersome at best. This makes labor markets rigid because the movement of the labor force between sectors is less fluid. Both public and private sectors could benefit from a flow of workers between employers.

Finally, benefit formulas and eligibility conditions vary considerably among the schemes. Fragmentation then becomes another source of inequalities, as the mandatory pension system treats workers in different sectors differently.

Much of the workforce remains uncovered by a formal pension scheme, reflecting the structure of labor markets. Around a third of the workforce in Middle East and North African countries is covered by the pension system. Coverage rates are higher in predominantly public sector economies, such as Libya, or in countries with special programs for agricultural workers and the self-employed, such as the Arab Republic of Egypt and Tunisia.

While better incentives for individuals to contribute and for systems to improve their administrative capacity to track contributions could expand coverage and reduce evasion at the margin, the main driver will be the capacity of the economy to generate jobs in the formal sector. Prospects today are not encouraging, and a considerable part of the labor force will continue to lack access to appropriate income security during old age.

Governance and administration of pension schemes are weak. In particular, pension reserves are not managed in the best interests of their members. Tripartite boards, with representatives of government, employers, and trade unions, are common. Nominated members often lack the expertise necessary to manage large and complex financial institutions, and responsibilities are blurred.

The result is that, where there are pension reserves, investment policies are risky, governed more by political influence than by the interests of pension scheme members. Most reserves are in the form of government debt, in part reflecting the state of development of capital markets. However, the debt is rarely formal or marketable. Holdings in private sector enterprises are often in companies managed directly by the pension fund. Their value is difficult to determine, the relative performance of the companies is difficult to assess, and the companies' solvency is often questionable.

In addition, administrative capacity is generally weak, amplifying the problems. Although no survey of administrative capacity has been conducted across countries, the quality of management raises issues regarding the administration of collection and record keeping, identification of plan members, payment of benefits, information technology infrastructure, and administrative costs. In particular, information technology systems are either outmoded or nonexistent. This makes it impossible for workers to check the accuracy of records and to know the pension entitlement that they have earned.

Finally, *pensions involve a long-term commitment: today's policies have implications for years and decades to come.* Middle East and North African countries are making pension promises that will be difficult or impossible to keep. With serious financial problems impending, the time for a change in pensions is now.

The Way Forward

Countries considering pension reform ought to differentiate policy discussions at two levels: (a) general principles and objectives for the pension system and (b) mechanisms for implementation.

Regarding the objectives, pension systems around the world concentrate on guaranteeing a basic level of income at retirement (adequacy function) and/or ensuring a minimum level of replacement of before-retirement income (insurance function). Middle East and North African countries will need to make explicit choices about the objectives of the pension system. Thus societies will need to determine the level of pension entitlements that the system will guarantee at various levels of income. These choices reflect social preferences and cultural factors (such as family structure and the capacity of individuals to save on their own for retirement). In all cases, choices need to be affordable. Replacement rates that require a 30 percent contribution rate are neither affordable nor sustainable. In general, there is little rationale for the pension system to be the only source of retirement income, particularly among middle- and high-income workers.

Regarding implementation, countries have a large pool of pension systems from which to choose. These systems can be classified along three dimensions: how they are financed (pay-as-you-go, fully funded, government budget, or some combination), how pensions are calculated and risks distributed (earnings-related schemes, defined-contribution schemes, or some combination), and how the system is managed (for example, private or public management, centralized or decentralized management). There is no unique model that should be implemented. Choices need to respond to local economic, political, and social conditions. These choices, however, need to be based on sound economic analysis. In all cases, basic norms for the proper operation of the system should be respected. In the Middle East and North Africa, the following principles should guide the reform:

- The pension system should provide benefits that are adequate and affordable to all workers.
- The pension system should be financially self-sustainable, thus guaranteeing that pension promises can be kept.
- If redistribution takes place, it should be transparent and progressive (that is, from high- to low-income workers).
- The pension system should not distort incentives, and this requires a closer link between contributions and benefits.

In most Middle East and North African countries, current defined-benefit schemes are likely to remain an important part of the mandatory pension system. An integrated reform strategy will then involve interventions in the following areas:

- *Improving financial sustainability, incentives, and equity of current earnings-related schemes.* This will imply realigning promised benefits with contribution rates and retirement rules and establishing a closer link between the earnings on which contributions are paid and the earnings on which pension entitlements are calculated.
- *Mitigate the impacts of the reforms on women and review policies that mitigate against them.* The necessary changes in benefit formulas and eligibility conditions are likely to affect more women than men. Thus it is necessary that adjustments for them will be more gradual. In addition, women should have the same rights when it comes to transferring pensions to their survivors. Special interventions will also be required to better protect the rights of divorced women and those married to men with multiple wives. Finally, it is important to identify and cost mechanisms to maintain a minimum level of contributions to the pension fund during the child-bearing years.
- *Identifying mechanisms to finance the current implicit pension debt in a transparent manner while making future liabilities explicit.* Pension reform will ensure that the pension rights accrued by new contributions will be sustainable. The reform, however, will not eliminate the current implicit pension debt—that is, the flow of pension promises to current

retirees and current contributors. It is important to make this implicit debt explicit (that is, in the form of formal government debt) and to design transparent financing mechanisms. In addition, to improve the credibility of the fiscal framework, it is desirable that new implicit pension liabilities be backed by explicit government debt.

- *Improving governance and administration.* Reforms include improving the mechanisms to select the governing body, accountability, and investment policies to ensure that pension schemes are run in the best interests of members. In addition, work is needed on improving institutional capacity and administration, which will include investments in information technology systems. Finally, it is important to review the institutional organization of the pension system to ensure a gradual integration of the various schemes. In the meantime, "bridges" are needed to facilitate mobility across schemes.
- *Expanding coverage.* Efforts are needed to explore ways of extending the formal pension system to vulnerable groups. However, this policy should follow reforms that put the pension system on a financially sustainable footing.
- *Diversifying the retirement-income provision.* Countries with a core of sound banks and insurance companies and a clear agenda to support financial sector development (for example, Jordan, Lebanon, and Morocco) should consider higher levels of funding in the mandatory scheme. It is also desirable to promote the development of voluntary private pensions, which implies having in place the appropriate regulatory and supervisory framework.

The report is organized in six chapters. Chapter 1 discusses motivations and objectives and details the main findings and messages of each of the chapters. Chapter 2 discusses the initial conditions for pension reform, including demographics, macroeconomic prospects, and the level of development of the financial sectors. Chapter 3 takes stock of the public pension system in the region and identifies the main problems that necessitate attention. Chapter 4 introduces a general framework for pension reform. It describes a set of minimum conditions that any reform program will have to meet: the specific content of these programs clearly will have to reflect local economic, social, and political conditions. Given the relevance for most countries in the region, chapter 5 treats separately the issue of how to improve the management of public pension funds to serve the interests of plan members. Finally, chapter 6 provides a brief overview of where Middle East and North African countries stand in the reform process and discusses future prospects.

Acronyms and Abbreviations

CASNOS	Caisse d'Assurance Sociales des Non-Salariés, Algeria
CDG	Caisee de Dépôt et de Gestion, Morocco
CIMR	Caisse Interprofessionnelle Marocaine de Retraite, Morocco
CMR	Caisse Marocaine de Retraite, Morocco
CNR	Caisse Nationale de Retraite, Djibouti
CNR	Caisse Nationale des Retraites, Algeria
CNRA	Caisse Nationale de Retraite et d'Assurance, Tunisia
CNRPS	Caisse Nationale de Retraite et de Prevoyance Sociale, Tunisia
CNSS	Caisse Nationale de Sécurité Sociale, Morocco
CNSS	Conseil National de Sécurité Sociale, Tunisia
CNSS	Conseil National de Sécurité Sociale, Djibouti
CPP	Canadian Pension Plan
CSEA	Comité de Suivi des Etudes Actuarielles, Morocco
CSRO	Civil Servant Retirement Organisation, the Islamic Republic of Iran
EOSI	End-of-service indemnity, Lebanon
GASS	Civil service pension fund, Yemen
GCC	Gulf Cooperation Council
GCSS	Private Pension Fund, the Republic of Yemen
GDP	Gross domestic product
GEPF	Government Employees Pension Fund, Egypt
GOSI	General Organisation for Social Insurance, Bahrain
IRR	Implicit rate of return
MPO	Management and Planning Organization, the Islamic Republic of Iran
NIB	National Investment Bank, Egypt
NSSF	National Social Security Fund, Lebanon
OECD	Organisation for Economic Co-operation and Development
OPS	Organisme de Protection Sociale, Djibouti

PFC	Pension Fund Commission, Bahrain
PPEEPF	Public and Private Enterprises Employees Pension Fund, Egypt
PPP	Purchasing power parity
PROST	Pension Reform Options Simulation Toolkit
RCAR	Régime Collectif d'Assurance et de Retraite, Morocco
RNS	Régime des Non-Salariés, Tunisia
RSA	Régime Salaries du Secteur Agricole, Tunisia
RSAA	Régimes Salaries Associés du Secteur Agricole, Tunisia
RSNA	Régime des Salariés Non-Agricoles, Tunisia
SSC	Social Security Corporation, Jordan
SSF	Social Security Fund, Libya
SSIU	Social Security Investment Unit, Jordan
SSO	Social Security Organization, the Islamic Republic of Iran
SSW	Social Security and Welfare, Iraq

BOX 1

Glossary of Key Technical Terms

Accrual rate. The share of the preretirement income (income measure) that the worker receives on retirement for each year of contribution.

Full-career worker. An individual who joins the system at age 20 and contributes until the normal retirement age or until the maximum replacement rate is reached.

Implicit rate of return. Technically, the rate of return that equates the present value of contributions to the present value of future pension payments. Since individuals pay contributions (an operation similar to depositing savings in a bank account) and, on retirement, receive pensions (an operation similar to withdrawing savings from a bank account), it is possible to compute the implicit rate of return on the contributions.

Income measure. The income used as the basis for computing the pension—for instance, the average of the last 10 years of salaries. Technically, the pension is equal to the income measure times the accrual rate times the number of years of contributions.

Pension wealth. The value at the time of retirement of discounted future pension payments.

Replacement rate. The pension divided by the last wage.

Vesting period. The number of years during which individuals have contributed and accumulated pension rights.

Indexation of pensions. The process by which the value of pensions is adjusted over time—for instance, as a function of inflation.

Revalorization of wages. The process by which the wages included in the calculation of the pension are adjusted—for instance, by inflation.

CHAPTER 1

Overview

More than 60 countries have introduced reforms to their mandatory pension systems in the space of 20 years (Schwarz and Demirgüç-Kunt 1999). The strategies have varied widely, but a common motivation has been the need to deal with the financial problems, and fiscal implications, of generous earnings-related schemes mostly financed on a pay-as-you-go basis. In doing so, reforms have often served other objectives, such as reducing adverse distributional transfers across and within generations, mitigating distortions in labor markets and savings decisions, and, in some cases, contributing to financial sector development and economic growth.

As has happened elsewhere in the world, pension systems in the countries of the Middle East and North Africa today are at a crossroads.[1] They all have earnings-related pension schemes, in essence financed on a pay-as-you-go basis, which in their current form go back to the late 1960s and early 1970s. These schemes cover, on average, 30 percent of the labor force. Despite these relatively modest coverage levels and the fact that only 5–10 percent of the elderly receive a pension, expenditures as a share of gross domestic product (GDP) are already in the 1–3 percent range, which in most cases is above expectations, given international patterns and current demographic structures. Most funds are accumulating large and unsustainable unfunded pension liabilities, and problems regarding equity, efficiency, governance, and administration are pervasive.

This report takes stock of current mandatory pension systems in the region, assesses the magnitude and nature of the main problems, and outlines the common components of an integrated reform strategy. As discussed in chapter 2, the region is highly heterogeneous. There is large variation across countries in size, level of income, productive structure, and political organization: from the Arab Republic of Egypt, with more than 60 million inhabitants, to Djibouti, with only 450,000 inhabitants; from the Republic of Yemen, with income per capita of $450, to oil-rich countries in the gulf, where per capita income surpasses $10,000; from oil-poor countries such as Jordan, Lebanon, and Morocco, where incentives to embrace market reforms are relatively strong, to oil-rich countries such as the Islamic Republic of Iran and Libya, which continue to be dominated by the public sector; from monarchies such as Saudi Arabia to nascent democracies such as Algeria and Lebanon. The idea of seeking a common strategy for pension reform could seem futile, yet the pension systems across the region share important features in design and face similar structural problems. Thus it is possible to formulate a set of minimum conditions that any reform program will have to meet; the specific content of these programs clearly will have to reflect local economic, social, and political conditions.

A preliminary assessment of pension systems in the region was undertaken five years ago (Boersch-Supan, Palacios, and Tumbarello 1999). With the limited data available at the time, the report identified several of the problems facing Middle East and North African countries and encouraged governments to initiate reforms while demographic conditions were favorable. Since then, the World Bank has been providing technical assistance in the area of pension reform to several countries in the region, new and more detailed information has become available, and various country studies have been prepared.[2] This report is thus able to deepen and expand the analysis as well as the policy recommendations.

The report is organized in six chapters. This first chapter provides a brief overview of the materials presented in the book. Chapter 2 discusses the initial conditions for pension reform, including demographics, macroeconomic prospects, and level of development of the financial sector. Chapter 3 takes stock of the public pension systems in the region and identifies the main problems that require attention. Chapter 4 introduces a general framework for pension reform and describes a set of minimum conditions that any reform program will have to meet. Given the relevance for most countries in the region, chapter 5 treats separately the issue of how to improve the management of public pension funds to serve the interests of plan members. Finally, chapter 6 provides a brief overview of where countries in the region stand in the reform process and discusses prospects for the future. The following sections present a detailed summary of the main findings and messages of each of the principal chapters.

Chapter 2: Initial Conditions for Pension Reform

The chapter looks at the demographic characteristics of countries in the Middle East and North Africa, macroeconomic prospects for growth and job creation, as well as the structure of the financial sector.

Developments in these three areas are important not only because they affect the functioning of the pension system but also because they can constrain the choice of reform.

Demographics Remain Favorable But Should Not Be a Cause for Complacency

Although there are important differences in demographic structure, all countries in the region share a relatively young population. A rapid increase in old-age dependency ratios will take place only after 15 to 20 years. Within the next decade, the average population growth rate for the region will remain at around 1.9 percent a year, declining to 1.5 percent for the period 2015–25. The expansion of the working-age population is expected to be accompanied by a continuous increase in female participation rates. This will produce dramatic effects on the size of the labor force, which is expected to grow 3.3 percent a year between 2002 and 2010, declining to 1.8 percent around the second half of the 2020s.

These apparently favorable demographics should not be a cause for complacency. First, it is not clear that the future expansion of the labor force will be accompanied by an expansion of employment in the formal sector and, therefore, an expansion of the covered population. Second, even if this were to occur, chapter 3 shows that, in the majority of cases, the implicit rates of return paid on contributions by the pension systems are too high to be sustainable. This being the case, expansion of the covered population will worsen the financial situation of the funds. Hence, independent of the aging process, pension systems will eventually run into trouble. The future aging of the population will simply make things worse.

Slow Growth and High Unemployment Remain Important Challenges

The majority of countries have made important progress toward achieving macroeconomic stabilization, which improves the operational conditions of pension funds. With only a few exceptions (the Islamic Republic of Iran and the West Bank and Gaza), inflation rates are generally below 5 percent a year. This creates a better environment for investors, including pension funds, but does not preclude the need for mechanisms that protect the income of retirees against price fluctuations. External balances have also improved, although capital controls persist and pension funds are restricted from investing abroad. Fiscal policies are the Achilles' heel. Among the countries surveyed, the fiscal outlook appears persistently delicate. Fiscal balances continue to be negative (between

5 and 12 percent of GDP), and public debt remains high (between 50 and 200 percent of GDP). This reinforces the need to control the accumulation of implicit pension debt in pay-as-you-go systems and to find appropriate and transparent financing mechanisms.

The main challenge remains to stimulate economic growth and job creation in the private formal sector. Not doing so implies that an important part of the labor force will remain outside the pension system and might not be accumulating sufficient savings to finance an adequate standard of living during old age. Moreover, better living standards for the elderly can result only from sustained economic growth. Unfortunately, the most recent forecasts put the average yearly growth rate of income per capita for the next decade in the 1–2 percent range for the region. Today, the region's unemployment rate is among the highest in the world, conservatively estimated at 15.9 percent.[3] The informal sector is also large and expanding (constituting between 42 and 55 percent of nonagricultural employment). Without growth rates of at least 5–6 percent a year, unemployment rates will remain high in most countries. It is important to emphasize that pension reform could have a role in facilitating economic growth and job creation if it (a) reduces distortions in labor markets, for instance, by not basing the financial sustainability of the pension system on increases in the contribution rate; (b) contributes to increased national savings; and (c) contributes to the development of the financial sector.

Financial Sectors Remain Underdeveloped But Offer New Opportunities for Pension Systems in Some Countries

The role of the public sector in providing pensions and the proper level of funding for the pension system depend, in part, on the level of development of the financial sector. As financial sectors develop, private (that is, voluntary) arrangements can be expected to assume a more prominent role in the overall pension system. The level of development of the financial sector also affects both the opportunities for investment (for earnings-related and defined-contribution schemes) and the choices regarding the level of funding. Important questions concern the existence of a core of sound banks and insurance companies, the level of development of debt markets, and the level of development of stock exchanges.

Banking Sector

The banking sector is quite heterogeneous across countries, with assets ranging from less than 20 percent of GDP (the Republic of Yemen) to more than 300 percent (Lebanon). In all cases, credit to the private sector represents less than 50 percent of total assets. Only Jordan, Morocco, and Tunisia have a core of commercial banks that seem to be relatively resilient to both interest rate and exchange rate shocks, although moderately exposed to deteriorating credit quality in the portfolio. These banks have the potential to channel pension fund savings to medium- and long-term investments. Elsewhere in the region, banking systems are more vulnerable to exchange rate shocks or deteriorating portfolio quality, have significant exposure to a single borrower (for example, government bonds in Lebanon), or are too weak to intermediate new funds effectively.

Insurance Sector

The insurance sector has expanded in the region, but assets remain below 5 percent of GDP; in most cases, the contribution to financial intermediation is small. No country has well-developed annuity markets, and the majority of assets relate to property and casualty insurance and therefore are invested in short-term, liquid instruments. The life insurance sector is better developed and regulated in Egypt, Jordan, Lebanon, Morocco, and Tunisia, with premiums ranging between 9 percent (Tunisia) and 30 percent (Egypt) of the total. In these countries, insurance companies could provide voluntary private pensions and compete for the management of public pension funds. In the other countries surveyed—Algeria, Djibouti, Libya, the West Bank and Gaza, and the Republic of Yemen—the insurance sector is weak or nonexistent and lacks expertise in the management of financial funds. In the Islamic Republic of Iran, the government has privatized the sector, and the regulator is committed to passing the necessary regulations and supporting the industry. Reputational risks, however, are hindering its expansion.

Debt Markets

Government debt in the form of bonds and treasury bills is a key component of debt markets, yet these represent a modest part of the total government debt in the region. Domestic debt tends to be short term—between one and five years—and benchmark yield curves have failed to develop (this is due, in part, to the fragmented issuance of public debt). In most countries commercial banks heavily dominate the purchase of domestic debt issues. A movement toward funded pensions or the shift of current reserves in the pension systems to more transparent asset classes would imply increasing the share of government debt held by domestic investors, lengthening maturities, and holding open and regular debt auctions.

Corporate bonds are the smallest component of the capital markets, with maturities between two and five years. Issuance is usually done through private placement rather than through auction. Only Tunisia has noticeable levels of corporate bonds, at 15 percent of stock market capitalization in 2002, although the majority is tied to financial institutions.

Equity Markets

Stock exchanges exist in all countries reviewed in this report with the exception of Djibouti, Syria, the West Bank and Gaza, and the Republic of Yemen. However, with the probable exception of Jordan, financing through the stock exchange is marginal, and the number of listed companies is very small. Egypt has the highest number of listed companies (1,000), but only 40 percent are traded.

Chapter 3: Taking Stock of Pension Systems in the Middle East and North Africa

Chapter 3 is the heart of the report. It summarizes the findings of a review of more than 30 pension schemes across 13 countries. The chapter presents the main features of pension systems in the region and the key challenges along five dimensions: (a) institutional organization and coverage; (b) the size and shape of the schemes; (c) incentive problems; (d) equity, including gender equity, problems; and (e) financial sustainability.

Pension Systems Are Fragmented and Coverage Is Modest

None of the countries surveyed has a national pension scheme that covers all categories of workers. Even Jordan, which has recently integrated the schemes for private sector workers, civil servants, and the military, excludes the self-employed and workers in the agricultural sector. Egypt, Morocco, and Tunisia have the largest number of schemes: six, five, and four, respectively. This fragmentation is an important policy issue because it constrains the mobility of the labor force within and across sectors, increases administrative costs, and generates an unequal treatment of different categories of workers.

There is a large variation in coverage rates among the countries included in the analysis (between 10 and 70 percent of the labor force) explained mainly by the structure of the labor market (for example, public or private sector) and institutional arrangements that cover different categories of workers. In Libya, for instance, coverage rates are high (above 70 percent of labor force) because a large majority of the labor force is employed in the public sector or state-owned enterprises. In Morocco, in contrast, a large agricultural sector keeps coverage rates depressed (around 20 percent of the labor force). Algeria, Egypt, and Tunisia achieve higher-than-average coverage rates through special schemes.

In general, the prospects for expanded coverage rates are limited, and governments need to think creatively about mechanisms to protect the old-age income of vulnerable population groups. Better incentives to enroll or better administrative capacity to track contributions could improve coverage at the margin, but the impacts are likely to be limited. Without an expansion of the formal sector of the economy, coverage rates are unlikely to increase substantially. In this context, noncontributory pensions (also called social pensions) could be used to guarantee a basic level of retirement income to vulnerable groups.

Pension Schemes Have Large Mandates

The chapter presents an assessment of targeted replacement rates across pension systems in the region. The replacement rate is defined as the pension divided by the last salary. It indicates the share of total gross income that is replaced or preserved at retirement. On average, the mandates of pension systems in terms of income replacement are more onerous in the Middle East and North Africa than in other regions. The Islamic Republic of Iran, Iraq, and the Republic of Yemen have the highest replacement rates in the world for the average full-career worker (above 100 percent).[4] The average gross replacement rate for the region is 75.7 percent. This is much higher than the pension promise in 24 high-income Organisation for Economic Co-operation and Development (OECD) countries, in 10 countries in Eastern Europe and Central Asia, and nine countries in Latin America and the Caribbean, where pension replacement rates average 57 percent.

Net replacement rates, which include the effect of taxes, are even higher. Hence, in Egypt, while the gross pension represents 80 percent of the gross wage, the net pension represents more than 100 percent. In essence, the average worker has more disposable income after retirement than while working!

Schemes for civil servants target, in general, higher levels of income replacement than schemes for private sector workers.

The targets for the basic pension also tend to be among the most generous in the world. Moreover, Middle East and North African countries rarely place ceilings on the covered wage or ceilings are high. As a result, replacement rates that are flat across levels of income. Basically, the pension system guarantees the same level of income replacement to a low- as to a high-income individual.

The problem with having large mandates is that few people will want to save for retirement outside the mandatory pension system, including middle and high earners. This means that retirement savings are not diversified, making them more risky for individuals than they need be and hampering the development of capital markets through long-term savings institutions. Finally, high mandates are simply unlikely to be affordable, since, to be financed, they will require contribution rates that the economies cannot sustain.

Benefit Formulas and Eligibility Conditions Damage Incentives

The mechanisms used to compute and award pensions affect the behavior of individuals, including retirement, labor supply, and savings decisions. Chapter 3 assesses incentive problems by reviewing implicit rates of return on contributions. Indeed, since individuals make contributions during their active life (an operation similar to depositing savings in a bank) and receive pensions when they retire (an operation similar to withdrawing savings from a bank), it is possible to compute the implicit interest rate (or rate of return) on the contributions (savings).

The results show that, across countries and schemes, current benefit formulas and eligibility conditions provide incentives for retirement over work. This is reflected in implicit rates of return that are higher for individuals retiring early than for individuals retiring late. The reason for this pattern is the lack of actuarially fair reductions in pensions for early retirement and actuarially fair compensations for delayed retirement.

Ceilings on replacement rates, or pensions, can also lower the rate of return for individuals retiring late and thus discourage additional years of contribution. Indeed, once the ceiling is reached, additional contributions do not bring additional benefits. These ceilings are pervasive in the region, since most countries use them to reduce costs.

The systems also provide incentives to manipulate salaries strategically, since only the last few salaries count toward the pension. With the exception of the RCAR (Régime Collectif d'Assurance et de Retraite) in Morocco, none of the schemes uses a full-career average of salaries to compute the pension. In general, the schemes use the last salary or an average of three to five years. The problem is that workers have an incentive to declare lower wages early in their career and higher wages late in their career.

All of the pension schemes in the region reward individuals who evade or game the system. This is again explained, in part, by the fact that only a few wages count toward the pension. Ceilings on replacement rates also contribute by reducing the implicit rate of return paid to workers who have long contribution periods (to avoid the ceiling, individuals might choose to delay enrollment). In general, a weak link between contributions and benefits reduces the incentives to enroll and contribute.

Redistribution within Pension Systems Is Nontransparent and Can Be Regressive

When it comes to redistribution, a primary source of inequality within generations is also related to the fact that only a few wages count toward the pension. Manual workers have relatively flat earnings across their career. Managerial and especially professional workers tend to see their pay rise more rapidly over their lifetime. Basing pension values on final salary favors workers with steeply rising earnings. In Algeria, for instance, a 25-year-old man whose salary grows at 2 percent a year will receive a rate of return one percentage point lower than a colleague whose salary grows at 4 percent a year.

In all pension schemes, there are implicit transfers from young to old workers, regardless of the level of income, because implicit rates of return on contributions are allowed to vary by the age of enrollment in the system. In Tunisia, for instance, a 20-year-old male retiring at age 60 will receive a 4.5 percent real rate of return, while a 30- and a 40-year-old male will receive a 7 and 9 percent real rate of return, respectively.

Regarding gender equality, pension laws across the region have attempted to provide women with more flexible retirement decisions and more secure survivor benefits, driven by the assumption that men are the principal breadwinners. Standard eligibility ages and vesting periods for pensions are either equal for men and women or favorable to women. Early-retirement rules tend to be more generous for women than for men. Thus, in general, women receive higher implicit rates of return on their contributions and a higher pension wealth.[5]

This special treatment, however, also makes women more vulnerable to pension reform. Indeed, if the goal is to have a pension law that treats women and men equally, then adjustments will tend to affect women more than men. Thus policy makers need to devise mechanisms that mitigate the impact of pension reforms on women. Some alternatives are discussed in chapter 4.

Pension Systems Are Financially Unsustainable

The sustainable implicit rate of return that a pay-as-you-go system can afford to pay on contributions is a function of the growth rate of the covered wage bill. Over the long run, a good proxy for this sustainable implicit rate of return is the growth rate of the economy (3–4 percent a year). In the large majority of cases, pension systems are paying rates of return well above these levels. These high implicit rates of return reflect a misalignment of the accrual rate, the retirement age, survival probability at retirement, and contribution rate. Basically, current replacement rates are too high given the retirement age, contribution rate, and life expectancy at retirement.

As a result, all pension funds have accumulated large implicit pension debts. Under conservative assumptions, normalized estimates of accrued-to-date pension liabilities range between 6 percent of GDP (RCAR in Morocco) and more than 170 percent (Social Security Corporation—SSC—in Jordan). The average implicit debt in the region is close to 80 percent of GDP, often linked to a small segment of the labor force. These liabilities refer to the present value of pension promises to current retirees and the pension rights accrued to date by current contributors. Large implicit pension debts threaten macroeconomic stability and the credibility of the fiscal framework. They also represent a potentially large intergenerational transfer. Indeed, in the absence of any intervention, future generations will have to finance the implicit pension debt in the form of lower pension benefits, higher taxation, or reductions in the budget for other items (for example, education and health).

Chapter 4: A Framework for Reform

Chapter 4 argues that it is important to differentiate between two types of questions when discussing pension reform: (a) questions regarding the objectives of the pension system and its mandate for income replacement and (b) questions regarding mechanisms with which to implement this mandate. The chapter starts by discussing factors that could guide choices regarding income replacement targets as well as international experiences in terms of system design. The subsections that follow cover six topics: the basic norms for the design of earnings-related schemes, such as the current systems in the region, the potential benefits and costs of higher levels of funding in the pension systems, the types of policies that could be considered to expand coverage, and the important issues related to institutional organization, regulation, and administration.

Choosing and Implementing the Mandate of the Pension System

The primary objective of a public pension system is to ensure that older people have a decent standard of living in retirement. However, there are different interpretations of this primary objective. The first is that the pension system should need to ensure only a basic standard of living. The main rationale for the existence of the pension system in this case is the need to reduce poverty (measured in relative terms), and the focus is on the "adequacy" of the pension benefit, which can be defined relative to economywide average earnings. The second interpretation is that the pension system should ensure a reasonable standard of living in retirement relative to the position before retirement. Under this interpretation, the pension system plays an insurance function in the context of imperfect financial markets and myopic individuals. The focus in this case is on the replacement rate: the value of the pension relative to individual earnings.

Across countries, there are various degrees of emphasis on these objectives. Countries such as Australia, Canada, Denmark, and the United Kingdom focus on adequacy. Pension systems in Finland, Italy, and Luxembourg emphasize the insurance function. In between, countries such as France, Germany, and the United States balance the objectives of adequacy and insurance. These countries guarantee both a basic pension and a replacement rate ranging between 25 and 50 percent of the last salary. In general, replacement rates fall with the level of income due to the existence of ceilings on the covered wage. Hence, the adequacy and insurance functions focus on low-income workers.

There are no formal rules to define the proper level of the basic pension or the average replacement rate. Choices need to take into account, first, cultural factors, such as family structures or the willingness of individuals to save for old age, and, second, economic factors, such as the general standard of living of the population, estimates about minimum consumption needs (for example, the poverty line), the existence of other formal and informal social assistance programs, and, of course, the costs. The targets for basic pensions and replacement rates need to be affordable.

Once the pattern of income replacement has been chosen, a large typology of pension schemes can be designed to achieve these targets. These pension schemes can be classified along three dimensions: (a) how the system is financed, (b) how the risks are distributed, and (c) how the system is managed. Around the globe, choices have been dictated by local economic, social, political, and cultural conditions. The chapter summarizes broad international trends. Choices, however, need to be based on sound economic analysis. In all cases, basic norms for the proper operation of the system should be respected.

Minimum Standards for an Earnings-Related Pension System

In most countries in the region, defined-benefit schemes will continue to be at the core of the public pension system. It is therefore important to review current benefit formulas and eligibility conditions with a view to promoting financial sustainability, efficiency, and equity. (See box 1 for a glossary of key technical terms.) In a nutshell, this implies having a sustainable system that pays an implicit rate of return on contributions, avoiding unnecessary variations in the rate of return across individuals to prevent adverse distributional transfers, and correcting distortions in labor supply, savings, and retirement decisions. To achieve these goals, countries need to converge gradually to the following standards:

- *Measure of income used to compute the pension.* Countries should gradually include all salaries in the calculation of the pension, but they should be appropriately revalorized—that is, past wages need to be adjusted by a given index. An index could be the growth rate of the average covered wage. The purpose of this policy is not to reduce the level of the pension but to improve incentives and equity.
- *The accrual rate.* The accrual rate of a well-designed pay-as-you-go system is linked intrinsically to the contribution rate, the retirement age, survival probabilities after retirement, and the rate used to revalorize wages. The accrual rate should be chosen to reflect the mandate of the pension system regarding income replacement for the average full-career worker at a given retirement age. If, for instance, the target replacement rate is set at 50 percent for an individual retiring at age 60 with 40 years of contributions, then the accrual rate should be equal to 1.25 percent. The contribution rate and the retirement age should then be adjusted accordingly.
- *Contribution rate.* Policy makers ought to be careful not to overtax labor, and this implies that the contribution rate should not be used as the parameter that "closes" the finances of the system. High contribution rates can reduce the demand for labor, expand the informal sector, or simply reduce individuals' well-being by forcing them to save well beyond their preferences. The preferred alternative is to set a contribution rate that is affordable once all components have been taken into account (for example, health insurance, unemployment insurance) and to keep it constant over time.
- *Normal retirement age.* Because there is a limit to how much an economy can afford to pay on contributions and because the accrual rate reflects the mandate of the pension system regarding income replacement—which presumably should also remain constant over the short and medium term—the normal retirement age ought to be the parameter that adjusts endogenously. Thus, for a given contribution rate, the choice of accrual rate would determine the choice of retirement age. The higher the accrual rate—and therefore the higher the pension that an individual receives—the longer the individual has to work. Clearly, there is a biological limit to how long individuals can work, and this depends on the economic sector. This

limit constrains the choices regarding the value of the accrual rate: there is a maximum level that a given economy can afford to pay.

- *Early retirement.* It is good policy to give some flexibility to individuals and allow them to retire earlier. However, in order to guarantee the same rate of return to all individuals, independent of the age when they retire, the accrual rate should be adjusted as a function of the retirement age. Individuals retiring before the normal retirement age should have a lower accrual rate, while individuals retiring after the normal retirement age should have a higher accrual rate.
- *Vesting period.* A minimum vesting period is not a necessary condition to receive the earnings-related pension as long as the accrual rate is set properly. On the contrary, the introduction of vesting periods becomes another source of variation in rates of return that can deter enrollment. Individuals who join the system late in their life can be penalized, since they are forced to contribute past the normal retirement age without adjustments to their pension. A vesting period should be enforced, however, to be eligible for a minimum pension guarantee.
- *Mechanism used to index pensions.* Practices vary around the world, but prudence and the aim of preserving a constant rate of return within and across generations suggest that the proper index should be inflation. The indexation process should be automatic, not subject to negotiation or political discretion.

The Case for Virtual Account Systems

Countries can also consider reforms of their defined-benefit schemes through the introduction of notional defined-contribution or virtual account systems. In essence, the virtual account system enforces the standards or best practices of traditional earnings-related pay-as-you-go systems. However, the benefit formula is operationalized differently. In the virtual account scheme, contributions are registered in individual accounts. It is only a registration on "book" because individuals do not have real funds accumulated in their account, contrary to defined-contribution schemes. The contributions are indexed by the sustainable rate of return of the system, again a function of the system's average wage and the covered population. When the individual retires, the pension is computed as an annuity of the sum of revalorized contributions. This is done by dividing the total contributions by a so-called G factor, which is simply the discounted sum of the survival probability at various ages after retirement.

The virtual account approach generates a more transparent link between contributions and benefits. Countries that have implemented virtual account systems have also invested in better procedures for reporting to plan members regarding their accrued rights. The virtual account system can also facilitate the political economy of reform. Changing the paradigm can help countries to implement the best practices in design discussed previously. Indeed, some of these reforms might be difficult to implement using the language of traditional defined-benefit schemes.

Costs and Benefits of Higher Funding

There are several ways to increase the level of funding of a pension system. Chapter 4 discusses alternative approaches, but the main focus is on switching (completely or partially) from a pay-as-you-go to a fully funded system (as was done in Chile and other countries, where basically all or part of the targeted replacement rate is financed on a capitalization basis).

International experiences suggest five potential benefits of higher funding: (a) higher rates of return on contributions and a better diversification of risks, implying higher pensions for the same contribution rate; (b) potentially higher national savings; (c) the development of security markets; (d) the reduction in financial risks confronting firms; and (e) a more stable and efficient banking sector. Each of these is discussed in chapter 4 in the context of countries in the region.

Costs, in contrast, are related to sourcing the funds and the risk of capital loss. Costs can be exacerbated in places with an unstable macroeconomic environment, a weak banking system, volatile capital markets, or a high risk of capital losses in the funded system as a result of weak institutional capacity to manage investments and inappropriate governance structures and regulations.

In most countries in the region, there are three constraints to higher levels of funding, although they are not necessarily binding. First, a frail fiscal position makes it difficult to finance the costs of transition, as part of new contributions can no longer be used to finance pensions. Second, investment opportunities are limited even in countries with more advanced financial sectors. Third, weak governance structures, weak institutional capacity, and limited expertise in the private sector for outsourcing make it difficult to conduct investment policies in the best interests of plan members.

Countries that are better placed to increase funding include Egypt, Jordan, Lebanon, Morocco, and Tunisia. These countries have a core of sound banks and are engaged in reforms in the financial sector. They have a nascent insurance industry with know-how in the management of funds that could serve as the basis for the development of private voluntary pensions. In Egypt and Jordan, particularly in the former, current occupational plans could also serve as the basis for the take-off of voluntary pension plans (the main constraints are still large mandates of the public sector and the average level of income of the population). The main risk regarding higher levels of funding in the mandatory system is related to weak governance and institutional capacity. In all cases, it would be important to promote the outsourcing of fund management and even administrative procedures. Given a frail fiscal stance, the transition to higher levels of funding would need to be gradual.

Countries where the benefits of higher funding are less evident and the risks and constraints are more severe include Algeria, Djibouti, the Islamic Republic of Iran, Iraq, Libya, the West Bank and Gaza, and the Republic of Yemen. A priority in these countries would be to bring the defined-benefit, pay-as-you-go system up to standards by improving administration, developing management and information systems, and, to the extent possible, improving investment policies. In parallel, governments would need to continue with structural reforms for private sector development, including the financial sector. These countries could then start by creating the conditions for voluntary private pensions. The constraint in this case is the low level of income per capita and the limited capacity to save. A more important role for voluntary schemes also would entail reviewing the mandate of the mandatory system, at least in the case of middle- and high-income workers.

Administration and Regulation

Several areas are not discussed extensively in the report and yet are critical for the proper functioning of a pension system: (a) the institutional organization, meaning the types of programs in place and the institutions in charge of managing them; (b) the way in which administration is designed and implemented; and (c) the way in which pension funds are regulated.

Ideally, the reform of pension systems in the Middle East and North Africa region should aim at full integration. Countries would basically converge to a unique pension system that covers all categories of workers, although there could be differentiated contribution rates to facilitate the voluntary enrollment of vulnerable groups. Countries such as the Islamic Republic of Iran would also need to seek the integration of occupational plans, which currently operate as substitutes to the main scheme (the Social Security Organization).

Success of any policy initiative aiming to reform the national pension program will depend heavily on administrative capacity and planning. Analysis of the existing systems, procedures, and institutions should be part of any comprehensive reform. The focus should be on the division of responsibilities of various public agencies involved in the process, the expenses associated with administering the system, and the administrative burden on employers and employees.

Another area where work is required concerns the regulation of mandatory and voluntary pension plans. In general, neither public pension funds nor occupational pension plans are formally regulated.

Chapter 5: Improving the Management of Pension Funds

Chapter 5 discusses policies that could be implemented to provide incentives to manage pension funds in the best interests of plan members. The question is highly relevant in the Middle East and North Africa. Indeed, most of the public pension schemes have accumulated reserves. Among the countries reviewed, these range between 4.2 percent (Djibouti) and 52.5 percent (Bahrain) of GDP. At the regional level, the reserves of the mandatory pension systems account for 14.4 percent of GDP. This level is among the highest in the world, second only to South Asia.

Unfortunately, weak governance and poor or no accountability to plan members have led to investment policies that are not designed and implemented in the best interests of plan members. Chapter 5 presents best international practices to improve the management of pension funds. However, these impose high standards that can be difficult to implement, in part, because of political constraints and governance problems at a broader level. Nonetheless, some realistic interventions could be feasible over the short and medium terms: (a) building technical capacity to design investment policies; (b) outsourcing the management of part of the funds; and (c) most important, improving transparency, which involves mandating full disclosure of pension fund operations.

Chapter 6: Progress to Date and Prospects

The final chapter assesses progress on pension reform across countries in non-gulf countries of the Middle East and North Africa and explores socioeconomic factors that could explain the observed differences. Three groups of countries are identified. The first includes countries that are in the very early stages of the reform process or have not yet initiated discussions: Algeria, Libya, and Syria. The second involves countries where policy discussions are more advanced but where a coherent strategy has yet to emerge: the Islamic Republic of Iran, Iraq, Tunisia, and the Republic of Yemen. The third group refers to countries that are leading pension reform and have either (a) developed detailed reform proposals or laws or (b) introduced important structural reforms, even if these affect only part of the pension system. These countries are Djibouti, Egypt, Jordan, Lebanon, Morocco, and the West Bank and Gaza.

A few patterns emerge from the review of regional experiences:

- *In countries that are leading reform efforts, the crises of civil servants and military pension schemes have been an important motivation for reform.* This is the case of Djibouti, Jordan, and the West Bank and Gaza. It has also been a push factor in Lebanon, although the lack of a proper pension system for private sector workers was the main driver of reform. In Egypt, the fact that the implicit pension debt of the pension fund is matched by explicit debt with the National Investment Bank (close to 50 percent of GDP) and that the government is already servicing this debt also creates incentives for reform.
- *Good analyses and diagnoses have played an important role in putting countries into motion.* This is definitely the case in the Islamic Republic of Iran, Jordan (in the case of the SSC), Morocco, and Tunisia. In all these countries, discussions about pension reform within and outside the government started with publication of reports highlighting the problems of the various pension schemes.
- *In all countries leading pension reforms, a high-level policy maker or institution has been driving the reform process.* Basically, an individual or a group of persons understands the issues, takes the initiative to create awareness about the need for change, proposes solutions, and generates consensus for reform within the government.
- *In countries lagging behind, these three elements are not present.* In Algeria and Libya, the availability of important oil revenues might be minimizing the magnitude of the financial problems facing the pension systems and their effect on fiscal stability.

There are also differences in the political process surrounding pension reforms in various countries. The Islamic Republic of Iran, Lebanon, and Morocco included the civil society in the policy dialogue from the outset. To this end, multisectoral commissions were put in place. Morocco, in addition, took a comprehensive approach to reform that included all pension funds and relevant institutions. On the contrary, in Djibouti, the policy dialogue and preparation of the reform strategy took place initially without consultations outside the government. Plan members were not involved until late in the process. No commission was set up to design the reform program. In Jordan, discussions are taking place within the SSC, with little coordination between the SSC and the various ministries and other relevant institutions (for example, the Insurance Commission).

There is also considerable variation in reform strategies. Djibouti and Jordan are developing an integrated earnings-related scheme, and Jordan is also developing voluntary private pensions. Morocco is developing two earnings-related schemes, with one integrated defined-contribution, fully funded scheme. Lebanon is proposing an integrated defined-contribution scheme with a basic pension guarantee. A similar approach is being taken in the West Bank and Gaza.

Challenges for the future are necessarily different in the three groups of countries. Among the countries in the early stages of reform, the focus ought to be on preparing the necessary baseline data to conduct a proper assessment of the financial problems facing the schemes. Without this baseline, it is not possible to initiate discussions about the costs and benefits of alternative reform packages. In the second group of countries, the immediate goal is to move from strategic guidelines to a detailed reform concept, which will require further analytical work and consensus building. The remaining group needs to consolidate an integrated reform strategy and move toward implementation.

In all cases, this report is intended to raise awareness about the need for prompt interventions, thus allowing governments to take a gradual approach toward reform and avoid drastic adjustments in the future. The report also provides an analytical framework to guide discussions about the options for reform as well as the implementation of new laws. In all countries of the region, the time for change is now.

Notes

1. For the purpose of this report, the Middle East and North Africa region refers to the following countries: Algeria, Bahrain, Djibouti, the Arab Republic of Egypt, the Islamic Republic of Iran, Iraq, Jordan, Kuwait, Lebanon, Libya, Morocco, Oman, Qatar, Saudi Arabia, the Syrian Arab Republic, Tunisia, the United Arab Emirates, and the Republic of Yemen. Also covered is the West Bank and Gaza Strip. Given the availability of data at the present time, however, the analysis concentrates on non-gulf countries (except for non-Arab gulf countries and Bahrain).

2. See World Bank (2002a) for Algeria; World Bank (2003f) for Bahrain; World Bank (2001b) for Djibouti; World Bank (2005c) for Egypt; World Bank (2003d)

for the Islamic Republic of Iran; Robalino, Sluchynskyy, and Bogomolova (forthcoming) for Iraq; World Bank (2003c) for Jordan; World Bank (2005a) for Lebanon; World Bank (2005b) for Libya; World Bank (2004a) for Morocco; World Bank (2003a) for Tunisia; World Bank (2002b) for the West Bank and Gaza; and Mitchell (1999) for the Republic of Yemen.

3. The unemployment figure refers to non–Gulf Cooperation Council countries.

4. A full-career individual refers to a plan member enrolling in the system at age 20 and contributing until the normal retirement age or until the maximum replacement rate paid by the system is attained.

5. Pension wealth is defined as the present value of future pension payments.

CHAPTER 2

The Initial Conditions for Pension Reform

This chapter sets the context for pension reform in the region by reviewing the main facts regarding demographic and macroeconomic dynamics as well as the level of development of financial sectors. The section on demographics focuses on trends, both within the region and worldwide, in population growth rates, life expectancies, and dependency ratios and discusses their potential effects on labor markets and the performance of pension systems. The section on macroeconomics assesses the recent economic performance of the region and the key structural factors likely to influence future prospects for economic growth and job creation and reviews indicators of macroeconomic stability. These factors not only affect current pension systems but can also constrain the choice of reforms. The final section presents a brief assessment of the level of development of financial sectors in the region, because decisions regarding the level of funding in the pension systems and the role of the public and private sectors partially depend on it.

Demographics

From a demographic perspective, there is often a tendency to treat the Middle East and North Africa as a homogeneous region, with a large youth population and high population growth rate. The fact, however, is that, beyond the obvious differences in size, countries in the region are quite heterogeneous in both population structure and dynamics. This section characterizes these dynamics across countries and assesses the impacts on labor markets and, through this channel, pension systems.

Key Demographic Characteristics

The Middle East and North Africa region brings together a population of approximately 300 million people or roughly 5 percent of the world population. This figure is divided among large countries such as Algeria, Egypt, the Islamic Republic of Iran, and Morocco, with populations

Figure 2.1 Average Population Growth Rate, by Region, 1960–2002

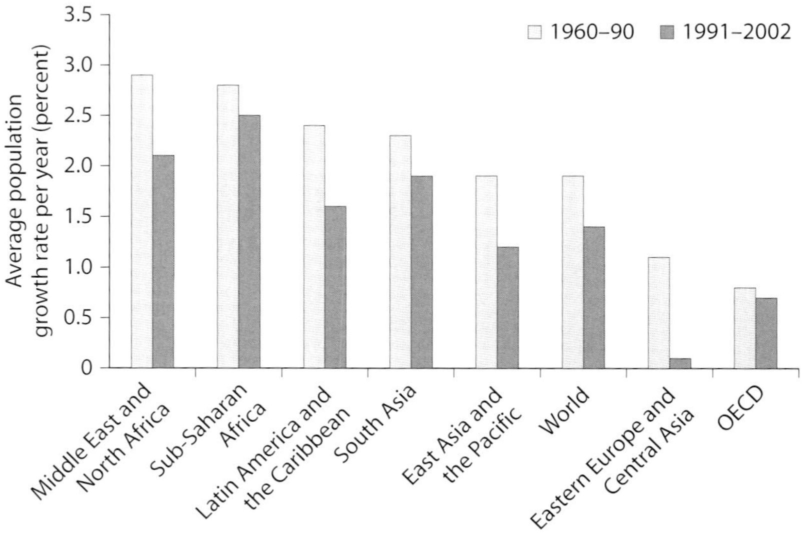

Source: Authors' calculations based on World Bank 2004f.

between 28 million and 60 million, and smaller countries such as Djibouti, the West Bank and Gaza, and most of the gulf countries, with populations of less than 4 million (see table A.1 in appendix A).

The region historically has shown exceptional population growth rates. Between 1960 and 1990, the population growth rate averaged 3 percent, one of the highest in the world. Although population growth rates declined in the second half of the 1980s, the average remains higher than that of other regions of the world, with the exception of Sub-Saharan Africa (see figure 2.1).

The Middle East and North Africa is one of the youngest regions in the world. The average old-age dependency ratio has been and remains one of the lowest, second only to that of Sub-Saharan Africa and far below the world average (see figure 2.2).

Nonetheless, comparisons among countries within the region highlight significantly different demographic dynamics and structures. The Middle East region has a younger population and faster rate of population growth, while the North African region has a relatively older population and a slower rate of growth. Djibouti, the Gulf Cooperation Council (GCC) countries,[1] and the Republic of Yemen exhibit significantly higher population growth rates, with figures ranging from 6.0 percent (the United Arab Emirates) to 2.1 percent (Bahrain and Djibouti), while Lebanon and the North African countries of Algeria, Egypt, Morocco, and Tunisia exhibit growth rates that are below the regional average (see figure 2.3). Nevertheless, even Tunisia, which has the lowest rate of population growth in the region, is just below the world average.

Figure 2.2 Old-Age Dependency Ratio, by Region, 1960–2003

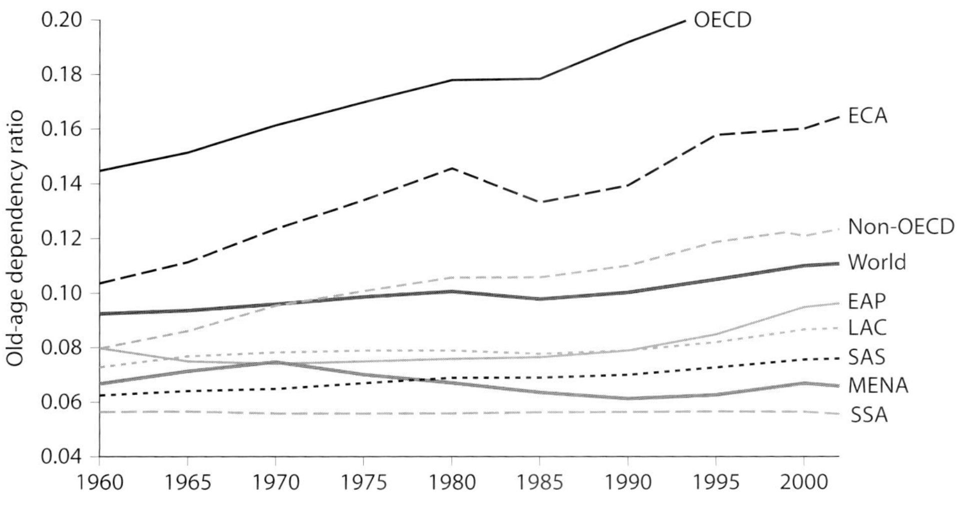

Source: Authors' calculations based on World Bank 2003f.

Note: The old-age dependency ratio is the ratio of the population age 65+ to the population age 15–64. EAP, East Asia and the Pacific; ECA, Eastern Europe and Central Asia; LAC, Latin America and the Caribbean; MENA, Middle East and North Africa; Non-OECD; SAS, South Asia; SSA, Sub-Saharan Africa.

Figure 2.3 Average Population Growth Rate in Middle East and North African Countries, 1960–2002

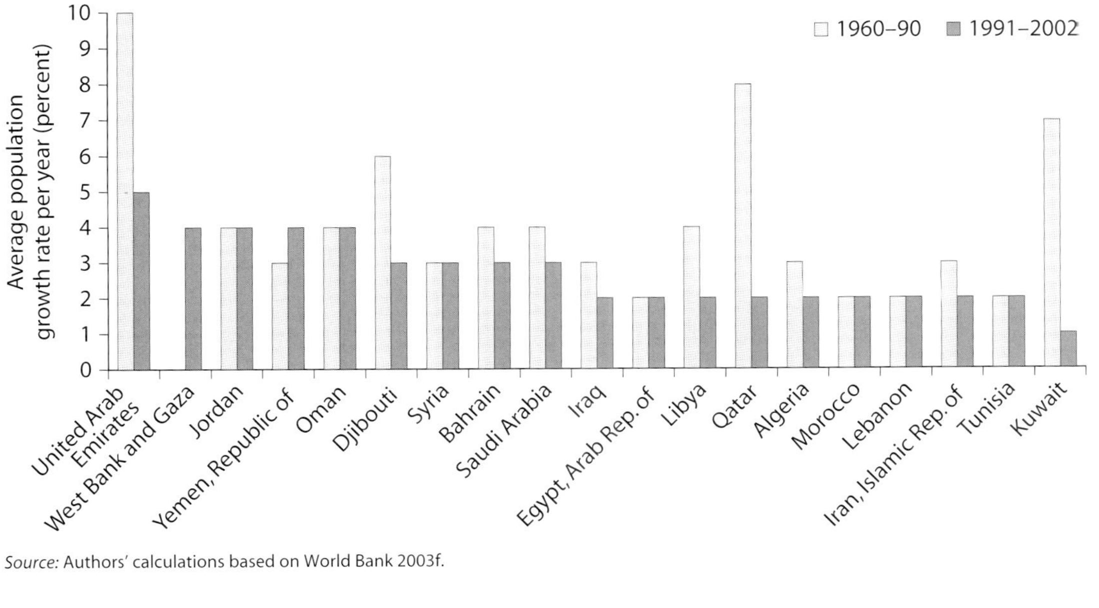

Source: Authors' calculations based on World Bank 2003f.

Figure 2.4 Young- and Old-Age Dependency Ratios in Middle East and North African Countries, 2000

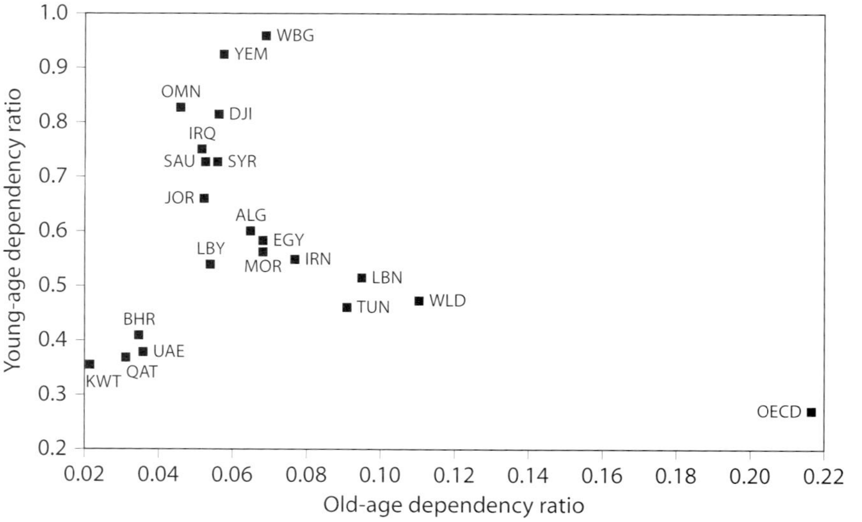

Source: Authors' calculations based on World Bank 2003f.
Note: ALG, Algeria; BHR, Bahrain; DJI, Djibouti; EGY, Arab Republic of Egypt; IRN, Islamic Republic of Iran; IRQ, Iraq; JOR, Jordan; KWT, Kuwait; LBN, Lebanon; LBY, Libya; MOR, Morocco; OMN, Oman; QAT, Qatar; SAU, Saudi Arabia; SYR, Syria; TUN, Tunisia; UAE, United Arab Emirates; WBG, West Bank and Gaza; WLD, World average levels; YEM, Republic of Yemen.

Regarding the structure of the population, countries exhibit differences in both their old- and young-age dependency ratios. These ratios are important economically because they indicate the existing burden on the working-age population required to sustain nonproductive, old, and young dependents.

The young-age dependency ratio is quite high for Djibouti, Jordan, Oman, Saudi Arabia, Syria, the West Bank and Gaza, and the Republic of Yemen (see figure 2.4). In many GCC countries—namely, Bahrain, Kuwait, Qatar, and the United Arab Emirates—a large part of the population is concentrated in working-age brackets, as both the old- and young-age dependency ratios are relatively low. North African countries such as Algeria, Egypt, Libya, and Tunisia, as well as the Islamic Republic of Iran and Lebanon, are characterized by slightly higher old-age dependency ratios and significantly lower young-age dependency ratios. Even so, the country with the oldest population structure in the region, Lebanon, still ranks below the world average.

Differences in age structure reflect differences in where countries stand in the demographic transition.[2] Indeed, while mortality rates exhibit only small differences, fertility rates vary considerably among countries. For virtually all countries in the region, the first stage of the demographic transition took place in the 1950s, when mortality rates

Figure 2.5 Life Expectancy and Total Fertility Rate in Middle East and North African Countries, 1985 and 2002

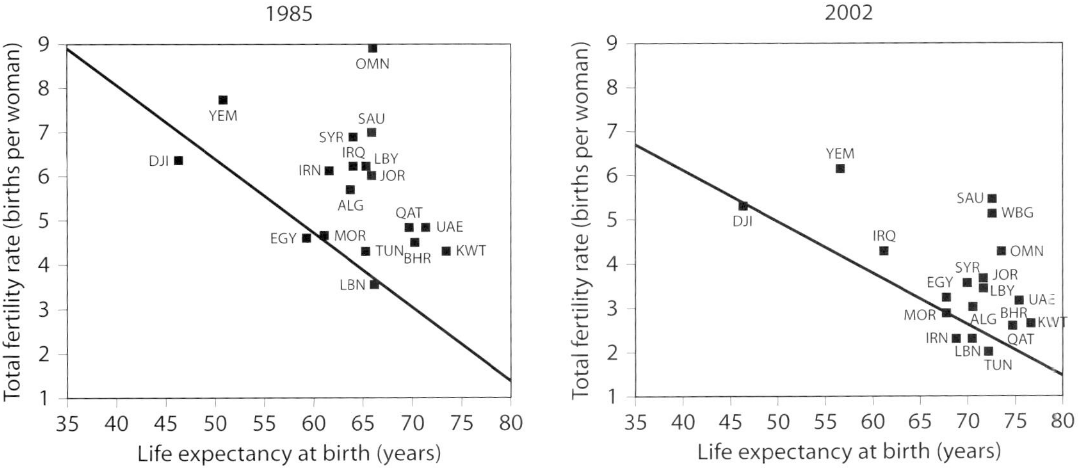

Source: Authors' calculations based on World Bank 2003f.
Note: The solid line shows the linear relationship between the total fertility rate and life expectancy calculated using world and country data. ALG, Algeria; BHR, Bahrain; DJI, Djibouti; EGY, Arab Republic of Egypt; IRN, Islamic Republic of Iran; IRQ, Iraq; JOR, Jordan; KWT, Kuwait; LBN, Lebanon; LBY, Libya; MOR, Morocco; OMN, Oman; QAT, Qatar; SAU, Saudi Arabia; SYR, Syria; TUN, Tunisia; UAE, United Arab Emirates; YEM, Republic of Yemen.

declined sharply and life expectancies increased gradually, triggered by recent progress in health care. The second stage of the demographic transition is still in progress and is characterized by a slow reduction in fertility rates. Current fertility rates remain high according to international comparisons.

The delayed reduction in fertility rates was the main driver of the sustained population growth between the 1960s and the 1990s (see figure 2.5, which compares life expectancy and the fertility rate in 1985 and 2002 against the world trend). With the exception of Djibouti, life expectancy has improved and attained higher-than-world-average levels in most countries. However, the fertility rate, despite an overall decreasing trend, has remained somewhat higher than the world average. Only Djibouti, the Islamic Republic of Iran, Lebanon, Morocco, and Tunisia rank at or below world-average levels. Overall, from 1985 to 2002, as the demographic transition progressed, fertility and life expectancy rates converged in the region.

Expected Demographic Dynamics

Survival and fertility rate forecasts imply a continuation of the demographic transition and a gradual convergence of rates in most countries.[3] Within the next 25 years, survival rates are expected to improve further throughout the region, while total fertility rates are expected to decline.[4] As a consequence, fertility rates and life expectancies will gradually become more homogeneous. Only Djibouti, Iraq, Saudi Arabia, the West Bank and Gaza, and the Republic of Yemen are expected to continue having relatively high levels of fertility.[5]

Projections imply a sustained but decreasing growth rate of the population. Within the next decade, the average population growth rate for the region is expected to remain around 1.9 percent a year, declining to 1.5 percent for the period 2015–25. Djibouti, Egypt, the Islamic Republic of Iran, Iraq, Jordan, Kuwait, Libya, Oman, and the United Arab Emirates are expected to experience higher-than-regional-average growth rates.

The aging process will be characterized by a sustained inflow of working-age population and in 15–20 years by a gradual outflow from working age to old age. As figure 2.6 shows, the rate of growth of the working-age population will exceed the rate of growth of the dependent population in the next 10–15 years for most countries in the region. Only after 2015 will the excess growth rate be significantly reduced, as the dependent population (mostly the elderly) starts to grow

Figure 2.6 Estimated Difference in the Average Growth Rate of the Working-Age and Dependent Populations in Middle East and North African Countries, 2000–20

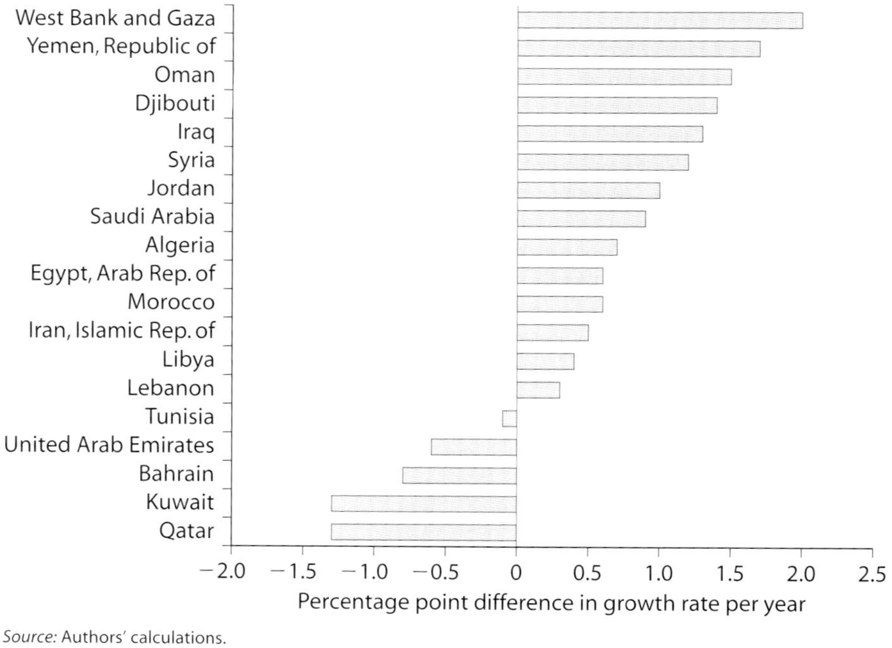

Source: Authors' calculations.

faster than the working-age population in countries such as Bahrain, Kuwait, Qatar, Tunisia, and the United Arab Emirates.

Both the increase in the working-age population and the gradual aging of the overall population are captured by increases in total and old-age dependency ratios, although the dynamics are clearly heterogeneous. Old-age dependency ratios are projected to increase only slightly between now and 2015–20 for all countries except the Republic of Yemen, where a further decrease is expected. After 2015–20 the old-age dependency ratio is expected to grow at a more sustained pace, and around 2040 or later most countries could reach the level observed in the Organisation for Economic Co-operation and Development (OECD) countries during the 1970s. Bahrain, Lebanon, and Tunisia would reach that level around 2030, while Kuwait, Qatar, and the United Arab Emirates would reach it around 2020.[6]

Expected Changes in the Labor Force

The expansion of the working-age population is expected to be accompanied by a continuous increase in female participation rates. This will produce dramatic effects on the size and growth of the labor force. Compared with international figures, the region has the lowest female labor force participation rates, despite the fact that for the past 15 years female participation rates have increased in every country of the region (see table A.4 in appendix A). The increase has been relatively moderate for Iraq, Libya, Morocco, Syria, Tunisia, and the Republic of Yemen but large—around 10 percentage points—for all other countries. On average, male participation rates have remained close to OECD levels over the past 25 years, with slight exceptions for certain countries. In the future, female participation rates in the labor market are expected to converge gradually to those of males (see figure B.3 in appendix B).

The labor force is projected to grow by more than 4 million on average each year between now and 2030, totaling more than 50 million new laborers between 2002 and 2015. The labor force growth rate is expected to decline gradually from 3.3 percent between 2002 and 2010 to 1.8 percent around the second half of the 2020s. Within the region, there are significant differences among countries. Algeria, the Islamic Republic of Iran, Iraq, Jordan, Oman, Saudi Arabia, Syria, the West Bank and Gaza, and the Republic of Yemen are likely to exhibit higher-than-average labor force growth rates in the near future, while Bahrain, Egypt, Kuwait, Lebanon, Libya, Morocco, Qatar, Tunisia, and the United Arab Emirates could experience lower-than-average growth (see figure 2.7).

Future demographic trends suggest that countries in the region have the potential to benefit from a "demographic dividend." Empirical

Figure 2.7 Projected Growth Rate of the Labor Force in Middle East and North African Countries, 2002–30

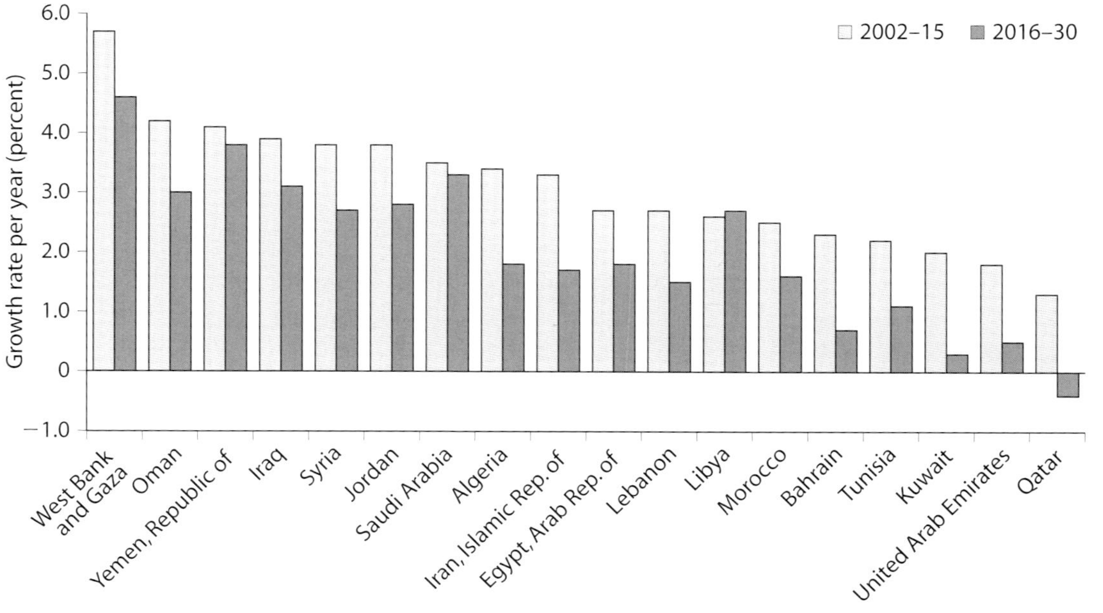

Source: Authors' calculations.

studies show that the combination of a low total dependency ratio and a rapidly expanding labor force is accompanied by a higher level of capital accumulation per capita, a higher saving rate, and a higher growth rate of output per capita (see Bloom, Canning, and Sevilla 2003). In addition, the rapid growth of the labor force creates conditions for increasing the growth rate of the contributory base of pension systems, thus allowing pay-as-you-go systems to pay potentially higher implicit rates of return on contributions and, hence, higher replacement rates for any given retirement age and contribution rate (see the second section of chapter 4 for a discussion of the conditions for the financial sustainability of a pay-as-you-go pension system).

The positive effects of this "demographic dividend," however, can be realized only if labor markets are able to absorb the new workers. Under current macroeconomic conditions (see the section on macroeconomics), the rapid expansion of the labor force instead could turn into a major development challenge: in the absence of private sector investment and growth, labor markets are unlikely to be able to absorb new entrants.

More important from the point of view of pension systems, if implicit internal rates of return paid on contributions are above sustainable levels, an expansion of coverage would worsen the financial situation of the pension funds. As discussed in chapters 3 and 4, the sustainable implicit rate of return on contributions that an earnings-related pension system financed on a pay-as-you-go basis can pay is a function of the growth rate of the covered wage. Hence, for a given growth rate of the average wage, the higher the growth rate of the covered population, the higher the implicit rate of return on contributions that the system can afford to pay. Within the region, a rapid expansion of the labor force could increase the sustainable implicit rate of return for pay-as-you-go systems. Unfortunately, even then, current implicit rates of return on contributions are likely to remain too high, so that new entrants to the pension system will actually worsen their financial situation.

A corollary is that expected financial problems are, to a large extent, independent of the future aging of the population. Even if current demographic structures remain constant, the pension systems could eventually run into trouble if an important misalignment were to occur between the sustainable and the observed implicit rate of return on contributions. Under these circumstances, population aging would only aggravate the problem. Moreover, given low coverage rates, currently favorable old-age dependency ratios do not necessarily translate into favorable pension system dependency ratios (see the fifth section in chapter 3).

Macroeconomics

The macroeconomy affects the performance of a pension system in various ways.[7] First, the *growth rate of the economy* ultimately determines the level of income that is available to distribute between the active and inactive populations. Also, over the long run, the growth rate of the economy is a good proxy for the sustainable implicit rate of return that defined-benefit schemes with pay-as-you-go financing can afford to pay on contributions and therefore the affordable level of benefits for a given retirement age and contribution rate.

Second, the *growth rate and the composition of the employed population* influence coverage rates and the finances of pension systems. A rising unemployment rate or an expanding informal sector implies that a large share of the labor force remains outside the contributory pension system and might not be accumulating the necessary savings to finance an adequate level of income during old age. High unemployment rates and a large informal sector also call for lowering, or at least not increasing, payroll taxes, thus affecting the finances of the pension fund.

Third, *macroeconomic stability* ultimately provides the enabling environment for the proper functioning of any pension system and the development of long-term financial instruments, including private pension savings and annuities. Inflation rates are important because they affect the real value of past wages and pensions and therefore the revalorization and indexation policies. High inflation rates can be an incentive for moving toward final-pay benefit formulas, which are a source of adverse distributional transfers and distorted incentives (see the third section of chapter 3). High inflation rates might also deter policy makers from committing to the automatic indexation of pensions, leaving pension funds—and retirees—vulnerable to ad hoc adjustments. Furthermore, the lack of price stability increases uncertainty and therefore the costs of investment. The fiscal position of the government affects its ability to support and finance the accumulation of implicit pension debt. Finally, the external balance of a country constrains or enables the diversification of pension funds' investments abroad. Countries with a fixed exchange rate and current account imbalances may have incentives to restrict or forbid investments abroad. This section further develops the analysis of each of these three channels in the context of Middle East and North African countries.[8]

Economic Growth: Past Trends and Future Prospects

During the past decade, all economies expanded, but incomes per capita grew modestly, in part due to decreasing total factor productivity.[9] Particularly weak performers were Djibouti and the West Bank and Gaza, where income per capita declined (see table 2.1). Only recently have GDP growth rates exceeded population growth rates in most countries, but economic growth rates remain below the levels required to reduce unemployment rates.

TABLE 2.1

GDP Growth in Select Middle East and North African Countries, 1990–2003

Percent

Country	Average, 1990–2003	Average per capita, 1990–2003	2002	2003
Algeria	1.9	0.1	4	6.8
Djibouti	−0.5	−3.2[a]	3	4
Egypt, Arab Rep. of	3.9	2.0	3	3
Iran, Islamic Rep. of	4.3	2.7	7	6.8
Jordan	5.0	1.0	5	3
Lebanon	5.8	4.1	2	3
Morocco	2.8	1.0	3.2	5.5
Tunisia	4.5	2.9	2	5
West Bank and Gaza	−1.7	−6.9[b]	−19	−2
Yemen, Republic of	4.6	1.6	4	4

Sources: Bank staff calculations; IMF 2004; World Bank 2003f, 2004f.
Notes: a. 1990–2002.
b. 1994–2002.

Falling total factor productivity itself reflects unfriendly business environments, public sector dominance of economic activities, lack of economic diversification, and inadequate levels of human capital. The lack of economic diversification and the dependence on commodities have exposed many countries to oil-price volatility. Human capital has failed to carry out its role as an engine of growth. A recent study finds that education, by gearing students toward public sector employment, has failed to contribute to economic growth (Pritchett 1999). On average, the expansion of schooling in the region has not expanded the output per worker.

Future growth will depend on the ability of countries to stimulate private sector investment. To date, some progress has been achieved in strengthening the institutional foundations of market-led economies by adopting structural reform programs that include privatization of state-owned enterprises, fiscal reform, trade liberalization, and deregulation. However, the reform agenda is largely unfinished at all levels. Key trade reforms, in particular, have not been implemented, and both tariff and nontariff barriers remain high (World Bank 2004e). Marginal tax rates on corporations and individuals are high across the region. The region also records the lowest levels of privatization as well as low levels of foreign direct investment inflows (Dasgupta, Keller, and Srinivasan 2002). The most recent IMF forecast for the region puts the annual average growth rate of income per capita during the next decade in the 1–2 percent range.

The Unemployment Challenge

The greatest development challenge facing countries in the region is addressing the unemployment crisis. The region's unemployment rate is among the highest in the world, conservatively estimated at 15.9 percent; unemployment is most pronounced in Algeria, Egypt, the Islamic Republic of Iran, and Morocco, which together account for two-thirds of the labor force in the region (see table 2.2).[10] In the Islamic Republic of Iran, for example, the labor force grew 4 percent in 2003; despite economic growth of more than 5 percent a year for the past three years, the unemployment rate is currently 13.8 percent and rising. The official unemployment rate is 9 percent in Egypt, although it is believed to be much higher in reality. Unemployment rates for individuals under 25 years of age are about twice as high as the national averages, in particular in Algeria and Tunisia, and up to three times higher in Lebanon and the Islamic Republic of Iran. Unemployment in the region is concentrated mainly among new entrants to the labor market and women at the middle and upper ends of the educational distribution. Due to the

TABLE 2.2

Distribution of Output and Employment in Middle East and North African Countries, by Sector, 2003

Percent

Country	Unemployment rate	As a share of GDP			As a share of employment		
		Agriculture	Services	Industry	Agriculture	Industry	Services
Algeria	28.4	11	24	65	12	30	58
Djibouti	60.0	4	82	14	—	—	—
Egypt, Arab Rep. of	9.0	16	50	34	30	21	49
Iran, Islamic Rep. of	13.8	11	53	37	23	31	45
Jordan	14.2	2	72	26	6	25	69
Lebanon	11.0[b]	12	68	20	—	—	—
Morocco	22.0	18	52	30	44	21	33
Tunisia	15.3	12	59	29	22	34	44
West Bank and Gaza	26.0	6	82	12	14	34	52
Yemen, Republic of	9.1	15	45	40	55	—	—

Source: World Bank 2003e; for the unemployment rate in Djibouti, World Bank 2004f; for the unemployment rate in Lebanon, St. Joseph University 2004.
Note: — = Not available.

demographics, the pressure of unemployment will continue to be exceptionally high for young workers at least until 2015.

The unemployment problem reflects, in part, the excessive reliance on the public sector as a source of jobs, which crowds out the private sector and results in a segmented labor market. Public sector employment as a share of total employment exceeds the averages for both industrial countries and other developing regions (World Bank 2004e). This is unambiguously the case in Algeria, Egypt, the Islamic Republic of Iran, and Jordan. The public sector also continues to dominate industrial activities through public enterprises. The preference for government employment stems from implicit and explicit employment guarantees as well as mismatched wage expectations resulting from relatively generous compensation and benefits policies, including pensions. In effect, the job security and social protection afforded by government employment distort career incentives.

High implicit and explicit labor costs can also contribute to the problem, and this is an issue to consider when reviewing the mechanisms for financing the pension system. Labor codes in the region continue to be rigid, particularly with regard to hiring and dismissal procedures. In fact, severance pay is among the most generous in the world. There is evidence that these programs protect jobs as opposed to income by reducing the incentives to dismiss workers (Robalino and Mataoanu forthcoming). In doing so, they also reduce the incentives to hire workers.

Current financing mechanisms for the pension system and for social security in general also increase labor costs and can reduce the demand for labor and encourage the movement to the informal sector.[11] Indeed, increasing contribution rates has been the preferred mechanism to improve the finances of social security systems; contribution rates now surpass 25 percent of wages in most countries. Weak linkages between contributions and benefits can also encourage evasion. Today, overall estimates of informal employment range between 42 percent of nonagricultural employment in Syria and 55 percent in Egypt.[12] The implication is that a large, and probably growing, share of the labor force remains outside the contributory pension system and might not be accumulating the necessary savings to cover a minimum level of income during old age.

Looking forward, the best-case scenarios suggest only gradual reductions in unemployment rates, implying that a significant part of the labor force will remain outside the pension system. Unemployment projections based on a simple accounting framework show that, with growth rates below 5 percent a year, unemployment rates will increase sharply in most countries (see figure B.4 in appendix B). In Lebanon, Morocco, and Tunisia, future dynamics will be more favorable, due mainly to slower expansion of the labor force. The situation is more worrisome in Algeria, the Islamic Republic of Iran, and Jordan and is particularly worrisome in the West Bank and Gaza and the Republic of Yemen.

Macroeconomic Stability

Important achievements in macroeconomic stability have occurred throughout the region. In general, countries have managed to control inflation, narrow current account balances, and reduce both fiscal deficits and public debt (see figure 2.8).

Inflation in most countries has decreased sharply but remains a social risk for vulnerable groups. Algeria, Egypt, Jordan, Morocco, and Tunisia have stabilized inflation rates below 5 percent. Algeria and Lebanon have succeeded in bringing inflation down from over 25 percent in the early 1990s to the single digits observed today. In the Islamic Republic of Iran inflation fell in excess of 30 percentage points from 1995 to 2003 (from 49 to 17 percent), although it remains stalled in double digits. Only in the Republic of Yemen and the West Bank and Gaza have inflation rates increased sharply since 2000, and they are now close to 6 and 10 percent, respectively. In general, the outlook is positive, but from a social protection point of view, mechanisms are needed to enable households to manage price volatility. In the case of mandatory pension systems, the *automatic* indexation of pensions should be a key policy objective.

Figure 2.8 Key Macroeconomic Indicators in Select Middle East and North African Countries, 1993–2003

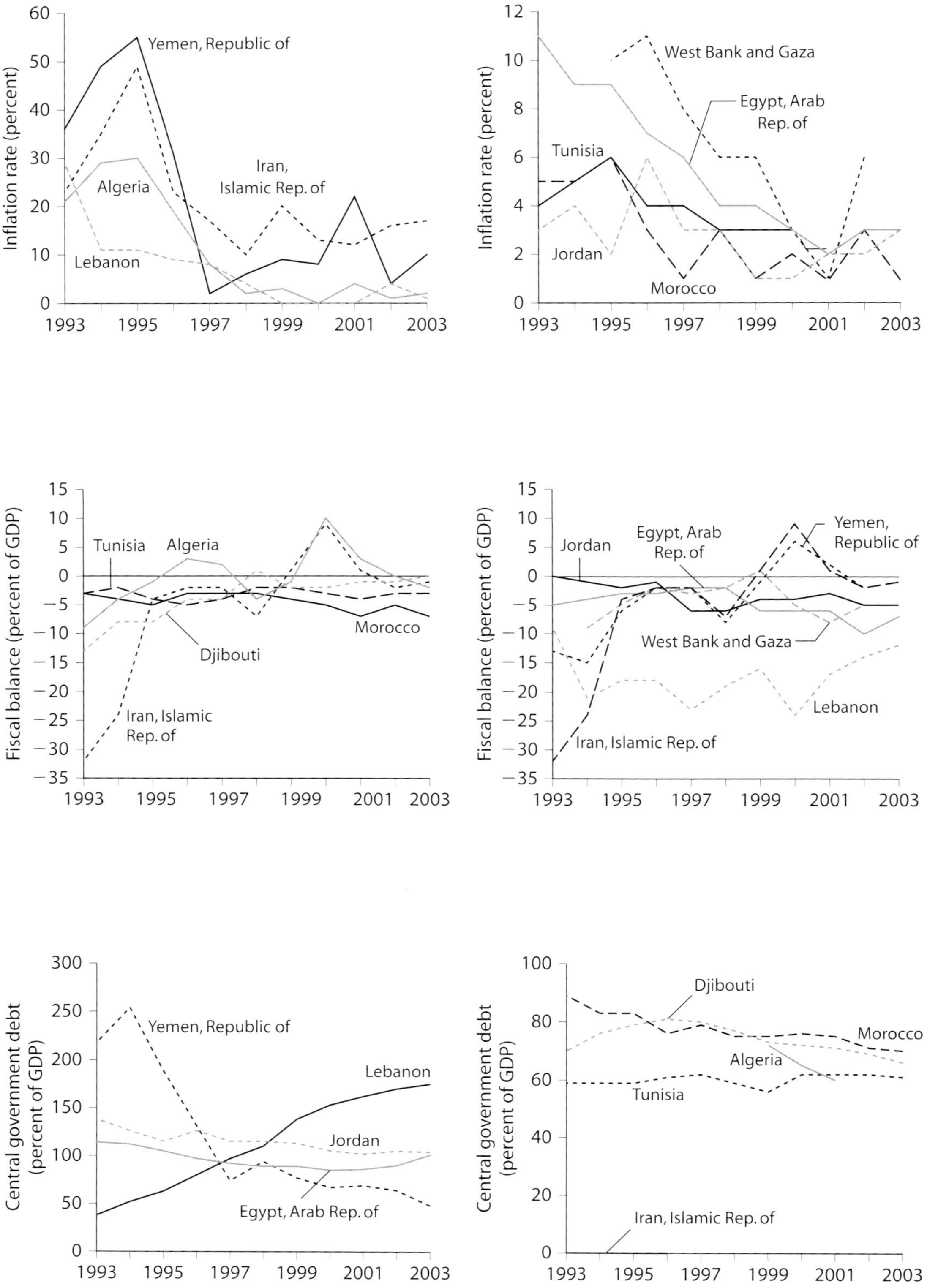

Figure 2.8 Continued

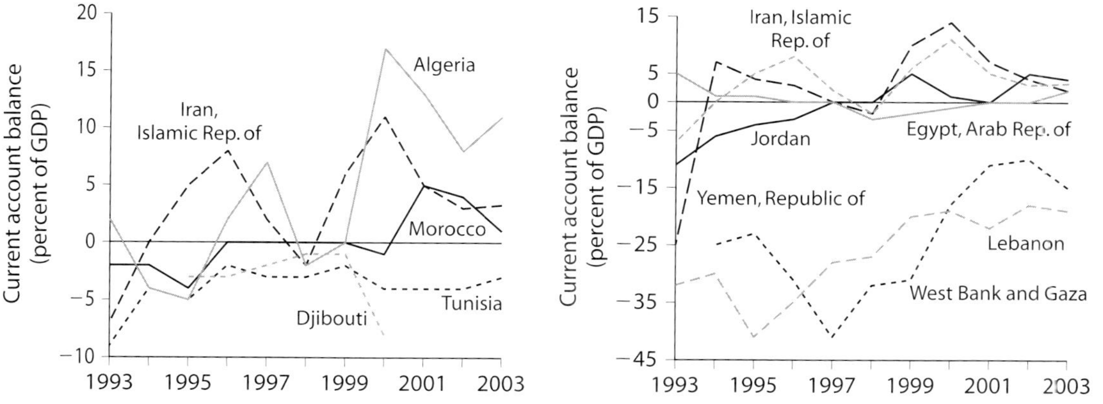

Source: Authors' calculations based on World Bank 2003f, 2004f.

Regarding the external balance, while current accounts are generating a surplus in most countries, the issue for pension systems concerns the restrictions on capital accounts. These go in parallel with tight regulation of trade quotas and tariffs. Paradoxically, self-imposed restrictions can result in uncertain capital inflows. Uncertain capital inflows, in turn, provide the incentive for governments to restrict private domestic savings within the confines of the country. Incentives are stronger given fixed or tightly regulated exchange rates, sometimes in conjunction with the domestic interest rate (for example, Egypt and Jordan).

Finally, despite improvements, the fiscal outlook appears persistently delicate for the countries surveyed. This reinforces the need to control the accumulation of implicit pension debt in pay-as-you-go systems but may also restrict the speed of reform. Fiscal balances continue to be negative (figure 2.8). The most worrisome cases are Lebanon (–12 percent of GDP), Egypt and Morocco (–7 percent), and Jordan (–5 percent). The exception is Algeria, due mainly to high oil revenues. Barring a few exceptions, the level of government debt across the region is also high, and trends are not positive. At 103, 121, and 214 percent, respectively, Jordan, Egypt, and Lebanon have the highest level of public debt to GDP. Moderately high levels are seen in Morocco (97 percent), Djibouti (66 percent), the Republic of Yemen (62 percent), and Tunisia (59 percent). The lowest levels are found in the Islamic Republic of Iran and the West Bank and Gaza, where the ratio of public debt to GDP is less than or equal to 20 percent. An issue of concern is that, in all cases, the analysis of the sustainability of the public debt excludes the implicit pension debt, which, as shown in chapter 3, can often be at least as high as the explicit government debt. In general, high explicit government debt should provide an additional incentive to reduce or at least stop the accumulation of implicit pension debt.

Overview of the Financial Sector

When discussing pension reform, countries often need to address two important questions: (a) What should be the relative roles of the public sector and individuals in financing a given level of income replacement for retirement? (b) How should the mandate of the public pension system be financed, meaning what should the level of funding be? The answers to these questions depend, in part, on the level of development of the financial sector. As financial sectors develop, private (that is, voluntary) arrangements can be expected to assume a more prominent role in the overall pension system. The level of development of the financial sector also has a role in determining the opportunities for investment as well as the risks of public pension funds. When appropriate regulations are not in place or a core of sound banks and insurance companies does not exist, increasing the level of funding of the pension system might not be desirable.

The level of development of the financial sector is also immediately relevant in the region, as several pension schemes have large reserves. In general, the ability of the financial system, including banks, insurance companies, capital markets, and other nonbank financial institutions, to intermediate savings and direct them toward productive investments is central to whether pension funds (either pay-as-you-go or funded schemes) will be able to invest assets prudently, contribute to the overall development of the economy, and generate long-term returns on behalf of beneficiaries.

This section provides an overview of the financial sectors of the non-GCC countries of the Middle East and North Africa, assessing whether the operations of the banking, insurance, and capital markets provide a sufficient foundation for pension fund investments.

The Banking Sector

Large variations in the size of the banking sector occur throughout the region, in part explained by the degree of openness of the economies to foreign capital. Banking sector assets range between less than 25 percent of GDP in the Republic of Yemen and more than 300 percent in Lebanon (see figure 2.9). Countries such as Jordan and Lebanon, which allow relatively free exchange of domestic and foreign currencies and

Figure 2.9 Banking and Credit as a Percentage of GDP in Select Middle East and North African Countries, 2002

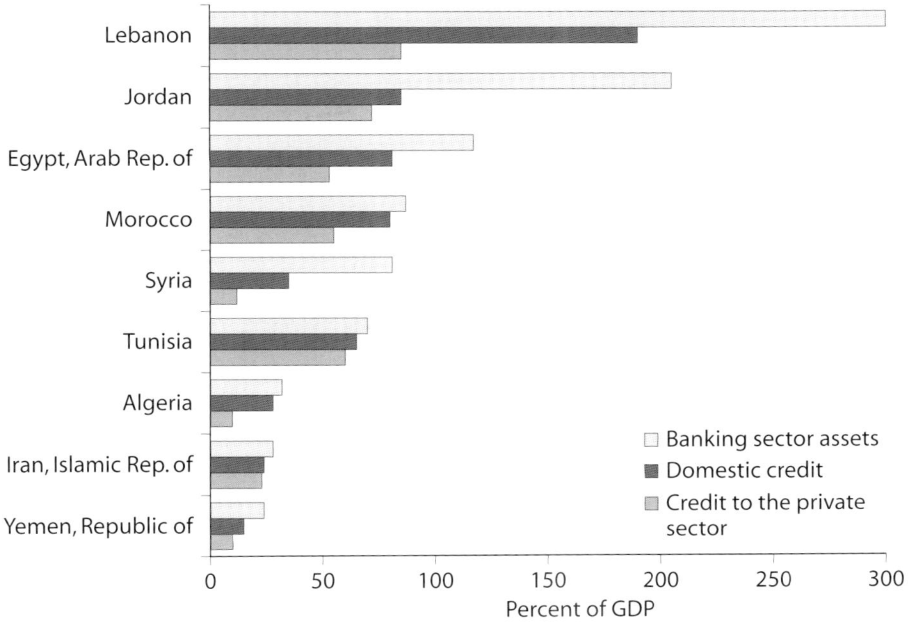

Sources: IMF 2004; Economist Intelligence Unit.
Note: Figures for Algeria and Islamic Republic of Iran are for 2001.

allow domestic residents to hold foreign exchange accounts, have much larger ratios of banking sector assets to GDP. Countries whose capital accounts, currency flows, or exchange rates are more restricted—Algeria and the Islamic Republic of Iran—have significantly smaller banking sectors relative to the economy.

A first question of interest regarding the banking sector regards the flow of credit. Indeed, investing pension funds in banks that are overexposed to government debt is not very different from lending directly to the government. In general, the relative allocation of credit between the public and private sector is explained by the ownership and financing needs of the government. Countries where the private sector dominates the ownership of banking and where domestic debt does not crowd out the private sector—Jordan and Tunisia—have higher rates of credit to the private sector. Egypt and Morocco have sizable state ownership of banks but are making efforts to achieve greater private sector orientation. Lebanon's banking sector has the highest exposure to government debt in the world, which is explained mainly by the size of its public debt. On the other end of the spectrum, the banking systems in several countries, including Algeria, the Islamic Republic of Iran, and Syria, remain government controlled, and only a small share of domestic credit goes to the private sector.

Still, even among countries moving to more private ownership, there is relatively high related-party lending, significant reliance on real estate collateral, and short-term maturities on loans. These factors point to financial intermediation that is not linked to long-term investment, relying instead on reputation, existing property, and trade-related credit. Supervisory regimes have made efforts to reduce bank lending to related parties or to ensure that such lending is conducted on an arm's-length basis, but lending based primarily on the medium- or long-term prospects of the corporate borrower is still not the norm. Banks are reluctant to lend at medium- or long-term maturities (that is, for investment) rather than for trade or working-capital purposes largely due to a heightened perception of risks. Very little maturity transformation takes place, which contributes to a truncated, and flat, yield curve.[13]

The second question of interest to pension funds relates to the solvency and stability of the banking sector. Countries where private banks are a significant part of the sector have sought to improve banking stability and private sector orientation,[14] while countries where the public sector dominates the banking sector exhibit weak incentives toward liberalization. Several of the banking systems have removed controls on interest rates, undergone significant restructuring, and strengthened supervisory and regulatory regimes so that published bank financial statements are reliable, nonperforming loans are recognized and provided for, and interest income is accrued correctly (see table 2.3). In these countries, banks are adequately capitalized.[15] In other countries, regulations such as controls on sector lending, directed lending, or centrally determined deposit and lending rates, which are generally

TABLE 2.3

Overview of Banking Sector and Financial Reforms and Stability in Select Middle East and North African Countries

Country	Interest rate deregulation	Private sector allocation of credit	Assessment of and provision for nonperforming loans	Reliance on treasury bills or other government assets
Algeria	Low	Low	Low	Low
Syria	Low	Low	Unknown	Low
Iran, Islamic Rep. of	Low	Low	Low	Low
Yemen, Republic of	Mixed	Good	Mixed	High
Egypt, Arab Rep. of	Mixed	Mixed	Mixed	Medium
Morocco	Strong	Good	Mixed	Medium
Tunisia	Mixed	Good	Mixed	Medium
Jordan	Strong	Good	Mixed	High
Lebanon	Strong	Good	Unknown	Excessive

Sources: Various World Bank-IMF Financial Sector Assessment Programs (FSAPs) conducted by the IMF, including: Morocco 2002b; Egypt 2002a; Algeria 2003; Tunisia 2001; Iran 2000; Jordan 2002.

recognized not to promote efficient intermediation, have not been lifted. The incentives to liberalize are also weak because of government ownership of the nonbanking real estate sector and the treatment of government-owned banks as conduits of funds to state-owned enterprises.

In conclusion, there are a few countries in the region where the banking sector appears sufficiently sound and regulated to form a base for both a funded pension pillar and investment of the reserves of state-run defined-benefit schemes.[16] Stress tests of banks in the region over the past several years, analyzing the effects of credit, interest rate, and exchange rate shocks, indicate that a core of commercial banks in Jordan, Morocco, and Tunisia are relatively resilient to both interest rate and exchange rate shocks but are moderately exposed to deterioration in portfolio credit quality.[17] Simultaneous shocks would likely have more serious impacts, which highlights the need for effective macroeconomic management. Banking systems elsewhere in the region exhibit somewhat stronger vulnerabilities to exchange rate shocks or deteriorations in portfolio quality, have significant exposures to a single borrower (for example, reliance on government bonds in Lebanon), or are too weak to intermediate new funds effectively. In all cases, the challenge remains the ability of banks to lend funds at medium and long terms for investment purposes.

The Insurance Industry

The insurance industry has experienced growth in many Middle East and North African countries over the past few decades, but with assets below 5 percent of GDP in most cases, the contribution to financial intermediation is still limited.[18] Annuity markets are underdeveloped across the board. In fact, a large majority of assets within the insurance sector are technical reserves of the property and casualty insurance business and therefore much more likely to have to be held in liquid instruments. Only Morocco can claim an insurance sector of any reasonable size (see table 2.4).[19] Life insurance, which has the potential to provide insurance companies with long-term funds for investment, represents only a small percentage of the total insurance market. Egypt and Morocco have the largest share of life insurance premiums, at 31 and 29 percent of total premiums, respectively, followed by Lebanon. In the other countries, life insurance premiums are below 15 percent. Factors such as ownership structure, fiscal incentives, cultural norms, and investment opportunities limit development of the market.

The structures of the insurance and banking industries have similarities: state dominance in a few countries, with correspondingly weak regulatory frameworks, and dispersed structures in others, with no clear

TABLE 2.4

The Insurance Sector in Select Middle East and North African Countries, Various Years, 2000–2

Percent

Country and year	Insurance sector assets as a share of GDP	Bank sector assets as a share of GDP	Insurance sector assets as a share of banking sector assets	Ratio of life premiums to total premiums
Algeria, 2001	2.3	36.9	6.2	—
Lebanon, 2001	2.6	295.9	<1.0	24
Egypt, Arab Rep. of, 2001	3.0	111.7	2.7	31
Jordan, 2002	3.9	200.8	1.9	15
Tunisia, 2000	4.8	71.6	6.7	9
Morocco, 2000	15.7	92.4	17.0	29

Sources: World Bank-IMF Financial Sector Assessment Programs (FSAPs) conducted by the IMF.
Note: — = Not available.

dominant company and several weaker companies. In Morocco, three private companies make up nearly 60 percent of the market, while in Egypt three state-owned companies form 90 percent of the system. In contrast, in Jordan and Lebanon the three largest companies constitute only one-third of the market. Where countries have opened up their insurance markets, supply (the licensing of insurance companies) has exceeded demand; yet, as firms begin to face increasingly rigorous regulations, consolidation will likely take place.

Reputational issues and lack of fiscal incentives constrain the development of the insurance industry throughout the region. A negative image of the insurance industry as a whole has emerged from the problematic settling of claims in the property and casualty business and the failure of a few insurance companies. Most countries do not have fiscal frameworks that favor long-term savings, while some impose taxes on insurance premiums—a clear disincentive and added cost to the industry.[20]

Limited long-term investment instruments also constrain development of the sector. Small and shallow equity markets, few new shareholding opportunities, and limited availability of corporate debt instruments clearly limit the investment opportunities for insurance companies.

Regulation and supervision of insurance are weak in the region, although progress has been made in a few countries. The past several years have witnessed an increasing commitment to improving the legal and regulatory framework, recognizing the potential role of insurance in risk mitigation and financial intermediation, and mitigating the potential harm from the failure of insurance companies, both to the industry and to the financial system as a whole, especially where cross-ownership is high. Jordan, in particular, has passed a strong insurance law and good regulations, increasing the capacity of the Insurance Commission. Morocco has also passed a good framework law but has not completed implementing regulations. Lebanon has drafted a new insurance law and initiated efforts to strengthen the insurance commission. Across the region, even where investments have been made in human resources, implementation and enforcement capacity are reportedly weak.

Taking into account the small size of the insurance sector, the lack of long-term savings and investment products offered by insurance companies, and the still-developing supervisory regimes, changes in the insurance environment will need to continue in order for the sector to play a role in a funded pension pillar or as a mechanism for investing the reserves of existing pay-as-you-go schemes. This will include strengthening the legal and regulatory framework, strengthening corporate governance and investment capacity, and providing fiscal incentives (or removing disincentives) for the use of life insurance or annuity products as long-term savings vehicles.

Debt Instruments

Medium- and long-term debt instruments and publicly traded equity instruments are available in most of the countries under review; however, even where corporate debt exists, short-term debt instruments are the norm and secondary markets are shallow. The cornerstone of debt markets in both developed and developing financial markets is generally government debt. In the Middle East and North Africa, domestic government debt in the form of treasury bills and bonds is generally only a modest portion of total government debt. External debt, often to international financial institutions or to bilateral donor countries, tends to be much higher due to lower costs and longer tenure (see figure 2.10). Only in Lebanon and Morocco do domestic debt levels approach external debt levels. Domestic debt tends to be short term—between one and five years—and yields are not fully market based. There appears to be a negative feedback mechanism between governments and investors with respect to returns and maturities. Investors demand high rates for longer maturities, presumably due to insecurity regarding domestic economic management, inflation, and currency depreciation. Governments, in turn, are unwilling to issue debt at the returns demanded by the market for longer maturities, contributing to a cyclical lack of a benchmark yield curve and investor mistrust. Finally, purchases of domestic debt issues in most countries are already heavily dominated by commercial banks (as well as by public pension schemes in some countries). A movement toward private funded pensions or the shift of public funds to more

Figure 2.10 Domestic and External Debt as a Percentage of GDP in Select Middle East and North African Countries, 2002

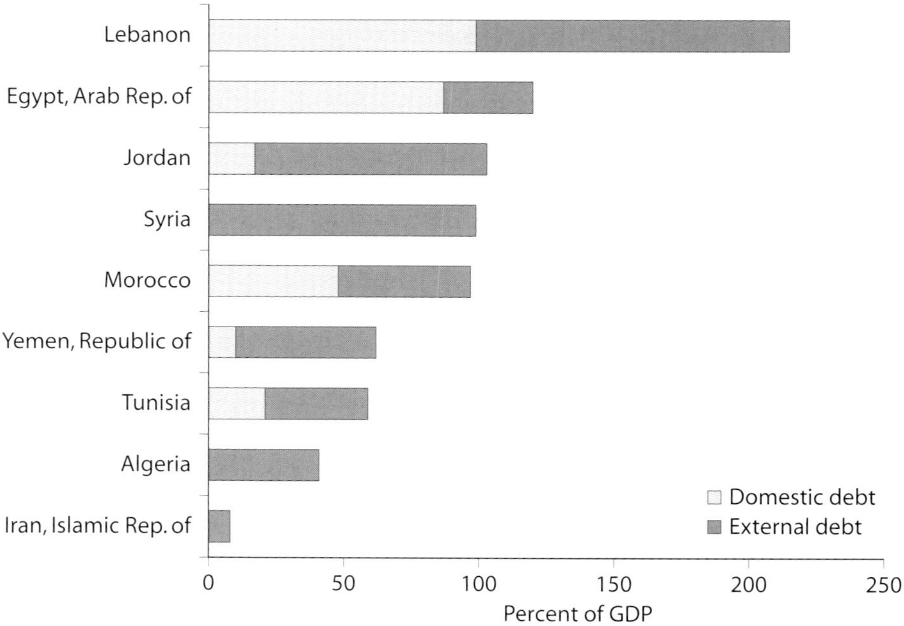

Sources: Alba, Al-Shawarby, and Iqbal 2004; Creane and others 2004; Economist Intelligence Unit; IMF 2004; Shatalov and others 2004.

transparent asset classes would imply increasing the share of government debt held by domestic investors, lengthening maturities, and holding open and regular debt auctions.

Corporate bonds are the smallest component of the capital markets. Only Tunisia has a noticeable level of corporate bonds, at 15 percent of stock market capitalization in 2002, although most bonds are tied to financial institutions. Jordan's corporate bonds represent 2 percent of stock market capitalization and are mostly government backed or tied to government-owned utilities. In Egypt, bonds appear to be issued predominantly by government agencies. In all countries, relative scarcity results in corporate bonds being bought and held to maturity rather than being traded after initial issuance. Corporate bond maturities remain relatively short—generally between two and five years—and issuance is usually done through private placement rather than through auction. This mirrors government practices with respect to treasury bonds (relatively short maturities and placement at agreed rates), resulting in a relatively flat yield curve. Indeed, growth of the corporate bond market has likely been slowed by lack of a medium- or long-term yield curve set through auction of government bonds, against which issuers and purchasers could price bonds. Finally, close relationships and often common ownership interests between corporations and banks result in a lack of incentives for corporations to look to the public for debt financing, especially where it will necessarily result in greater public disclosure.

Stock Markets

With the exception of Djibouti, Syria, the West Bank and Gaza, and the Republic of Yemen, stock exchanges exist in all countries reviewed in this report. However, with the exception of Jordan, financing through the stock exchange plays a much smaller role than borrowing through banks (see figure 2.11). The number of listed companies on local exchanges remains quite low, despite government incentives. Only 3 companies are listed in Algeria, 11 in Lebanon, approximately 50 in Tunisia and Morocco, 161 in Jordan, and around 1,000 in Egypt.[21] Listing a company, however, does not necessarily mean that shares trade or that private investors own the shares. For example, Telecom Egypt represents approximately 10 percent of market capitalization in Egypt but remains entirely government owned. Of the 100 largest stocks in Egypt, 60 are "almost untraded" and free float for the remaining 40 is less than 30 percent. Cross-shareholdings among related companies also are reported to reduce the number of shares available to outsiders. For example, a single conglomerate controls more than 50 percent of market capitalization in Morocco, while in the Islamic Republic of Iran two-thirds of total market capitalization is owned by the 12 largest investors. Low turnover ratios and low free float of shares magnify investor sentiment during

Figure 2.11 Market Capitalization and Credit to the Private Sector as a Percentage of GDP in Select Middle East and North African Countries, Various Years, 2000–2

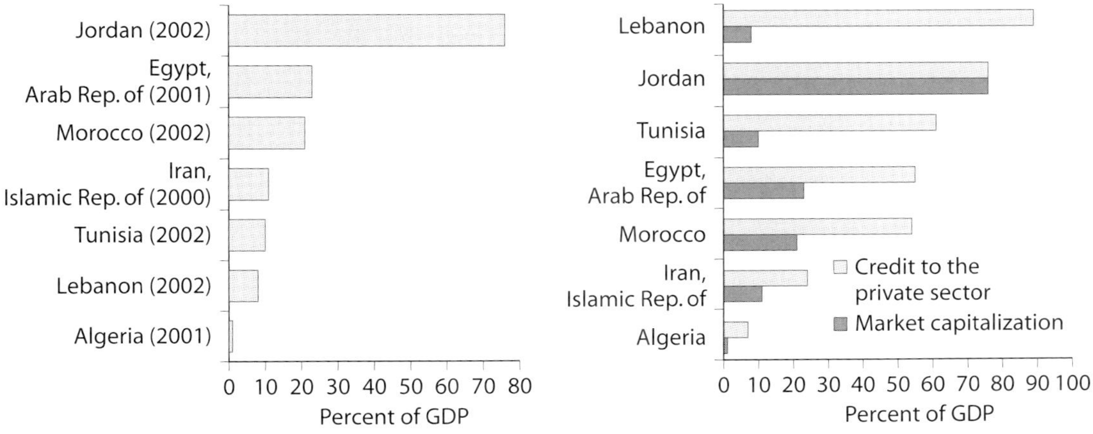

Sources: Financial Sector Assessment Program (FSAP) Morocco 2002; FSAP Egypt 2002; FSAP Algeria 2003; FSAP Tunisia 2001; FSAP Iran 2000; FSAP Jordan 2002.

Figure 2.12 Turnover as a Percentage of GDP in Select Middle East and North African Countries, Various Years, 2000–2

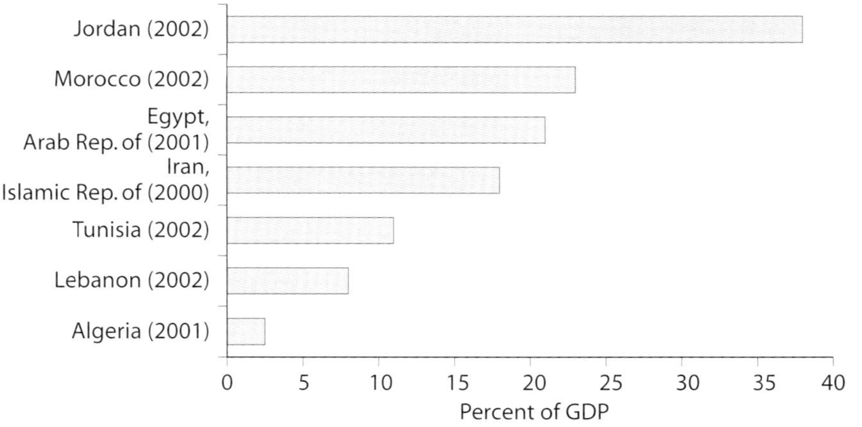

Sources: Financial Sector Assessment Program (FSAP) Morocco 2002; FSAP Egypt 2002; FSAP Algeria 2003; FSAP Tunisia 2001; FSAP Iran 2000; FSAP Jordan 2002.
Note: Annual turnover is based on the average of two years of market capitalization.

booms and busts (see figure 2.12). Finally, financial corporations play a large role in several exchanges and contribute to low sectoral diversification, increasing the risks to investors seeking a balanced portfolio.[22]

On a more positive side, countries have absorbed the lessons of the relative market booms and busts in the late 1990s and early 2000s: capital market laws, regulations, and supervisory authorities have been or are being strengthened significantly. Tunisia, in particular, has strengthened the regulatory framework with clear rules regarding insider trading, market manipulation, takeovers, public offers, and so forth, while Egypt, Jordan, and Morocco are in the process of updating their securities laws and strengthening the capacity of their regulatory agencies.

Collective investment schemes have only recently come into being in the region and are thus far active only in Egypt, Morocco, and Tunisia.[23] Where they exist, countries have worked to upgrade the professional capacity and the quality of regulations, although enforcement of regulations is relatively weak due both to a lack of capacity within supervisory agencies and to a desire not to stifle potential investment. In all countries where collective investment schemes have been established, banks, insurance companies, and other financial institutions are the primary sponsors. Depending on the ownership structure of the local financial sector (that is, whether sponsoring banks are part of larger conglomerates), investments under collective investment schemes may be tied to the underlying promoters, reducing the diversification of funds and increasing the risks to investors and the system as a whole.

Conclusions

This chapter reviews the initial conditions for pension reform in terms of demographic structures, macroeconomic prospects, and level of development of the financial sector. The main messages from the discussion are summarized as follows.

The region has a very young population with sustained rates of growth due to relatively high fertility rates. Because the labor force is expanding rapidly and total dependency ratios are declining, countries in the region have the potential to benefit from a demographic shift, with positive effects on the economy as well as on pension systems. A rapid aging of the population is likely to occur only two decades from now.

These favorable demographic developments, however, should not give room for complacency, as the aging of the population is not the main factor behind the financial problems facing pension systems. First, given low coverage rates, favorable demographic structures are not reflected in pension systems where old-age dependency ratios are high. Second, given structural problems in the labor market and weak private sector growth, it is uncertain that rapid expansion of the labor force will be accompanied by rapid expansion of employment in the formal sector. Finally, even if this were the case and the growth rate of the covered population did increase, it is unlikely to grow enough to align current implicit rates of return on contributions with sustainable rates. Hence, even in the absence of demographic changes, pension systems will run into trouble eventually. The future aging of the population will simply make matters worse.

The unemployment challenge facing Middle East and North African countries also has important implications for pension reform. First, policy makers need to rethink current financing mechanisms to avoid a sustained increase in payroll taxes, which can further reduce the demand for labor. High labor costs can also reduce the competitiveness of countries, discouraging private investment and job creation. Second, because an important part of the labor force is expected to remain outside the pension system, countries need to think creatively about mechanisms to protect those who are not accumulating the necessary savings to provide an adequate level of income during old age.

Regarding the macroeconomic environment, three messages need to be emphasized. First, already high levels of public debt reinforce the need to control the accumulation of implicit pension debt of pay-as-you-go systems, which can threaten the credibility of the fiscal framework. Clearly, frail fiscal balances constrain the repayment of this debt over the short term. Nonetheless, it is desirable for countries to make implicit liabilities explicit and to start exploring transparent financing mechanisms. Second, inflation rates have fallen significantly, which improves the prospects for long-term investors, including pension funds, as well as for the adoption of best practices in the design of benefit formulas in earnings-related schemes. Finally, improved external balances should allow countries to consider more flexible regulations regarding capital accounts and the investment of pension fund assets abroad.

With respect to the ability of the financial sector to absorb and intermediate pension assets, the outlook is mixed. Two groups of countries emerge. First, countries such as Jordan, Morocco, and Tunisia have incomplete financial markets, but the operating segments are stable and there is commitment to further reforms. The financial sector in these countries meets the minimum conditions for diversifying sources of savings for retirement by increasing the level of funding of the mandatory pension systems through a fully funded, defined-contribution tier and the development of privately funded voluntary pensions.

At the other end of the spectrum, countries such as Algeria, Djibouti, the Islamic Republic of Iran, and the Republic of Yemen have incomplete financial markets, with nonexistent or very small segments outside the banking sector and weak operating segments. Introduction of mandatory funded pensions and annuities is more controversial in these countries, at least over the medium term. Further progress in economic and financial sector development is necessary before complex pension reform programs can be put in place.

In between these groups, Egypt and Lebanon face structural factors that limit the degree to which the financial sector can play a role in intermediating pension assets. In Egypt, the public sector still plays a significant role in both the banking and insurance sectors; financial and operational restructuring programs will need to be completed. In Lebanon, the reliance of the banking sector on government debt means that banks are not appropriate vehicles for additional placement of pension assets—at the end of the day, funds are likely to be reinvested in government bonds.

Finally, outside of the spectrum are countries such as Libya and Syria. With nearly entirely state-controlled financial sectors, there is no rationale for shifting pension assets to the banking sectors or for introducing a funded pension pillar.

Notes

1. Countries in the Arabian Peninsula established the Gulf Cooperation Council (GCC) in 1981 to promote cooperation. The following countries are included in the GCC: Bahrain, Kuwait, Oman, Qatar, Saudi Arabia, and the United Arab Emirates.

2. A demographic transition consists of a shift from high to low mortality and birth rates. The initial stage of the demographic transition is characterized

by a rapid decline in mortality rates, while the final stage exhibits a slow reduction in birth rates.

3. See appendix B for a description of the methodology used to generate demographic projections.

4. See figure B.1 in appendix B for a description of current and projected survival probabilities across countries. Fertility rate forecasts are associated with rather large confidence intervals, as future fertility choices are associated not only with current demographic variables but also with future social and economic factors.

5. It could be argued that fertility rates in the Middle East and North Africa are structurally higher than in other regions because of the cultural and societal organization. Nonetheless, many of the determinants of fertility choices, such as health status, female education levels, female participation in the labor market, and urbanization levels, are correlated with income. Hence, as GDP per capita increases, it is reasonable to expect fertility rates to decline.

6. Bahrain, Kuwait, Qatar, and the United Arab Emirates have roughly constant or mildly increasing total dependency ratios, reflecting their more advanced stage in the demographic transition.

7. Clearly, the pension system itself influences macroeconomic dynamics. Some of the mechanisms are discussed in chapter 5.

8. Given data constraints, the discussion focuses on non-GCC countries.

9. Several studies identify decreasing total factor productivity growth as a primary reason for low GDP growth. The 1970s were marked by two conflicting dynamics: increasing accumulation (human and physical capital per labor) and declining growth. By the 1980s accumulation had collapsed and continued to fall during the 1990s as both public and private investment declined (see Bosworth, Collins, and Chen 1995; Dasgupta, Keller, and Srinivasan 2002; Keller and Nabli 2002; Sala-i-Martin and Artadi 2002).

10. The unemployment figure refers to non-GCC countries.

11. For a review of the literature and evidence for Algeria, see Robalino and Marouani (*forthcoming*). For simulations of impacts in Morocco, see Agénor and El Aynaoui (2003). Lax enforcement of labor and social security laws, in part given weak administrative capacity and negative incentives for enrollment embedded in pension laws, contribute to the problem.

12. The informal sector encompasses small and medium enterprises, part-time wage or seasonal workers, and various survival activities. Moreover, in Egypt, Morocco, and Tunisia, most informal employment occurs in broad services, manufacturing, mining, and utilities.

13. Despite a surplus of funds, most remain in relatively short-term time deposits. Because of flat or nonexistent yield curves, depositors have no incentive to place funds for longer periods in the domestic currency. The inability or unwillingness of governments to issue medium- and long-term government bonds, especially at yields demanded by the market, results in the inability of banks and other intermediaries to price long-term deposits or lend at fixed rates and longer maturities. Lack of competition among large potential depositors contributes to this. In Jordan, depositors and investors report extremely high demand for long-term, fixed-rate investments. However, they also demand extremely high premiums to lend funds for longer than a few years—premiums that seem out of line with past experience with inflation and currency movements. Lack of a truly competitive market for funds results in the placement of funds for shorter periods of time.

14. Jordan, Morocco, and Tunisia have made positive changes to monetary policy and banking supervision, and the quality of banking operations has improved as a result. Egypt, Lebanon, and the Republic of Yemen have also

made positive regulatory changes, but other issues in these three countries prevent banks from contributing significantly to the economy. In the Republic of Yemen, the key issues are the weak economy and weak judicial system. In Lebanon, excessive public debt crowds out private borrowing. In Egypt, structural issues and heavy government involvement in the sector prevent the system from operating efficiently.

15. The Bank for International Settlements sets the minimum risk-weighted capital adequacy ratio at 8 percent.

16. In Jordan, for example, the banking sector already intermediates a large percentage of the reserves of the Social Security Corporation, which manages the mandatory public pension program.

17. Stress tests measure vulnerabilities at a particular point in time and may not be relevant if there are changes in balance sheets.

18. Information related to the capital markets and nonbank financial intermediaries is not collected in a systematic manner in the region. The information provided here is based on miscellaneous World Bank reviews. Some information used here comes from reports produced under the joint World Bank-International Monetary Fund Financial Sector Assessment Program. To the extent that the FSAP reports have been made public by the participating countries, these are listed in the References. Although common assessment standards are used in reviewing regulatory frameworks, quantitative assessments of the nonbank financial sector vary from report to report, depending on the level of development of the system.

19. There may be some overstatement of total insurance assets in Morocco as a result of significant cross-ownership of insurance companies and banks, largely within a few key groups of private shareholders.

20. For example, in Egypt property and casualty premiums are subject to a 20 percent tax, while life insurance premiums are subject to a 4 percent tax. Even the lower rate places investment products linked to life insurance at a distinct disadvantage to deposits at a bank.

21. In Egypt, about 85 percent of listed companies are on a secondary listing for companies not meeting ownership diversification, accounting and auditing, or disclosure requirements of the primary list.

22. In Jordan, indexes for financial services are more than half the total market index, and trading of financial services approximates 40 percent of total trading on the exchange. In Lebanon, 6 of the 11 listings are banks. In Tunisia, 54 percent of market capitalization is related to banks, while financial institutions as a whole make up 63 percent of market capitalization.

23. In francophone North Africa, these are known as the Sociétés d'Investissement à Capital Variable and the Organismes de Placement Collectif en Valeurs Mobilières.

CHAPTER 3

Mandatory Pension Systems in the Middle East and North Africa

All of the countries in the Middle East and North Africa have earnings-related pension schemes, essentially financed on a pay-as-you-go basis. In most cases, the schemes as we know them today go back to the last quarter of the twentieth century. For this report, close to 30 pension funds were surveyed across 13 countries. This chapter presents an overview of the main features of those plans and the key issues they face.[1] The discussion is organized in five sections. The first section characterizes the institutional organization of the various schemes and discusses issues of coverage. The second reviews the mandates of the systems with regard to pension entitlements and introduces international comparisons. The third and fourth sections assess, respectively, the effects of current benefit formulas and eligibility conditions on incentives and the type of redistribution that takes place within the systems. The final section discusses issues regarding financial sustainability and the fiscal impacts of current pension systems.

Institutional Organization and Coverage

This section starts by describing the structure of the pension systems, including the number of funds and the schemes implemented for various categories of workers (for example, civil servants, the military, private sector wage earners, the self-employed). It then analyzes coverage rates and likely future dynamics.

Structure of the Pension Systems

Most pension systems in the region are fragmented, raising issues regarding administrative costs and labor mobility. None of the countries surveyed has a national pension scheme that covers all categories of workers (see table 3.1). Even Jordan, which recently integrated the

TABLE 3.1

Structure of the Pension System in Middle East and North African Countries

Country	Number of funds[a]	Integrated funds for civil servants and the private sector	Contractual workers in the public sector	Military	Workers in state-owned enterprises	Self-employed and others	Number of schemes
Algeria	2	Yes[f]	General	General[b]	General	Own fund	4
Bahrain	2	No	Public sector	Public sector[b]	Public sector	Not covered	3
Djibouti	3	No	Private sector	Own fund	Private sector	Not covered	3
Egypt, Arab Rep. of	3	No	Private sector	Own fund	Private sector	Private sector (three schemes)[b]	6
Iran, Islamic Rep. of	3	No	Public sector	Own fund	Private sector	Private sector[b]	4
Iraq	2	No	Public sector	Public sector[b]	Public sector	Not covered	3
Jordan[c]	2	Yes	General	General	General	Not covered	3[c]
Lebanon	2	No	Public sector	Public sector[b]	Public sector	Not covered	3
Libya	1	Yes[f]	General	General[b]	General	General[b]	3
Morocco	3	No	Own fund	Public sector[b]	Own fund	Not covered	4
Tunisia	2	No	Public sector	Public sector[b]	Public or private	Private sector (three schemes)[b]	6
West Bank and Gaza	2	No	Not covered	Not covered[d]	Not covered[d]	Not covered	2
Yemen, Republic of	4	No	Public sector	Own fund[e]	Public sector[e]	Private sector	4
Total	31						44

Source: Authors' calculations.

Notes:

a. Refers to the institution managing pension plans (schemes). It excludes occupational funds in public and private companies but includes pension funds for the military and security forces.

b. Within the fund plan, members have a special scheme.

c. Schemes for civil servants and the military are closed to new entrants.

d. New law has just been promulgated.

e. There are two separate funds: one for the military and another for the security forces.

f. Special provisions apply.

schemes for private sector workers, civil servants, and the military, excludes the self-employed and workers in the agricultural sector. Countries like Morocco and Tunisia have the largest number of schemes and funds. This fragmentation is an important policy issue because, in the absence of bridges that facilitate the transfer of rights between plans, it constrains the mobility of the labor force within and across sectors. A different scheme for civil servants and other workers in the public sector can also add distortions in labor supply. Indeed, when these schemes are more generous, they crowd out labor from the private sector. In the past, when economies were centrally planned and dominated by the public sector, fragmentation was not an issue. As countries embrace markets as a means to allocate productive resources across sectors and seek integration into the world economy, fragmented pension systems are likely to become an important problem. Fragmentation also increases administrative costs and can be a source of inequities, as workers in some sectors are favored relative to others.

One level of differentiation is between civil servants and private sector employees. Only Algeria, Libya to a certain extent, and Jordan of late have an integrated system for civil servants and private sector workers. In Algeria, one scheme, managed by the Caisse Nationale des Retraites (CNR), applies to all wage earners. In Libya, civil servants and private sector workers are also in the same scheme, managed by the Social Security Fund (SSF), although there are some differences in eligibility conditions. The last exception among the countries surveyed is Jordan, where the civil servant scheme was closed to new entrants in 1995.[2] New civil servants now join the Social Security Corporation (SSC), which before was the scheme for private sector workers. In all the other countries, a dual system exists. In Egypt, Law 79 of 1975 regulates a single scheme for civil servants, employees in the private sector, and employees in public enterprises, but special provisions apply to these three groups, and two separate funds manage the scheme: the Government Employees Pension Fund, in charge of civil servants, and the Public and Private Enterprises Employees Pension Fund (PPEEPF).[3] Lebanon and the West Bank and Gaza do not provide pension coverage to workers in the private sector.

In part, dualism is explained by the fact that schemes for civil servants evolved first. When coverage was expanded to private sector workers, the civil servant schemes prevailed in most countries. Lebanon is a special case: employees in the private sector are covered not by a pension plan but by an end-of-service indemnity. When employees leave a company, they receive the capital accumulated in their individual account with past employers plus a lump sum proportional to the number of years spent with the last employer. There is no mandate to transform the resulting capital into an annuity.

A second level of differentiation concerns contractual workers in the public sector and workers in state-owned enterprises. In Morocco, contractual workers have their own separate pension fund, the Régime Collectif d'Allocation et Retraites (RCAR). Until recently, workers in large public enterprises had company pension plans, but most of these have closed, at least to new entrants, who now join the RCAR. In Bahrain, Iraq, Lebanon, and the Republic of Yemen, contractual workers and employees in public companies enroll in the scheme for civil servants. In Tunisia, all contractual workers join the scheme for civil servants, but rules are less clear for workers in state-owned enterprises. Some companies join the scheme for civil servants; others join the scheme for private sector employees. In Djibouti and Egypt, workers in public companies without internal regimes and contractual workers join the regime for private sector employees. In the Islamic Republic of Iran, contractual workers join the scheme for civil servants, but workers in state-owned enterprises join the scheme for private sector workers. Finally, in the West Bank and Gaza, these two categories of workers are not covered.

For the military, countries have taken one of two approaches. In Djibouti, Egypt, the Islamic Republic of Iran, and the Republic of Yemen, the military have their own fund. In the other countries, they join either the general system (for example, Algeria and Libya) or the fund for civil servants (for example, Lebanon, Morocco, and Tunisia). In all cases, they enjoy special provisions. Jordan is an exception. The scheme for the military was closed to new entrants, who now join the SSC and are subject to the same benefit formulas and eligibility conditions as other members. However, given that the retirement age is generally lower for the military than for other workers, the budget is expected to finance individual accounts that will top up the benefits paid by the SSC.

Several countries also have set up special schemes for the self-employed, part-time workers, and workers in the agricultural sector. Algeria has a separate fund for independent workers, Caisse d'Assurance Sociale des Non-Salariés (CASNOS), which charges a lower contribution rate but offers benefits similar to the core scheme. Egypt has a mandatory pension plan for employers and the self-employed, a special regime for individuals working abroad, as well as a scheme for casual workers (all managed by the PPEEPF). The latter is basically a noncontributory scheme where members pay a symbolic flat rate and receive a flat benefit upon retirement. In the Islamic Republic of Iran, the self-employed and employees in small enterprises (fewer than 10 employees) join the regime for private sector workers and pay a lower contribution rate, although benefits are the same. In the Republic of Yemen, the same holds true, although there seem to be no differences in eligibility conditions or benefit formulas. In Libya, the self-employed join the general SSF scheme but pay higher contribution rates. Tunisia has a scheme for agricultural workers in cooperatives (Régime Salariés Associés du Secteur Agricole), another for wage earners in the agricultural sector employed at least 45 days per quarter by the same employer (Régime Salariés du Secteur Agricole), and a scheme for the self-employed (Régime des Non-Salariés, RNS). At the other extreme, Djibouti, Iraq, Jordan, Lebanon, Morocco, and the West Bank and Gaza do not offer coverage to the self-employed or part-time workers.

Beyond mandatory pension systems, occupational plans that often substitute for the main schemes are common across the region. These occupational plans contribute to the fragmentation of the labor market.

At least 20 occupational pension plans exist in the Islamic Republic of Iran, all defined-benefit arrangements. In Jordan there are 40 plans, all earnings-related. In Morocco, the Caisse Interprofessionnelle Marocaine de Retraite and the Caisse Nationale de Retraite et d'Assurance manage several regimes (World Bank 2004a). In Egypt, there are close to 600 occupational plans, but these complement the mandatory scheme. In general, the occupational plans are not subject to regulations or supervision by the government, disclosure is opaque, management standards presumably cannot be considered as "best practices," and many are facing financial difficulties. This is an issue of concern, first, because several of these plans are part of state-owned enterprises and add to the contingent liabilities of the government and, second, because plan members face a considerable risk of not receiving promised benefits.

The remaining sections of this chapter focus on the mandatory pension schemes and, in particular, on schemes for private sector employees and civil servants. The special schemes for various categories of workers are not reviewed in depth, and readers are referred to the country reports cited in chapter 1 (note 2).

Coverage

The degree to which today's workers are covered by formal pension systems concerns policy makers for two reasons. First, low coverage rates imply that large segments of the population might have insufficient income to support themselves in old age. In Middle East and North African countries, strong family and kinship ties are an important informal way of protecting older people. However, their effectiveness in the future is being called into question, in part, by the effects of rural-urban and international migration. Second, the coverage of the pension system affects its finances. For example, an expansion of coverage brings greater revenues over the short term, and as a result many governments see the expansion of coverage as the solution to financial problems. Unfortunately, as discussed in chapter 1 (section on demographics), the opposite could likely occur. The expansion of coverage brings higher revenues today but also higher expenditures in the future. When pension systems are unbalanced—benefit promises are too high relative to contributions—bringing in new plan members worsens their financial position. Hence policies regarding the expansion coverage need to balance social objectives with financial constraints.

This subsection assesses the level of coverage of current pension schemes and the factors likely to influence future dynamics. In all cases, the military is excluded from the calculations, since it often is covered by a separate fund or scheme for which little information is available.

There are two main structural influences on the extent to which the working population is covered by a mandatory, formal pension scheme: (a) the institutional arrangements for pension provision, particularly the extent to which different labor market groups are covered by the mandate, and (b) the level of employment and its distribution among different sectors of the economy. Other things being equal, countries that do not provide pensions to the self-employed or seasonal workers in the agricultural sector or where occupational plans are substituting for the mandatory system tend to have lower coverage rates. Countries with high unemployment rates, a large share of nonwage earners in the labor force, or a large agricultural sector also tend to have lower coverage rates. In contrast, countries with a large public sector (including the civil service and state-owned enterprises) or a more industrial private sector tend to have higher coverage rates.[4]

Coverage among the countries included in the analysis varies between 8 and 87 percent of the labor force. On average, the mandatory schemes cover 34 percent of the labor force. There is, however, little information on the characteristics of those covered (family status, earnings, and so forth) or on the industries and occupations in which they work. Libya has the highest level of coverage, in part, because a large majority of the labor force is employed in the public sector or state-owned enterprises (see figure 3.1). The other countries with coverage rates above 40 percent (Algeria, Egypt, the Islamic Republic of Iran, and Tunisia) offer special pension schemes to the self-employed or workers

Figure 3.1 Coverage of the Mandatory Pension System in Select Middle East and North African Countries

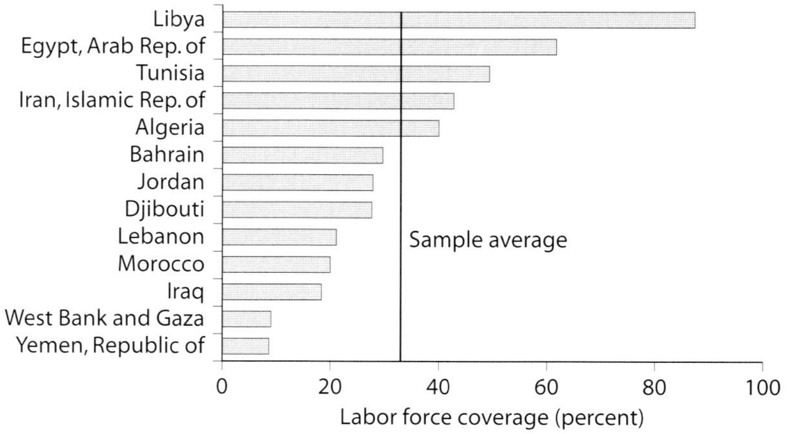

Source: Authors' calculations.
Note: Excludes military and security forces. Countries were selected based on the availability of data. The figure for Egypt excludes workers covered under Law 112/1980, basically a noncontributory scheme. Given, sometimes, important variations in labor force estimates across sources, numbers need to be interpreted with caution.

in the agricultural sector. In Egypt, the reported figure would be higher if the scheme for casual workers were included; this is basically a quasi-noncontributory system enrolling close to 30 percent of the labor force (close to 6 million workers). In the Islamic Republic of Iran, the self-employed also have access to the Social Security Organization (SSO), the mandatory scheme for private sector workers. Given the size of the public sector (including state-owned enterprises), the coverage of the mandatory pension system could be higher, except that numerous occupational plans operate as substitutes for the main scheme. A similar phenomenon is observed in Jordan, where coverage rates are around 30 percent. Moreover, coverage is not offered to the self-employed or seasonal workers in the agricultural sector. Lebanon and Morocco have low coverage rates (around 20 percent) relative to their level of income. In Morocco, one of the main reasons is that 45 percent of the employed population are workers in the agricultural sector who are not covered.[5] Indeed, in this sector seasonal jobs and multiple employers are frequent, and access to a formal pension scheme is less likely. Djibouti, Iraq, the West Bank and Gaza, and the Republic of Yemen also have the lowest coverage rates, and the factors explaining the outcome are similar. In Iraq, the formal private sector is small (only 1 percent of the labor force is enrolled.) The West Bank and Gaza does not provide coverage to private sector workers. Djibouti has the highest unemployment rate in the region (60 percent of the labor force), and the Republic of Yemen has the largest share of workers in the agricultural sector (55 percent).

Coverage rates might also be affected by the incentives for individuals to enroll in the mandatory pension systems and for employers to comply with the mandate. Individuals are affected by the cost of contributions, by their expectations about the level of pension benefits eventually received (and their links to the contributions paid), as well as by the transaction costs, such as complying with complex bureaucratic procedures. Employers also face compliance costs that might prevent them from covering their workers, particularly if they have only a small number of employees.

In most countries, tensions already exist among employers, employees, and the government regarding the level of the contribution rate to the social security system—often above 25 percent of gross wages, which is considered high. Although most countries provide generous benefits that could stimulate enrollment, pessimistic expectations about the ability of the system to deliver on these promises can reduce the incentives to enroll and contribute. As discussed in the section on incentives in this chapter, choices regarding benefit formulas and eligibility conditions can also provide incentives to evade enrollment and contributions—for instance, when only the last few salaries count toward the pension.

Working in the opposite direction, penalties for noncompliance and effective enforcement of the mandate to contribute tend to increase coverage. In the Middle East and North Africa, countries generally impose penalties for noncompliance, but enforcement capacity is weak. Hence problems regarding evasion and the insufficient declaration of wages are pervasive (see the section on administration in chapter 4).

What are the prospects for the expansion of pension coverage in the region? Cross-sectional studies show a correlation between the level of income per capita in a country and the coverage rate (Palacios and Pallarès-Miralles 2000). One explanation is that higher levels of income can be correlated with stronger administrative capacity and better-designed systems that improve the incentives to contribute. However, higher levels of income will not necessarily be accompanied by structural changes in labor markets or the institutional organization of schemes. As previously discussed, these are important factors that can explain deviations from the expected coverage rates. For instance, Algeria, Egypt, and Tunisia, the countries with special regimes, have coverage rates above the expected values for their level of income (adjusted for purchasing power parity). In Morocco, the coverage rate is below expectations (figure 3.2).

What happens to coverage in the future will depend mainly on how institutional arrangements evolve, how the parameters and rules of the pension system affect incentives to enroll, and, most important, how labor markets and industrial structures change. Over the short term, the structural reforms that are engaged in many countries of the region (for example, privatization, civil service reform) are likely to imply important reallocation of resources, both capital and labor between sectors, and could induce lower coverage rates. Over the medium and long term, without institutional and economic change that generates jobs in the formal sector, coverage is unlikely to expand much. This is the "pessimistic" scenario shown in figure 3.2. This scenario assumes that coverage among the employed population remains constant in different sectors and that new jobs, resulting from assumptions regarding economic growth and labor productivity, are distributed proportionally in each of these sectors. In this case, the share of the labor force covered by one of the mandatory systems will remain roughly constant and, in some cases, will even decline. This is because the total number of new contributors will be growing at the same rate as or slower than the labor force.

A more optimistic scenario considers changes in the structure of the labor market and industrial organization along with improvements in incentives to enroll and in enforcement capacity. In figure 3.2, this "optimistic" scenario is illustrated by assuming that current coverage rates among new employees gradually increase to 100 percent over a

Figure 3.2 Projected Coverage Rate in Middle East and North African Countries, 2003–30

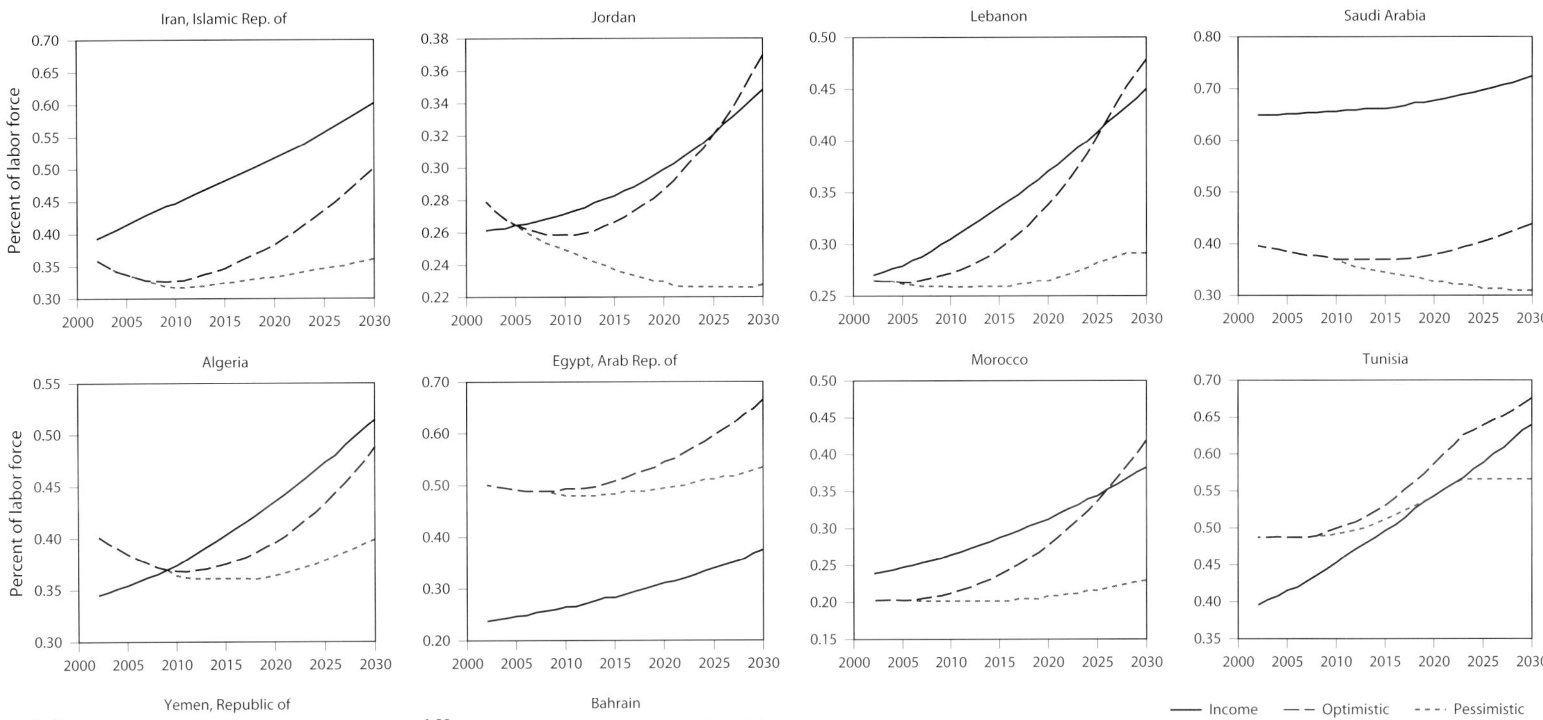

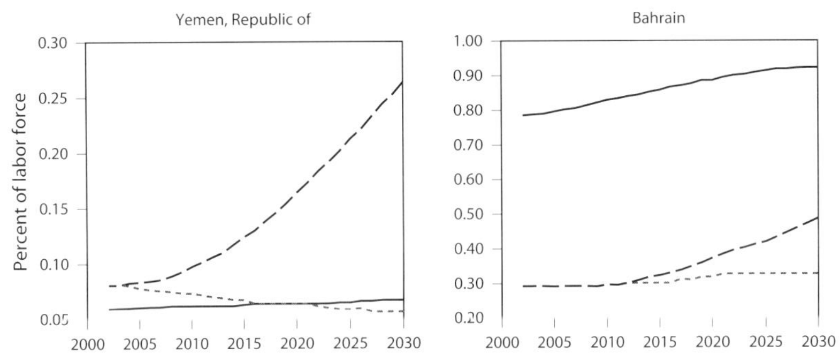

Source: Authors' calculations.

Note: The projections assume that GDP grows at 3.5 percent a year and labor productivity at 1 percent a year. These assumptions determine the growth rate of the employed population and, given the country-specific population growth rates, the GDP per capita. The income approach links coverage and income per capita with the formula estimated in Palacios and Pallarès-Miralles (2000). The pessimistic approach assumes that current enrollment probabilities for the employed population are constant. The optimistic scenario assumes that these probabilities gradually increase, reaching 100 percent of *new* employees in 30 years. See appendix B.

30-year period. This results in average coverage rates of 40–50 percent of the labor force. The truth is likely to lie somewhere in between the pessimistic and optimistic scenarios.

Size and Shape of the Schemes

All pension systems embody a set of retirement-income objectives, which, because of the complexity of the parameters and rules, is often implicit. This section aims to compare these implicit objectives for retirement income both among countries in the region and between the Middle East and North Africa and other regions of the world. This is done by simulating replacement rates for various pension schemes. The replacement rate is defined as the pension divided by the last salary. It indicates the share of total income that is replaced or preserved on retirement. The calculations are made for full-career workers at different income levels. Full-career here means that individuals join the system at age 20 and contribute until the normal retirement age is reached, or the maximum replacement rate paid by the system is attained.[6]

The simulations are not meant to predict the replacement rates that systems will deliver in practice—in fact, few plan members are full-career workers, and therefore many will deviate from the rates discussed here. The objective of the simulations is to isolate differences in parameters across countries.

The first two parts of the section explore income replacement for private sector workers and civil servants, respectively, within the region. The third part compares the key parameters that determine income replacement patterns in Middle East and North African countries with a range of pension systems in OECD, in Eastern Europe and Central Asia, and in Latin America and the Caribbean. Given data constraints, this comparison is done only in the case of schemes for private sector workers.

Income Replacement Patterns in Schemes for Private Sector Workers

There is a large variation in the level of income replacement targeted by pension systems in Middle East and North African countries. Figure 3.3 shows the gross replacement rate as a function of income expressed as a share of the economy-wide average earnings. Income ranges from 30 percent up to three times average earnings. The highest level of income replacement in the region is observed in the Islamic Republic of Iran, where the average full-career worker receives a gross replacement rate of 116 percent. The gross replacement rate is defined as the gross

Figure 3.3 Gross Replacement Rate as a Percentage of Average Earnings in Select Middle East and North African Countries

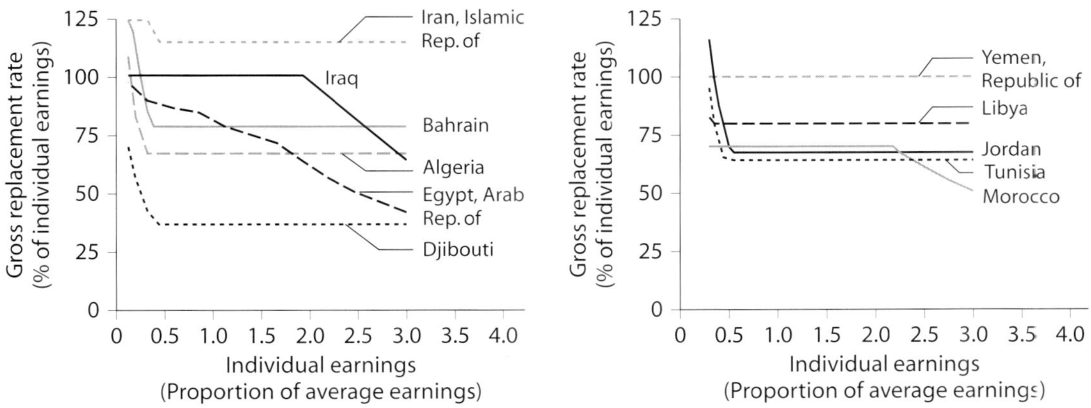

Source: Authors' calculations.

(that is, before taxes) pension divided by the gross salary. At the other extreme, in Djibouti, the average full-career worker receives a gross replacement rate close to 50 percent. Iraq and the Republic of Yemen target average gross replacement rates of 100 percent, Bahrain and Libya have average gross replacement rates of around 80 percent, while Algeria, Jordan, Morocco, and Tunisia target average gross replacement rates in the 60–70 percent range (see figure 3.3).

Two important parameters influence income replacement patterns: the minimum pension and the ceiling on the covered wage. The retirement incomes of low- and often middle-income workers depend on the value of the minimum pension rather than the parameters of the earnings-related scheme. Moreover, at high earnings, pensions can sometimes be affected by ceilings on pensionable earnings or maximum pension values. Both of these policies have substantial effects on pension values and the costs of the pension system that are not captured by looking at the entitlements of average-income workers.

The effect of the minimum pension is seen at lower levels of earnings except in the Republic of Yemen, where there is no minimum pension, and in Morocco, where it is very small. It is useful to note the earnings at which a full-career worker is entitled to the minimum pension. In Algeria, Bahrain, Djibouti, Jordan, and Tunisia, full-career workers with earnings below 50 percent of the average are eligible to receive the minimum pension and therefore receive higher replacement rates than the average full-career worker. In Libya, the minimum pension is set at 29 percent of the economywide average earnings. With an average replacement rate of 80 percent for the full-career worker, only individuals earning less than 36 percent of average earnings are eligible. In Morocco, the minimum pension represents only 18 percent of average earnings, and only individuals with incomes below 26 percent of the average are eligible. At the other end of the spectrum, in Bahrain the relatively low replacement rate for workers claiming the pension at the earliest age for eligibility means that a worker would need to earn 85 percent of the average not to receive the minimum pension. The high minimum pension in the Islamic Republic of Iran and in Jordan means that a worker would have to earn more than 70 percent of average earnings not to be eligible.

The ceiling on the covered wage has the effect of gradually reducing replacement rates for those with earnings above the ceiling. Indeed, the higher the wage, the smaller the proportion that is used to pay contributions and calculate the pension and therefore the smaller the ratio between this pension and the total wage. In Morocco, for instance, there is a ceiling of close to 2.3 times the average wage. Individuals with earnings above this ceiling receive lower gross replacement rates. In Egypt, the pension is computed on the basis of two different salaries: the basic salary and the variable salary. The first has a ceiling that is close to the average wage, while the second represents 1.8 times the average wage. In Iraq, there is no ceiling, but there is a maximum pension of close to two times the average wage; hence replacement rates also fall for higher incomes.[7] In the other countries, there are no ceilings, or the ceilings that exist are quite high. For instance, in the Islamic Republic of Iran the ceiling is close to eight times the average wage. As a result, replacement rates are flat across most levels of income.

When taxes on pensions and wages are taken into account, replacement rates increase considerably. Contrary to the gross replacement rate, the net replacement rate refers to the ratio between the net pension (that is, after taxes) and the net wage.[8] In all cases reviewed, net replacement rates are higher than gross replacement rates. This is because income taxes on pensions are generally lower than income taxes on wages and because pensioners no longer pay social security taxes. Hence, in Egypt, while the gross pension for the average full career worker represents 80 percent of the gross wage, the net pension represents more than 100 percent of the net wage (see figure 3.4). Basically, in Egypt, the average worker has more disposable income after retirement than while working! Libya is an interesting case because net replacement rates increase with the level of income. This is because pensions are not taxed, while income taxes on wages follow a progressive schedule.

Income Replacement Patterns in Civil Servant Pension Schemes

There is also a large range of variation regarding income replacement patterns for civil servant schemes. The most ambitious of the schemes is, once again, that of the Islamic Republic of Iran, followed by the

Figure 3.4 Net Replacement Rate as a Percentage of Average Earnings in Select Middle East and North African Countries

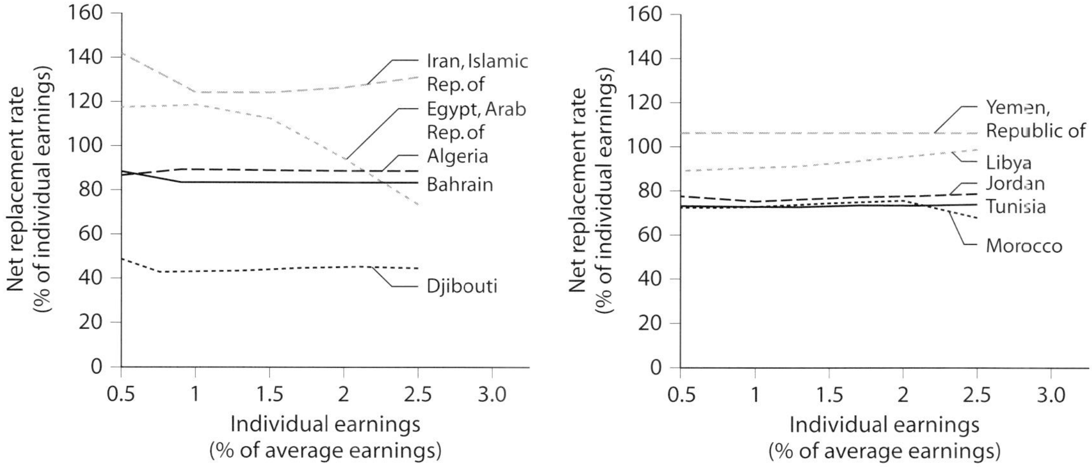

Source: Authors' calculations.

Figure 3.5 Gross and Net Replacement Rates as a Percentage of Average Earnings in Schemes for Civil Servants in Select Middle East and North African Countries

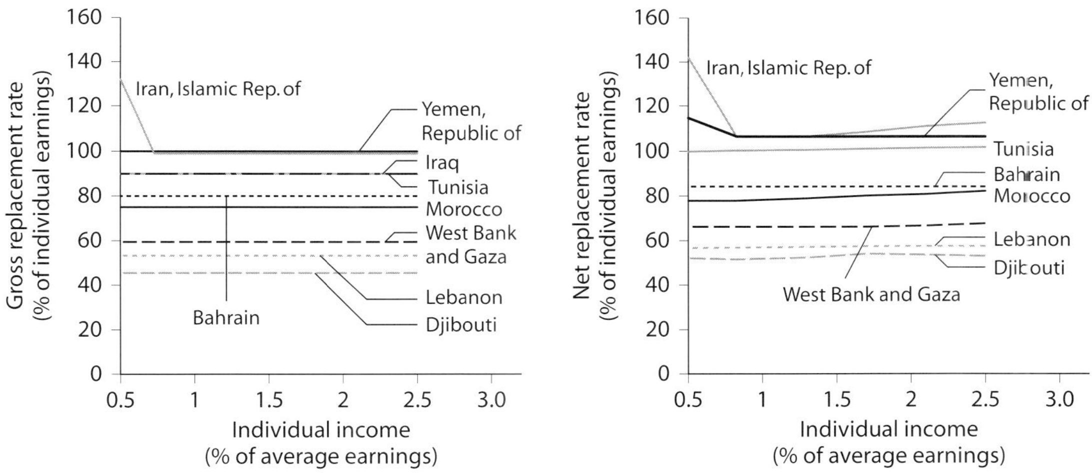

Source: Authors' calculations.

Republic of Yemen, which offers replacement rates for full-career workers of 100 percent or higher. Bahrain, Iraq, Morocco, and Tunisia target replacement rates for full-career workers in the 75–90 percent range. A third group includes Djibouti, Lebanon, and the West Bank and Gaza, with targeted replacement rates for the average full-career worker below 60 percent (see figure 3.5). In Lebanon the lower replacement rate reflects a shorter career, since workers can retire after 20 years of contributions without restrictions on the age. As in the scheme for private sector workers, net replacement rates are higher in all cases.

None of the schemes imposes a ceiling on the covered wage, and only the Islamic Republic of Iran guarantees a minimum pension that affects workers with earnings equal to or above 50 percent of the average. Out of the nine specialized schemes for civil servants, five offer basic pension guarantees: Bahrain, Djibouti, the Islamic Republic of Iran, Morocco, and Tunisia. The value of these guarantees expressed as a share of average earnings is 12.6, 21.3, 66.0, 18.0, and 31.8 percent, respectively. In Bahrain and Morocco only workers with earnings equal to or below 15 and 25 percent of the average, respectively, benefit from the basic pension. Tunisia has a more generous scheme that benefits workers with incomes equal to or below 48 percent of average earnings.

In general, schemes for civil servants target higher levels of income replacement than schemes for private sector workers; income replacement rates are flat. Only in the Islamic Republic of Iran is the gross replacement rate for the average full-career worker lower for civil servants than for private sector workers. In Bahrain, it is the same; in Morocco and the Republic of Yemen, it is 10 percent higher for civil servants; in Djibouti, it is 20 percent higher; and in Tunisia, it is 40 percent higher (see table 3.2).

An important measure of the relative generosity of a pension system is pension wealth. Pension wealth, which is also discussed in the next subsection, refers to the net present value of future pension benefits. Contrary to replacement rates, this indicator takes into account differences in life expectancy and in the age at which people become entitled to the pension. The indicator is also expressed as a proportion of

TABLE 3.2

Replacement Rate and Pension Wealth in Public and Private Pension Schemes in Select Middle East and North African Countries

	Gross replacement rate			Gross pension wealth		
Country	Civil servants	Private	Ratio of public to private	Civil servants	Private	Ratio of public to private
Bahrain	80.0	79.0	1.0	13.7	14.5	0.9
Djibouti	45.5	37.0	1.2	7.9	7.4	1.1
Iran, Islamic Rep. of	99.0	115.5	0.9	21.9	20.9	1.0
Morocco	75.0	70.0	1.1	15.1	10.3	1.5
Tunisia	90.0	64.0	1.4	16.1	18.0	0.9
Yemen, Republic of	100.0	90.0	1.1	16.7	13.4	1.2
Average	75.2	76.1	1.03	14.6	13.8	1.1

Source: Authors' calculations.

Note: Calculations are for average full-career workers. The individual is assumed to join at age 20 and retire at age 60. The discount rate of the calculation of the pension wealth is set at 3.5 percent per year. The numbers were generated based on existing legal provisions in each country.

Figure 3.6 Gross Pension Wealth as a Multiple of Average Earnings in Schemes for Civil Servants in Select Middle East and North African Countries

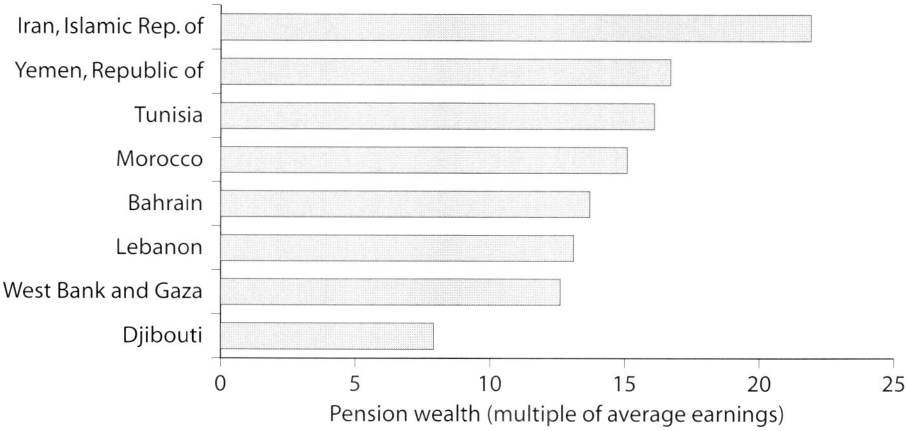

Source: Authors' calculations.
Note: Calculations are based on country-specific mortality rates. The discount rate is set at 3.5 percent a year.

individual earnings. For instance, in the scheme for civil servants in the Islamic Republic of Iran, pension wealth is equivalent to more than 20 times the preretirement income of the average full-career worker. Pension wealth in the case of the schemes for civil servants is, in general, 10–50 percent higher than in the schemes for private sector workers. The exceptions are Bahrain, the Islamic Republic of Iran, and Tunisia (table 3.2 and figure 3.6).

International Comparisons of Income Replacement Targets for National Schemes

Just as it is useful to compare the countries of the Middle East and North Africa with one another, so there are valuable lessons to be learned from comparing them with countries in other regions of the world. Consistent simulations of pension entitlements have now been carried out for the 30 member countries of the OECD, 13 countries in Eastern Europe and Central Asia, and 9 countries in Latin America and the Caribbean (see Whitehouse 2004).

These countries have more diverse pension systems than the countries of Middle East and North Africa, including:

- *Resource-tested schemes*, where the pension benefit is targeted on lower-income retirees. These can be pension-income tested (depending on pension income only), income tested (depending on pension, capital, and employment income), or means tested (depending on broad income and assets).

- *Basic schemes*, where the pension is a flat rate amount per year of contributions or residency.
- *Earnings-related schemes*, where the pension depends on past earnings. Different countries have adopted different variants, including the traditional defined-benefit model (which is the standard in Middle East and North African countries), notional accounts, or points systems.
- *Defined-contribution schemes*, where the pension depends on the value of contributions made, the investment returns earned, and the rate at which accumulated capital is converted into a retirement-income stream.

Furthermore, there is greater variability in the institutional structure of pension provision in these other countries. First, some OECD countries and many countries in Eastern Europe and Central Asia as well as in Latin America and the Caribbean have mandatory provision of private pensions. In Eastern Europe, Central Asia, and Latin America and the Caribbean, these are mainly defined-contribution plans operated by financial service companies. In OECD countries, there is often mandatory coverage by employer-based or industrywide occupational pension plans, which can be either defined-contribution or defined-benefit schemes. Furthermore, some OECD countries have occupational plans based on collective agreements between employees and employers. Since these cover 90 percent or more of the labor force, they are best thought of as quasi-mandatory. The calculations that follow are comprehensive in that they include all of these different types of mandatory and quasi-mandatory schemes.

In general, the mandates of pension systems regarding income replacement are more onerous in the Middle East and North Africa than in other regions. Figure 3.7 looks at the gross replacement rate that the average full-career worker can expect in the future under today's pension rules in Middle East and North African countries and a select group of countries in other regions of the world. Most readily apparent is the vast range of the results. The targeted replacement rate in Ireland is close to 30 percent, while the average full-career worker in the Islamic Republic of Iran receives a replacement rate of 116 percent. Clearly, Middle East and North African countries stand out, with 10 of the 11 countries that have schemes for private sector workers targeting gross replacement rates for full-career workers above the average in the sample. The highest replacement rates in the world are observed in three countries: the Islamic Republic of Iran, Iraq, and the Republic of Yemen. Comparing all countries for which calculations are available in the four regions, the average replacement rate is 77.9 percent in the Middle East and North Africa, compared with 56.4 percent in the OECD countries and in

Figure 3.7 Gross Replacement Rate as a Percentage of Average Earnings in Select Countries around the World

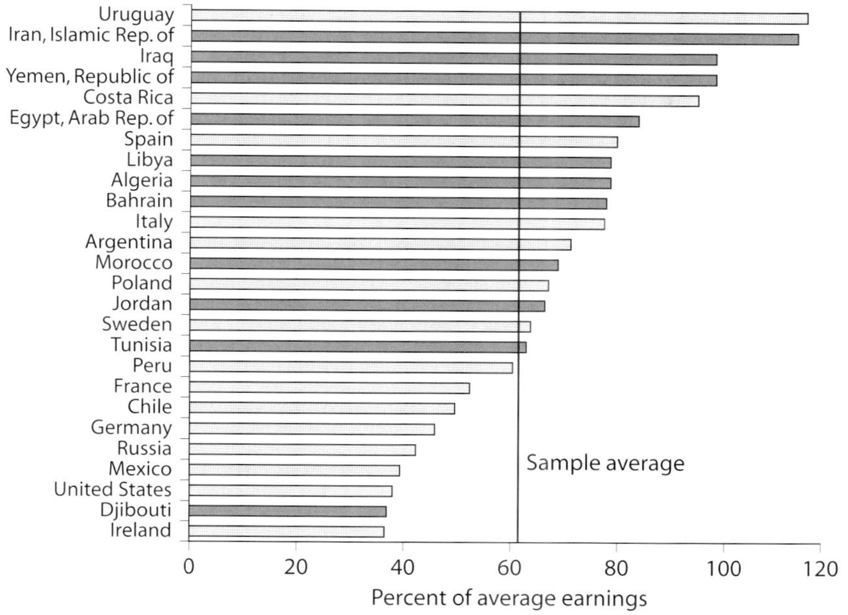

Sources: For Middle East and North African countries, authors' calculations; for other countries, Whitehouse 2004.

Note: The average of 61 percent was calculated based on a sample of 50 countries in 4 regions: OECD (23 countries); Europe and Central Asia (7); Latin America and the Caribbean (9); and the Middle East and North Africa (11).

Eastern Europe and Central Asia and 57.2 percent in Latin America and the Caribbean. The relative pension value at average earnings is thus 38.1 percent higher in the Middle East and North Africa than in the OECD countries and Eastern Europe and Central Asia and 36 percent higher than in Latin America and the Caribbean (see figure 3.7).

Targets for the basic pension guarantee in the Middle East and North Africa also tend to be above those observed in the other regions. For the countries considered in the sample, minimum pensions vary widely, between 14 and 66 percent of average earnings, with an average of 30 percent. Among the schemes for private sector workers in the Middle East and North Africa, only the Republic of Yemen does not guarantee a minimum pension. Seven of the remaining 10 countries target a minimum pension above or very close to 30 percent of average earnings (see figure 3.8). Only in Djibouti, Iraq, and Morocco is the minimum pension below or close to 20 percent of average earnings. The Islamic Republic of Iran guarantees the highest minimum pension, representing 66 percent of the average wage or 100 percent of the minimum wage.

Only four countries in the Middle East and North Africa implement ceilings on the covered wage. Two have very high ceilings; the other two

Figure 3.8 Minimum Pension Guarantee as a Percentage of Average Earnings in Select Countries around the World

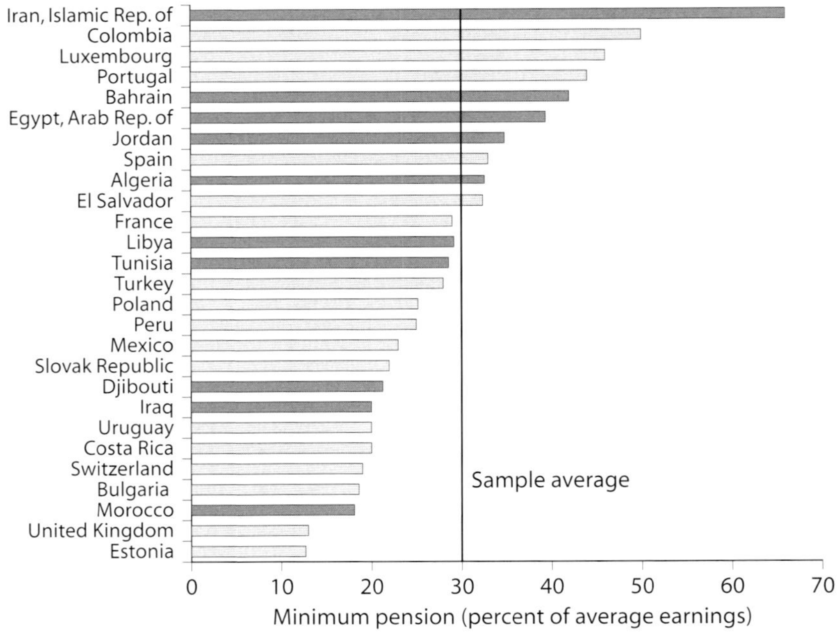

Sources: For Middle East and North African countries, authors' calculations; for other countries, Whitehouse 2004.

Note: The average of 29.4 percent was calculated based on a sample of 27 countries in 4 regions: OECD (8 countries); Europe and Central Asia (3); Latin America and the Caribbean (6); and the Middle East and North Africa (10).

have ceilings equal to or below the average in the sample. In this sample, ceilings range between 1.5 times the average wage (Sweden) and 10 times the average wage (Colombia). A majority of countries have ceilings below 3 times the average wage, but the average is closer to 3.5 times (see figure 3.9). Out of the four pension schemes for private sector workers in the Middle East and North Africa, Algeria and the Islamic Republic of Iran implement very high ceilings relative to the world average (six and eight times the average wage, respectively). The ceiling in Egypt is closer to the sample average, while the ceiling in Morocco represents only half of the sample average.

The pension systems in Middle East and North African countries offer the highest level of pension wealth. In the sample of countries analyzed, the six countries with the highest level of pension wealth are from the region: Algeria, Egypt, the Islamic Republic of Iran, Jordan, Tunisia, and the Republic of Yemen (see figure 3.10). In these countries, pension wealth surpasses 15 times the average wage, relative to a sample average of 11 times the average wage. Libya and Morocco have levels of pension wealth in line with the sample average. Only Djibouti has pension wealth significantly lower than the sample average. Average pension wealth for the Middle East and North African countries is 14 times average earnings,

Figure 3.9 Ceiling on the Covered Wage as a Multiple of Average Earnings in Select Countries around the World

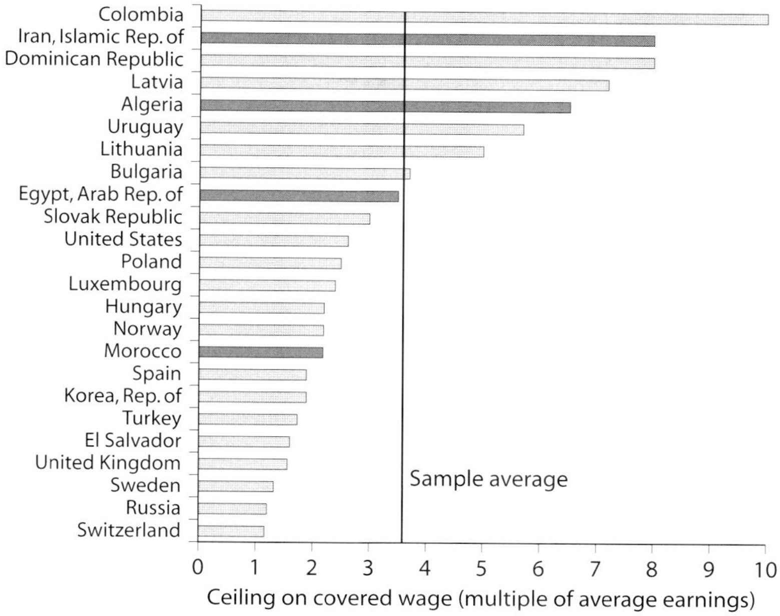

Sources: For Middle East and North African countries, authors' calculations; for other countries, Whitehouse 2004.
Note: The average of 3.58 was calculated based on a sample of 25 countries in 4 regions: OECD (11 countries); Europe and Central Asia (6); Latin America and the Caribbean (4); and the Middle East and North Africa (4).

Figure 3.10 Gross Pension Wealth as a Multiple of Average Earnings in Select Countries around the World

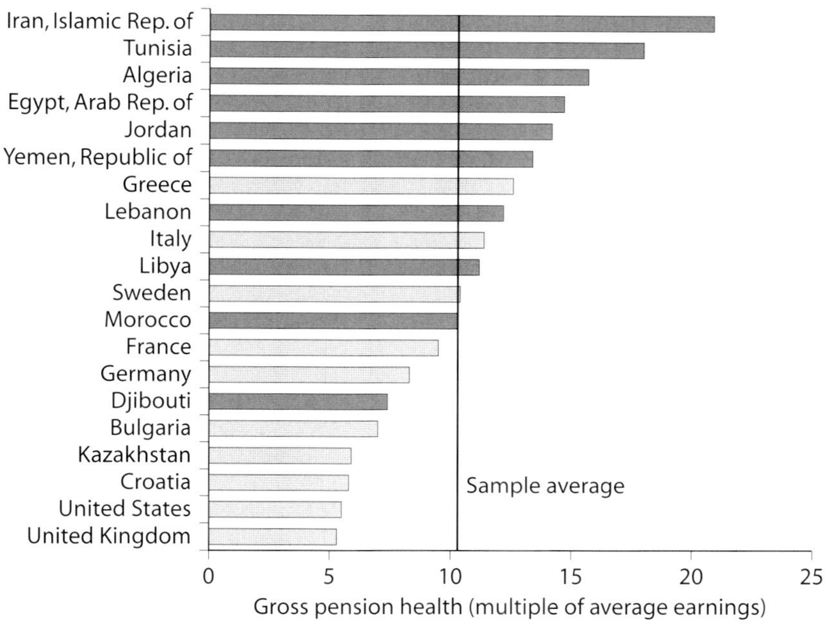

Source: Authors' calculations.
Note: Calculations are based on country-specific mortality rates and assume a 3.5 percent discount rate. The average of 10.3 was calculated based on a sample of 43 countries in 3 regions: OECD (23 countries); Europe and Central Asia (8); and the Middle East and North Africa (12).

compared with 9 times average earnings in 30 high-income OECD countries (most not shown on the chart), 8.5 times in the nine Latin America and the Caribbean countries, and zero times in the 13 Eastern Europe and Central Asia countries for which information is available. Thus pension wealth for workers with average earnings is 54 percent higher in the Middle East and North Africa than in OECD countries. The gap is 72 percent with Eastern Europe and Central Asia countries and 64 percent with Latin America and the Caribbean countries.

It is also important to consider the pension entitlements of workers at different earnings levels. These are summarized across the regions in tables 3.3 and 3.4. The first looks at gross replacement rates for workers with average earnings and those with low (half the average) and high (double the average) earnings. At all levels of income, average gross replacement rates in the Middle East and North Africa are higher than in other regions of the world. The difference is more important among average- and high-income individuals. As seen before, for workers with average earnings, pension values are around 38 percent higher in the Middle East and North Africa than in other regions. Among high-income individuals, pension values are between 50 and 63 percent higher. However, among low-income workers, pension values are only

TABLE 3.3

Gross Replacement Rate around the World, by Level of Earnings and Region

Percent of individual earnings

Level of earnings and region	Mean	Minimum	Maximum
Average earnings			
Middle East and North Africa	77.9	37.5	115.5
OECD	56.4	30.6	101.9
Eastern Europe and Central Asia	56.4	38.4	87.2
Latin America and the Caribbean	57.2	36.0	102.6
Low earnings			
Middle East and North Africa	81.3	42.5	132.0
OECD	74.6	47.3	115.5
Eastern Europe and Central Asia	63.7	47.3	96.2
Latin America and the Caribbean	77.7	39.1	105.3
High earnings			
Middle East and North Africa	75.7	37.5	115.5
OECD	46.4	15.3	95.2
Eastern Europe and Central Asia	50.4	25.4	75.4
Latin America and the Caribbean	48.3	29.4	89.0

Source: Authors' calculations.
Note: Results based on 23 high-income countries in the OECD, 13 countries in Eastern Europe and Central Asia, 9 countries in Latin America, and 10 countries in the Middle East and North Africa. Low earnings are defined as half the average; high earnings are defined as double the average. These simulations are based on currents laws and regulations.

TABLE 3.4

Gross Pension Wealth around the World, by Level of Earnings and Region

Multiple of individual earnings

Level of earnings and region	Mean	Minimum	Maximum
Average earnings			
Middle East and North Africa	14.0	7.4	20.9
OECD	9.1	5.5	18.3
Eastern Europe and Central Asia	8.1	5.5	12.2
Latin America and the Caribbean	8.5	4.8	16.6
Low earnings			
Middle East and North Africa	7.3	4.2	12
OECD	6.0	3.5	10.3
Eastern Europe and Central Asia	4.6	3.4	6.1
Latin America and the Caribbean	5.7	3.2	8.3
High earnings			
Middle East and North Africa	27.3	14.8	41.8
OECD	14.8	5.4	34.1
Eastern Europe and Central Asia	14.5	6.6	24.4
Latin America and the Caribbean	14.3	8.5	28.8

Source: Authors' calculations.
Note: Results based on 23 high-income countries in the OECD, 13 countries in Eastern Europe and Central Asia, 9 countries in Latin America, and 10 countries in the Middle East and North Africa. Calculations are based on country-specific mortality rates. The real discount rate is set at 3.5 percent a year. These simulations are based on current laws and regulations.

5 percent higher relative to Latin America and the Caribbean, 9 percent higher relative to OECD countries, and 27 percent higher relative to Eastern Europe and Central Asia.

The overall pattern of replacement rates by level of earnings is therefore very different among regions. In OECD countries and in Latin America and the Caribbean, replacement rates decline significantly with income. In Eastern Europe and Central Asia and in the Middle East and North Africa, in contrast, replacement rates tend to be much closer across the earnings range. OECD and Latin American systems tend to be more redistributive, giving higher replacement rates to lower-income workers than to higher earners. In Eastern Europe and Central Asia and in the Middle East and North Africa, the systems are more strongly insurance based, aiming to give broadly similar replacement rates to workers with different levels of earnings.

The earlier eligibility age for full-career workers means that pension wealth is higher in the Middle East and North Africa than in the other regions. For workers with average earnings, pension wealth is 55–70 percent higher in the Middle East and North Africa. For workers with high earnings, pension wealth is twice as high. For workers with low earnings, pension wealth is only between 16 and 40 percent higher (table 3.4).

Incentives

The mechanisms used to compute and award pensions affect the behavior of individuals (for example, retirement, labor supply, and savings decisions), the type of redistribution that exists within the system, and ultimately the system's financial sustainability. This section assesses incentive problems by looking at patterns in the real implicit rate of return (IRR). Indeed, since the pension schemes receive contributions from plan members and eventually pay benefits, it is possible to compute the implicit return on these contributions. The goal is to compare the rate of return received by individuals who follow different strategies, for instance, regarding enrollment and retirement. It thus becomes possible to identify the types of strategies that are rewarded by the scheme and those that are penalized.

Because implicit rates of return ultimately are determined by the choice of benefit formulas and eligibility conditions, the analysis illuminates the main problems regarding these choices. In relation to benefit formulas, key parameters discussed in this section include (a) the measure of income used to compute the pension (for example, last salary, full-career average); (b) the accrual rate; (c) the existence of a maximum replacement rate or pension; and (d) the level of the minimum pension. In relation to eligibility conditions, the analysis focuses on (a) the contribution rate, (b) retirement ages, and (c) vesting periods. As previously mentioned, all the main parameters of the various pension schemes in the region are summarized in appendix C. The methodology used to compute IRR is presented in appendix F. The main findings follow.

Across countries and schemes, current benefit formulas and eligibility conditions provide incentives for retirement over work: the IRR is allowed to vary widely as a function of the retirement age, with those retiring early receiving higher rates of return. This is illustrated in figure 3.11 for Jordan and Morocco, but the pattern is observed in the majority of the other schemes as well.[9] In Jordan, the SSC will pay a 25-year-old male who joins the system today and retires at age 55 an implicit real rate of return on contributions of 6 percent a year. The same individual retiring at age 65 will receive a 3.5 percent rate of return on contributions. In Morocco, the Caisse Nationale de Sécurité Sociale (CNSS) will pay similar rates of return to these two hypothetical individuals.

The reason for this pattern in the majority of schemes is the lack of "actuarially fair" reductions in pensions for early retirement and "actuarially fair" compensations for delayed retirement.[10] Most of the schemes under review (the exception is the CASNOS in Algeria) allow individuals to retire before the "normal" age. Among the seven

Figure 3.11 Changes in the Internal Rate of Return as a Function of Retirement Age in the SSC in Jordan and the CNSS in Morocco

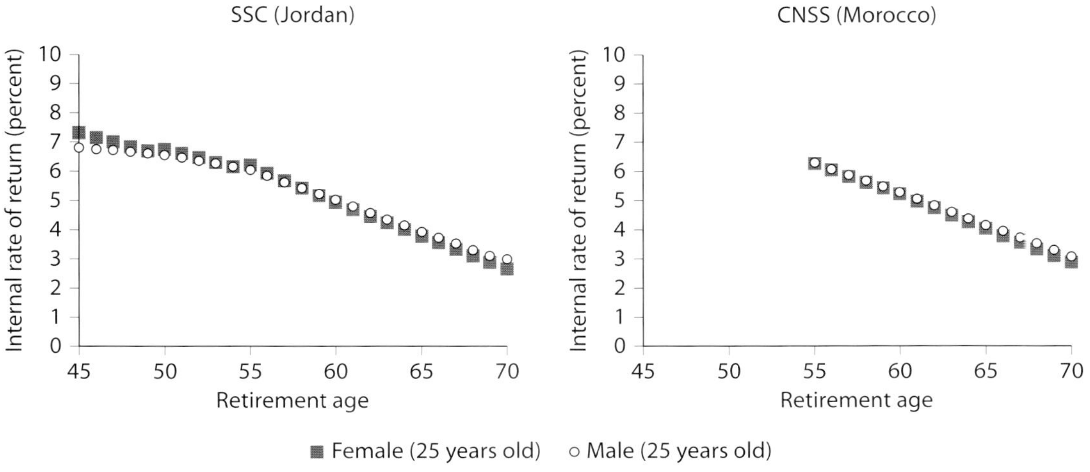

Source: Authors' calculations.
Note: Refers to both males and females age 25 when joining the system, earning the average wage, married, and retiring at various ages. Mortality tables are country and sex specific.

specialized schemes for public sector workers, four (Djibouti, the Islamic Republic of Iran, Tunisia, and the Republic of Yemen) do not impose any reductions. Among the schemes for private sector workers, the SSO in the Islamic Republic of Iran, the CNSS in Morocco and the RNS in Tunisia do not impose reductions either. All other schemes with early-retirement programs have reductions, but they are below actuarially fair levels. The exception is the RCAR in Morocco, where reductions are above actuarially fair levels. Regarding compensation for delayed retirement, again only the RCAR has a formal mechanism that encourages deferred retirement (that is, compensation is above actuarially fair levels).

Maximum replacement rates can also reduce the rates of return for those retiring late and thus discourage additional years of contributions. Indeed, once the maximum is reached, additional contributions do not bring additional benefits. These maximums are pervasive in the Middle East and North Africa, since most countries use them to reduce costs in the presence of high accrual rates. The RCAR in Morocco is again the only system without a maximum. In most countries and schemes, the maximum can be reached after 30–35 years of service. The Organisme de Protection Sociale (OPS) and the Caisse Nationale de Retraite (CNR) in Djibouti have the highest maximum replacement rates, reached only after 54 and 62 years of contributions, respectively.

The systems also provide incentives to strategically manipulate salaries because only a few count toward the pension.[11] With the exception of the RCAR in Morocco, none of the schemes uses a full-career average of salaries to compute the pension. In general, the schemes use the last salary or an average of three to five years. The OPS in Djibouti and the Régime des Salariés Non-Agricoles (RSNA) in Tunisia use the average of the last 10 years, the CNSS in Morocco uses the average of the last 8 years, while the CASNOS in Algeria uses the average of the best 10 years. Two possible explanations for why defined-benefit schemes deviate from the full-career average are high inflation rates and poorly developed information systems. Indeed, in the absence of appropriate revalorization for past salaries, high inflation rates would reduce the value of the pension. Without well-developed information systems, in contrast, it is impossible to track the wage history of workers. As discussed in chapter 2, however, inflation rates have been considerably reduced. Moreover, the movement to a full-career average does not have to take place overnight, thus giving information systems time to catch up gradually. In fact, in several of the countries, the necessary information systems are already in place.

The problem is that workers have an incentive to declare low wages early in their career and declare high wages late in their career. To mitigate this problem, Egypt, Jordan, and the Republic of Yemen have implemented restrictions in the calculation of the average that is used as reference for the pension. In Jordan, for instance, if the ratio between the last wage and the wage five years prior to retirement is higher than 1.6, the difference is subtracted from the average used to compute the pension. In the Republic of Yemen, the average of the last two years of salaries cannot be higher than 1.5 times the average of the last five years. These measures, however, are only partial solutions to the problem, since workers can still underdeclare wages that do not count toward the pension. Moreover, the measures can penalize workers facing legitimate wage increases at the end of their career.

All of the pension schemes reward individuals who evade or game the system. This phenomenon is illustrated in figure 3.12 for Bahrain and Egypt. In Bahrain, an individual who joins the system at age 25 will receive a 6 percent real IRR if he retires at age 60; if he delays enrollment by 10 years, his rate of return will be close to 8 percent a year. This same person will receive an IRR of 7 percent a year if he enrolls at age 25, contributes 5 years, leaves the system for 25 years, and returns to the system at age 55. This is again explained, in part, by the fact that only a few wages count toward the pension. Ceilings on replacement rates also contribute by reducing the IRR paid to workers who have long contribution periods. To avoid the ceiling, individuals might choose to delay enrollment.

Finally, current systems could also discourage individual savings by offering generous implicit rates of return on contributions. Theoretically, other things being equal, the higher the rate of return on mandatory

Figure 3.12 Internal Rate of Return and Enrollment and Evasion Strategies in the GOSI in Bahrain and in Egypt

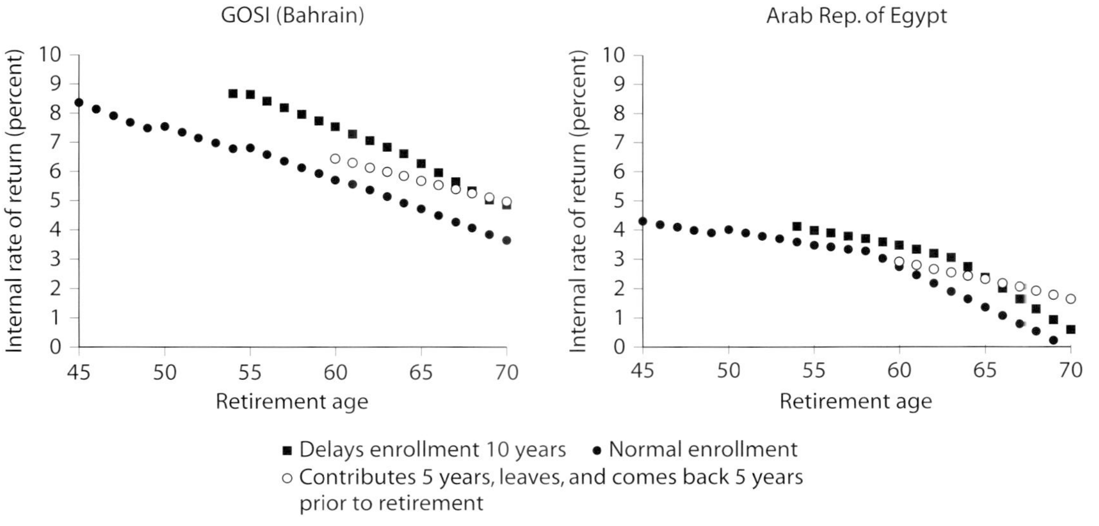

Source: Authors' calculations.
Note: Refers to males age 25 when joining the system, earning the average wage, married, and retiring at various ages. Mortality tables are sex and country specific.

contributions, the lower the incentive to save (see Lindeman and others 2003). If individuals expect to receive high pensions when they retire, they can be less motivated to save elsewhere. This would preclude the diversification of savings for retirement, which is desirable to mitigate financial risks, and the development of long-term savings schemes, which are known to contribute to financial sector development and economic growth (see chapter 4). By reducing individual savings, a high IRR could also reduce the aggregate level of savings in the economy. The literature on this issue, however, is mixed and no evidence is currently available in the case of Middle East and North African countries.

Equity within and across Genders

Implicit rates of return also indicate the type of redistribution that takes place within the pension system. In a pension system with no internal redistribution, all individuals of a given age cohort should receive the same rate of return, regardless of their gender or wage history. When some individuals receive higher rates of return than others, then redistribution is taking place. By looking at the IRR received by various groups of plan members, it is possible to assess the nature of the redistribution: Are middle- or high-income individuals benefiting more from the system than low-income individuals? Are men benefiting more than women?

Equity within Genders

In all the schemes in the region, redistribution occurs, but it is not transparent. One source of inequality within generations is also related to the fact that only a few wages count toward the pension. Manual workers have relatively flat earnings across their career. Managerial and especially professional workers tend to see their pay rise more rapidly over their lifetime (Whitehouse 2004). Basing pension values on final salary favors workers with steeply rising earnings. In Algeria, for instance, a 25-year-old man whose salary grows at 2 percent a year will receive a rate of return one to two percentage points lower than a colleague whose salary grows at 4 percent a year (see figure 3.13).

Minimum pensions can, to a degree, offset the adverse redistribution by increasing the rate of return of employees at the bottom of the income distribution. In Jordan, for example, a 25-year-old entrant with earnings of half the average, retiring at age 50, can expect an IRR above 8 percent a year due to the minimum pension. However, the same individual, but with a longer vesting period, would not benefit from the minimum pension. He could even receive a lower rate of return than a middle- or high-income worker with a short career who benefits from the minimum pension or who experiences a faster rise in salary (figure 3.13).

Figure 3.13 Internal Rate of Return and Wage History in the CNR in Algeria and the SSC in Jordan

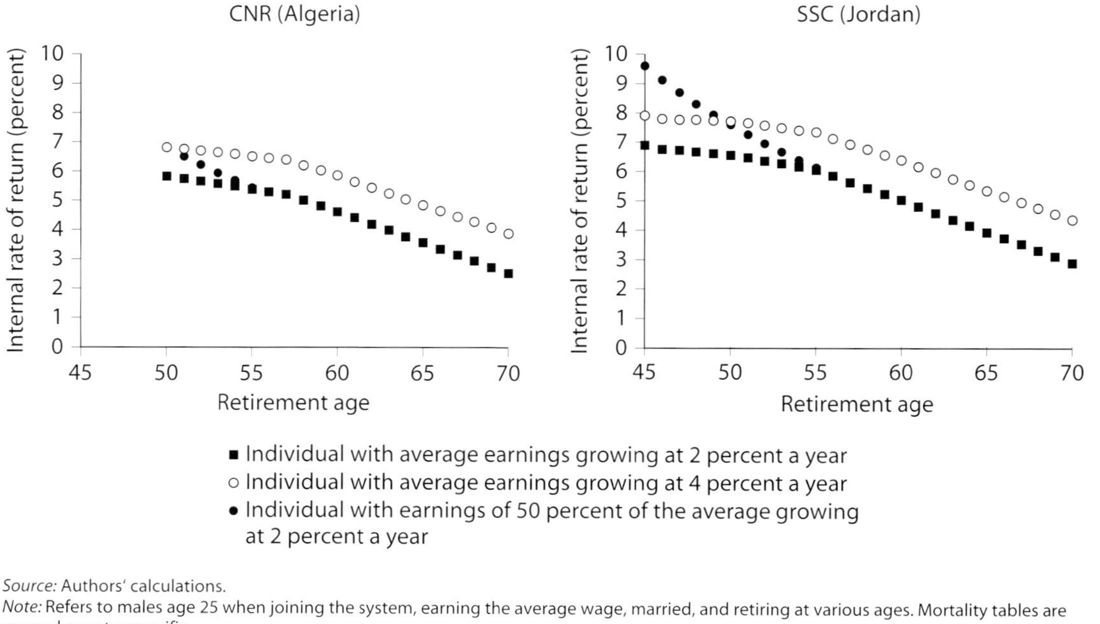

Source: Authors' calculations.
Note: Refers to males age 25 when joining the system, earning the average wage, married, and retiring at various ages. Mortality tables are sex and country specific.

Figure 3.14 Internal Rate of Return and Enrollment Age in the SSO in the Islamic Republic of Iran and the RSNA in Tunisia

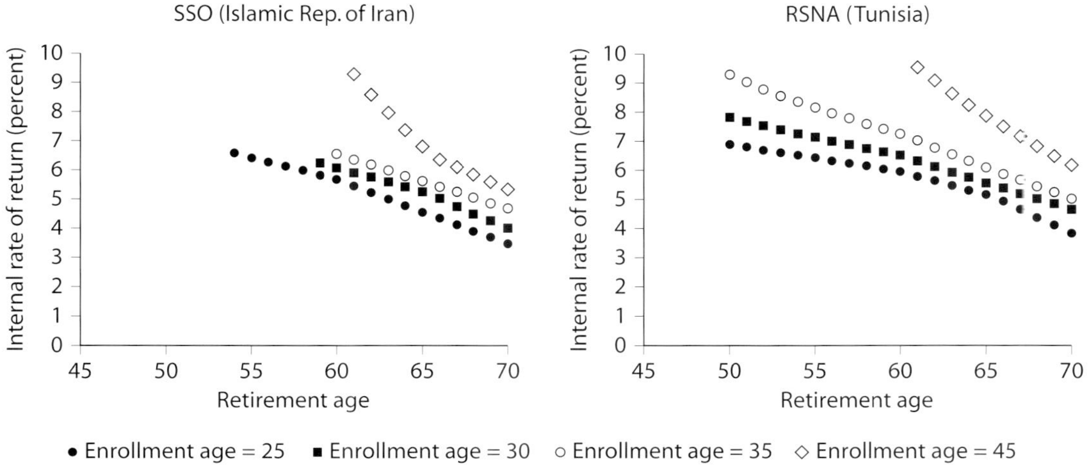

Source: Authors' calculations.
Note: Refers to males, earning the average wage, married, and retiring at various ages. Mortality tables are sex and country specific.

In all pension schemes, there are implicit transfers from young to old workers, regardless of the level of income, as the IRR is allowed to vary by the age of enrollment in the system. In the Islamic Republic of Iran, for instance, a 25-year-old male entrant who retires at age 60 will receive a 4 percent real rate of return on his contributions, a 30-year-old male entrant will receive 5.5 percent, and a 45-year-old male entrant will receive close to 6 percent (see figure 3.14). In Tunisia, the differences are even more striking. The 25-year-old male entrant retiring at age 60 will receive a 5.5 percent real rate of return, while the 35- and 45-year-old entrants will receive 7 and 9 percent, respectively.

There are various reasons for this pattern. First, when the accrual rate is too high relative to contributions, for a given retirement age, older individuals with shorter vesting periods benefit from a higher IRR.[12] Second, when accrual rates are not constant over the contributory period, (meaning that they are higher for the first few years of contributions) older workers usually receive higher replacement rates for the same vesting period and thus a higher IRR. This type of accrual rate is used in Morocco's CNSS and in all Tunisian pension funds. Third, the ceilings on the replacement rates tend to penalize young workers with a longer career. Minimum pensions can also increase the IRR of older workers with a shorter vesting period, regardless of their level of income. Minimum vesting periods have been introduced to mitigate these problems, but at the risk of reducing incentives for enrollment among older workers. In Djibouti, for instance, where the vesting period is set at

25 years, workers who enroll in the system after age 40 can receive negative implicit rates of return on their contributions. These vesting periods basically imply a "moving" retirement age. Workers who enroll in the system late in their life face considerably higher retirement ages (see the discussion in chapter 4).

A final source of adverse redistribution, and probably the most severe, is related to the current accumulation of unfunded pension liabilities. As discussed in the last section of this chapter, all pension schemes in the region are accumulating large pension debts. These can be seen as "bonds" that the government is issuing to cover the pensions of a modest share of the labor force: a segment of relatively well-off individuals employed in the formal sector. Future generations of workers, including those at the bottom of the income distribution, will have to repay these bonds.

Gender Equity

The issue of gender equity in pension systems has been described as "controversial and unsettled" (Steinhilber 2002; see also ILO 2000). This report argues that gender inequality can be assessed by looking at two indicators: the relative pension wealth of men and women and the relative implicit rates of return that the pension system pays on contributions. This approach then abstracts from gender inequalities that emerge outside the pension system, in particular, in the labor market.

An important finding is that, in most countries, pension wealth is higher for women than for men, even when replacement rates and eligibility ages are the same.[13] Here pension wealth is computed at the earliest possible retirement age, assuming that the individual enrolls at age 20 and is an average, full-career worker. Across the countries, average pension wealth is 22 percent higher for women than for men (see table 3.5). This is because retirement rules tend to be more flexible for women and because women live longer, on average, than men. Across these countries, at age 50, for example, women can expect to live 34.1 more years, on average, and men can expect to live an additional 26.5 years, a difference of 7.6 years. This gap between male and female life expectancy is largest in Bahrain (9.2 years) and the Republic of Yemen (8.6 years). It is smallest in Djibouti (5.2 years).

The calculations of implicit rates of return for men and women confirm these results: the IRR is higher for women than for men in all of the schemes analyzed (see table 3.5).[14] Clearly, when the pension of a surviving spouse is included in the calculations, the difference between the IRR paid to women and the IRR paid to men is reduced. This is, first, because men tend to die before their wives and, second, because women who outlive their husbands tend to do so for a longer period than men

TABLE 3.5

Earliest Eligibility Age and Pension Wealth for Full-Career Workers, by Gender, in Schemes for Private Sector Workers in Select Middle East and North African Countries

	Earliest eligibility age		Pension wealth (proportion earnings)		Difference in Implicit rates of return between women and men by retirement age (%)		
Country	Men	Women	Men	Women	Age 45	Age 55	Age 60
Algeria	50	45	13.9	15.2	6.30	0.35	0.17
Bahrain	40	35	11.8	14.3	0.23	0.54	0.41
Djibouti	50	50	7.4	8.7	—	0.14	0.06
Egypt, Arab Rep. of	40	40	7.3	8.7	0.18	0.26	0.30
Iran, Islamic Rep. of	50	40	20.4	24.7	8.08	0.13	0.15
Jordan	45	35	12.1	15.4	0.57	0.40	0.23
Libya	62	60	13.1	15.5	—	0.25	5.76
Morocco	55	55	10.3	13.5	—	—	0.29
Tunisia	50	50	18.0	22.7	0.09	0.22	0.24
Yemen, Republic of	50	45	15.5	18.7	—	0.15	0.16

Source: Authors' calculations of replacement rates and pension wealth.
Note: Assumes that individuals enroll at age 20; — = not applicable.

who outlive their wives. Moreover, in some schemes, women can only pass their pension to the surviving husband if he is unable to work due to disability and if he is not receiving a pension of his own. This reduces the proportion of women who can pass on a survivor pension. From the point of view of the system, on average, a male plan member is more expensive than a female plan member.

In summary, four components of benefit formulas and eligibility conditions explain most of the relative variation in IRR between women and men: the retirement age, the vesting period, the rules for early retirement, and the rules regarding the survivor pension. They are discussed below.

In all the schemes reviewed, except Morocco's Caisse Marocaine de Retraite (CMR) and the Islamic Republic of Iran's SSO, the rules for transferring survivor rights to children are the same for men and for women. However, under the assumption that men are the principal breadwinners, the rules for receiving a survivor pension are more flexible for women than for men. In Djibouti's civil service scheme, for instance, surviving husbands are not entitled to a pension. In Bahrain, Egypt, and the Republic of Yemen, husbands can only receive the survivor pension if they are unable to work. Women also lose their survivor pension if they work, but they can choose not to. In all cases, survivor benefits cannot be combined with a regular old-age pension. In Jordan, surviving husbands also have the right to their wife's pension if they are unable to work, but, if ineligible, their share of the pension is transferred to the children. In Morocco's CMR, the survivor benefit for children is halved if the father is alive, but not if the mother is the survivor. In the Islamic Republic of Iran's SSO, children cannot receive a survivor pension from their mother if the father is alive. In the other schemes in Algeria, Djibouti, the Islamic Republic of Iran, Morocco, and Tunisia, the rules for survivor pensions are the same for men and for women.

Standard eligibility ages and vesting periods are either equal for men and women or favorable to women. In the majority of schemes, the normal retirement age is 60 for men. The exceptions are in Algeria's CASNOS and Tunisia's RNS, where the normal retirement age is 65 for men, and in Djibouti's OPS and CNR, where it is 55. In the first two schemes, the normal retirement age is 60 for women; in Djibouti, it is 55, the same as for men. In 7 of the 19 remaining mandatory schemes for public and private sector workers—Algeria's CNR, Iraq's Social Security and Welfare (SSW) and the scheme for civil servants, Bahrain's General Organisation for Social Insurance (GOSI), the Islamic Republic of Iran's SSO, Jordan's SSC, and both of the Republic of Yemen's pension funds—the normal retirement age is 55 for women. In the others, it is 60. There is more variation in vesting periods, which range between zero and 40 years. In the majority of cases, the statutory vesting period is the same for men and for women. The three exceptions are Algeria's CNR, Bahrain's GOSI, and the scheme for civil servants in the Republic of Yemen, where women have shorter vesting periods.

Early-retirement rules tend to be more generous for women than for men. In the CNR in Algeria, women can apply for early retirement at age 45 with 14 years of contributions, compared with age 50 and 20 years of contributions for men. The adjustments to benefits are the same. In the Civil Servant Retirement Organisation (CSRO) in the Islamic Republic of Iran, women can retire with no minimum age after 20 years of contributions, while men need 30 years. In the Islamic Republic of Iran's SSO, women can retire at age 42 with 20 years of service, while men need to be 50 years of age and have 30 years of contributions. Jordan has the most generous retirement rules for women: they can apply for early retirement at any age with 15 years of contributions, while men need to be at least 45 years of age and have 18 years of contributions. Moreover, early-retirement reductions are half of those that apply to men. In Morocco's CMR, women can apply for early retirement at any age with 15 years of service, while men need to contribute 21 years. In Bahrain's GOSI, women can retire at any age with 15 years and men with 20 years of contributions. In the West Bank and Gaza, the same treatment is given to men and women.

An important gender issue is the pension treatment in cases of divorce. All systems entitle a woman to a survivor pension only if she is married at the time of the husband's death. The exception is Egypt, where divorced women are entitled to a survivor pension if they did not initiate the divorce. Although divorced women have rights over the pension of their father in all schemes, they remain vulnerable to poverty during old age.

The conclusion from this analysis is that pension laws across the region have attempted to provide women with more flexibility in their retirement decisions and more security in their survivor benefits, driven by the assumption that men are the principal breadwinners. However, this special treatment also makes women more vulnerable to pension reform. If the systems are to be balanced, pension benefits for women need to be adjusted downward as a function of the retirement age (see chapter 4). This might induce, women to defer retirement in exchange for a higher pension, choosing to have less time for leisure and family and receiving a lower IRR. At the extreme, in the case of a defined-benefit, pay-as-you-go system, where all members receive the same implicit rate of return on contributions, regardless of gender, at a given retirement age, the replacement rate ought to be lower for women than for men, simply because women live longer. Thus policy makers need to devise mechanisms to mitigate the impact of pension reform on women. Some alternatives are discussed in chapter 4.

Pension Costs, Financial Sustainability, and Fiscal Implications

Pay-as-you-go systems are, in essence, contracts issued by the government that promise to pay pensions in the future in exchange for contributions in the present. Hence, governments are receiving money today and creating an unfunded obligation in the future, which is a financial operation very similar to issuing regular debt.[15] If the implicit interest rate paid on this debt is too high, the pension system will run into trouble eventually.

It can be shown that the sustainable implicit rate of return on contributions that a pay-as-you-go system can pay on contributions is a complex function of the growth rate of the covered wage bill. Over the long run, a good proxy for this sustainable rate is the growth rate of the economy.[16] In general, simulations for several countries in the region show that real implicit rates of return on contributions above 3 percent a year are unlikely to be sustainable. The essence of the financial problem across pension systems in Middle East and North African countries is that implicit rates of return on contributions are too high.

Therefore, all pension systems in the region are financially unsustainable, even in the absence of a future aging of the population. In the

Figure 3.15 Real Implicit Rate of Return for a Representative Plan Member in Select Middle East and North African Countries, by Fund

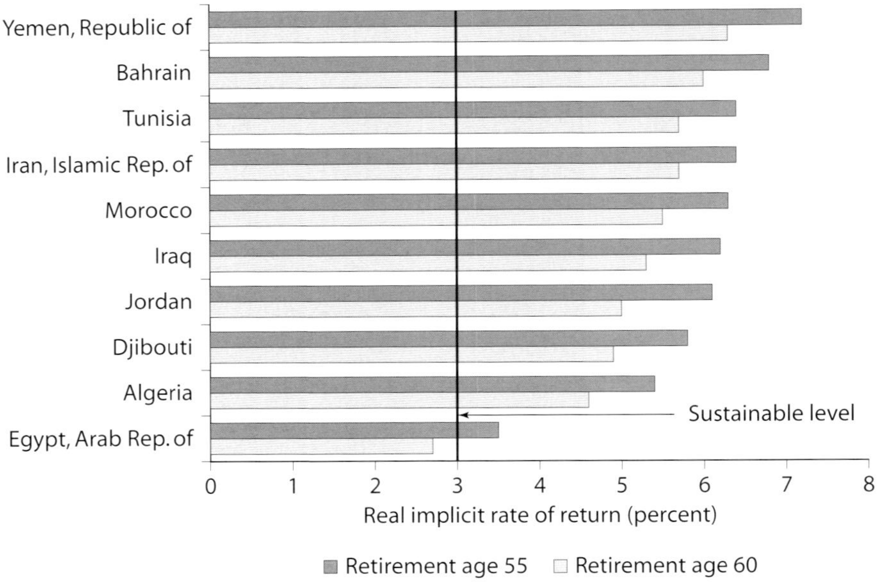

Source: Authors' calculations.
Note: Calculations are for an individual male entering the system at age 25 and retiring at age 55 or 60. At lower retirement ages, IRR would be higher.

large majority of cases, pension systems are paying real rates of return well above 5 percent a year.[17] This can be seen in figure 3.15, which graphs the IRR for a male who enters the system at age 25, is married, earns the average wage during his whole career, and retires at age 55 or 60 with a pension indexed to inflation. Rates of return vary from more than 7 percent a year to zero. The most generous schemes are in Bahrain and the Republic of Yemen. The least generous schemes are in Egypt, given a high contribution rate (25 percent), and Djibouti, after the recent parametric reform. However, one needs to be careful with the comparisons since the classification depends on who is chosen as the representative plan member (for example, men or women); as well as the retirement age. For instance, in Jordan and Bahrain, rates of return at age 45 can be above 8 percent (real) per year (see figures 3.12 and 3.13).

Schemes for civil servants and the military are particularly vulnerable to financial instability. Public sector employment has declined relative to the labor force in the past two decades. These pension schemes are also more demographically mature than schemes for private sector workers, because they have had a smaller influx of new contributors to hold down the dependency ratio. They also are more mature in the sense that they typically predate programs for private sector workers and already have a higher proportion of retirees. If public sector employment continues to grow less rapidly than the workforce as a whole, the sustainable rate of return on these schemes will be below the rate of growth of the economy. Moreover, fiscal pressures often have resulted in slower growth of pay in the public sector than in the economy as a whole, which again reduces the sustainable rate of return.

High and unsustainable IRRs basically reflect the misalignment of accrual rates, retirement ages, and contribution rates. In a well-designed and financially self-sufficient pay-as-you-go scheme, the sustainable accrual rate is a precisely defined function of the retirement age and the contribution rate, given the survival probabilities at retirement and the expected sustainable IRR.[18] From an equilibrium situation, increases in life expectancy imply a lower accrual rate, a higher retirement age, or a higher contribution rate. Similarly, given survival probabilities and the contribution rate, the lower (higher) the retirement age, the lower (higher) the accrual rate. None of the pension schemes in the region, unfortunately, follows this approach in calculating accrual rates.

In the majority of countries surveyed, pension expenditures are already above expected levels given the current demographic structure (see figure 3.16).[19] In half of the sample, pension expenditures already have reached or surpassed 2.5 percent of GDP, and this excludes the military. This level of spending is close to the average expenditure of public health systems in the region. Countries such as Djibouti and the Republic of Yemen have relatively high expenditures, but coverage rates are below the average. Lebanon is an exception because it does not provide pensions to private sector workers. Expenditures on civil servant pensions represent 0.5 percent of GDP, while expected expenditures capture 1.2 percent of GDP.[20]

Figure 3.16 Pension Expenditures as a Percentage of GDP in Mandatory Schemes in Select Middle East and North African Countries

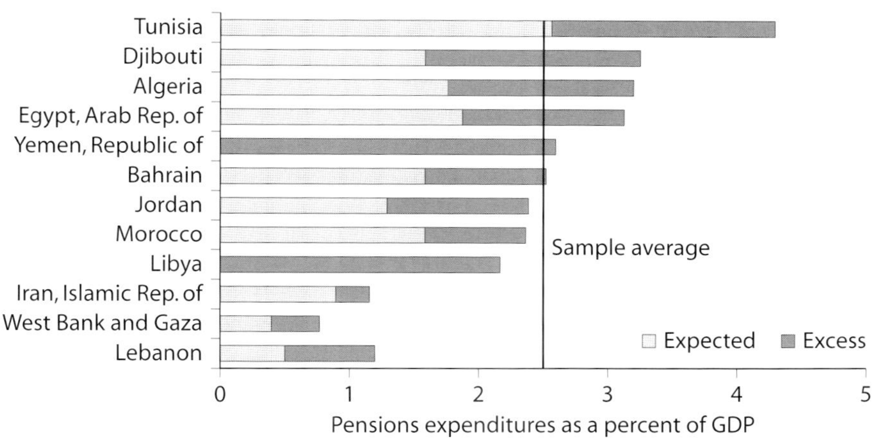

Source: Authors' calculations based on information provided by pension funds.

Note: Expected refers to predicted levels given the share of the elderly population (see endnote 19). Excess is the difference between assured and predicted expenditures. For Libya and the Republic of Yemen, there are no estimates of expected expenditures as a function of the share of the population age 65+ years. In all cases, pension expenditures include only old-age, disability, and survivor pensions.

Figure 3.17 Normalized Implicit Pension Debt in Select Countries around the World

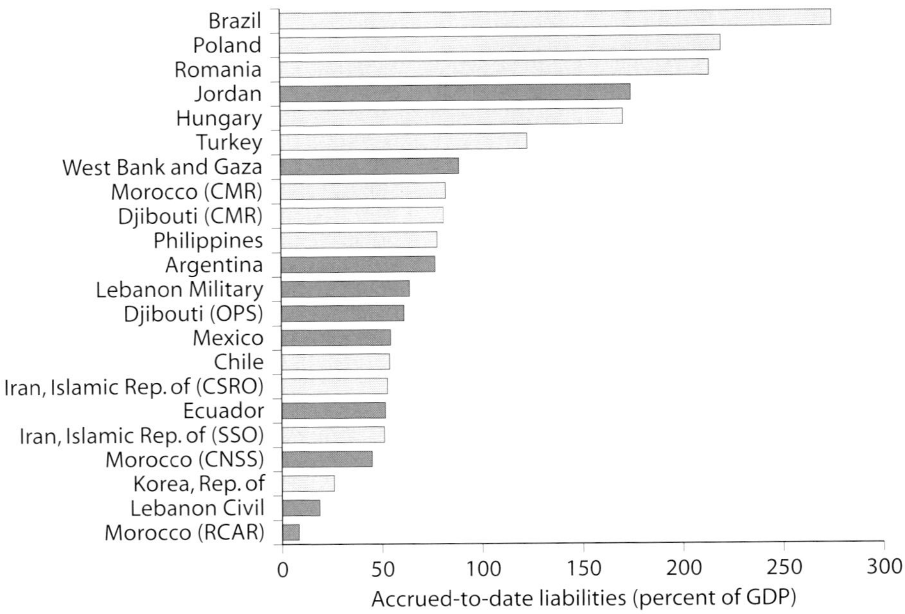

Sources: For Middle East and North African countries, see Robalino and Bogomolova forthcoming; for other countries, see Holzmann, Palacios, and Zviniene 2004.
Note: The implicit pension debt is defined as accrued-to-date liabilities (termination measure). It is the present value of pension promises to current retirees and the pension rights accrued to date of current contributors. Calculations assume that pensions are indexed with prices. The discount rate is set at 4 percent.

Most schemes are accumulating implicit pension debts that are not sustainable (see figure 3.17). Under conservative assumptions, normalized estimates of accrued-to-date pension liabilities range between 6 percent of GDP (RCAR in Morocco) and more than 170 percent (SSC in Jordan).[21] These liabilities refer to the present value of pension promises to current retirees and the pension rights accrued to date by current contributors. The measure can be interpreted as the total payments that the pension systems would need to make to plan members if they were liquidated today. For the majority of schemes in the Middle East and North Africa that have been analyzed, the implicit pension debt has already surpassed 50 percent of GDP. Aggregating across schemes for public and private sector workers, the implicit pension debt is 90 percent of GDP in the West Bank and Gaza, 96 percent in the Islamic Republic of Iran, 130 percent in Morocco, and 137 percent in Djibouti. Jordan has an implicit pension debt approaching 175 percent of GDP, among the highest in the world. These numbers represent more than two times the explicit public debt. Although no information is currently available for Algeria, Egypt, Iraq, Libya, and

Tunisia, it is expected that the implicit pension debt has reached a similar order of magnitude: 50–100 percent of GDP.[22]

Unfortunately, the value of the implicit pension debt is not included in standard fiscal accounts. This is a problem for at least three reasons.[23] The first reason, and perhaps the most important, is that this omission severely biases the analysis of the sustainability of the public debt and resulting policies regarding revenues and levels of spending. Basically, governments would be ignoring an important spending item, which compromises the credibility of fiscal and monetary policies. Indeed, with rising implicit pension debts, governments might face incentives to raise taxes sharply, default on public debt, or reduce the real value of this debt through higher inflation. Second, foreign investors are increasingly aware of these linkages, and this increases the country risk premiums, given uncertainties regarding the true level of the public debt, its future dynamics, and policy implications. In countries that are more integrated with the world economy, governments have less flexibility to adapt fiscal policy to domestic financing needs, which means that an uncontrolled accumulation of pension debt eventually would need to be financed through drastic cuts in benefits, which could severely disturb social stability and harm social cohesion. Finally, studies have shown that the implicit pension debt influences individual consumption and savings decisions. Ignoring this debt, therefore, also biases the policy analysis of interventions aiming to influence these decisions, such as the promotion of voluntary, private, long-term savings.

These large implicit pension debts also represent the source of a potentially large intergenerational transfer. Indeed, in the absence of any intervention, the implicit pension debt will have to be financed by future generations in the form of lower pension benefits, higher taxes, or a smaller government budget for other items (such as education and health).

Clearly, several schemes in the region have reserves, but these are usually small relative to the implicit pension debt and do little to improve financial sustainability.[24] Reserves range between 4.2 percent in Djibouti to more than 50 percent of GDP in Bahrain. At the regional level, reserves represent 14 percent of GDP, which is among the highest in the world. With the exception of the RCAR in Morocco, however, the pension funds are not managed as prefunded systems. Reserves are basically treated as a source of revenue of last resort—a buffer stock that, in a well-designed pay-as-you-go system, should be used to mitigate unexpected demographic and macroeconomic fluctuations. Moreover, across countries, there are important challenges to ensure that these reserves are managed in the best interests of plan members (see chapter 5).

The fact that the Middle East and North Africa remains a young region—the labor force is expected to continue growing at an average of 3.3 percent a year during the next decade—should not be a cause for complacency. First, it is not clear that, given the current unemployment problem, the expansion of the labor force will be accompanied by a similar expansion of the population employed in the formal sector of the economy, thus bringing higher revenues to the pension funds. Second, and more important, even if this were the case, higher revenues today also imply higher pension expenditures in the future. Because implicit rates of return on contributions are too high (that is, the pension systems are "borrowing" contributions at a rate that they cannot afford), new entrants worsen rather than improve the financial situation of the funds.

Even without changes in the demographic structure of the population, the pension systems sooner or later will run into trouble, and the future aging of the population will aggravate the problem. In most countries, old-age dependency ratios in the population are expected to start increasing around 2025. Old-age dependency ratios in the pension systems are already increasing rapidly, particularly in the schemes for civil servants. This will accelerate the financial crisis (see figure 3.18).

The projected dependency rates presented in figure 3.18 were conducted using PROST (Pension Reform Options Simulation Toolkit). PROST is a computer-based pension model developed by the Social Protection Unit of the World Bank. The model is designed to simulate

Figure 3.18 Projected Dependency Ratio in Private and Public Pension Schemes in Select Middle East and North African Countries, 2002–74

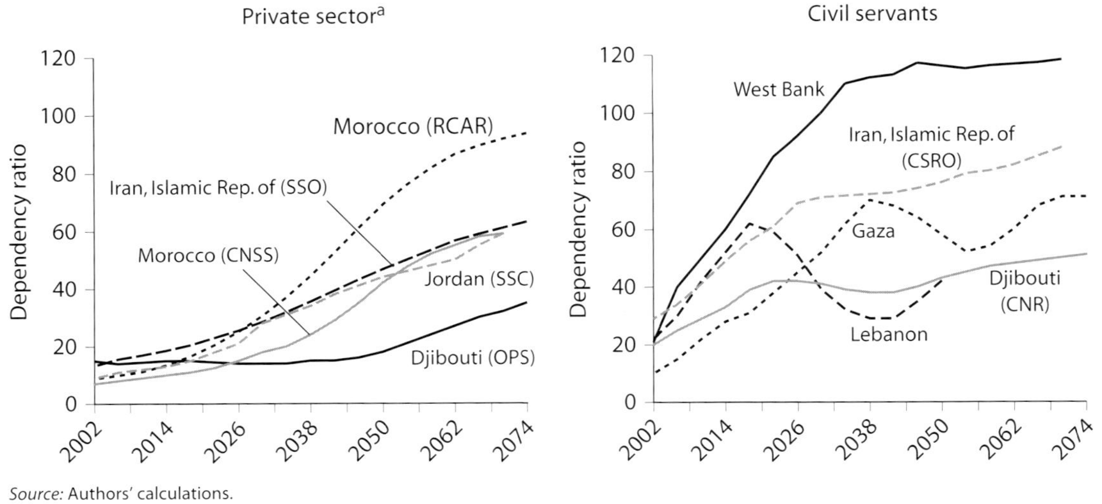

Source: Authors' calculations.
a. Or contractual workers for the public sector (RCAR).

the behavior of pension systems and to assess their financial sustainability under different sets of assumptions over a long time frame. It allows us to model different pension reform options—from "parametric" reforms of pay-as-you-go, defined-benefit schemes to systemic reforms, such as the introduction of fully funded, defined-contribution or notional defined-contribution schemes. The program can be adapted to a wide range of country circumstances and can handle simulations up to 100 years and more. PROST has been used in more than 80 countries to provide quantitative input for pension policy discussions. Key output from PROST was satisfactorily benchmarked against a number of countries where micro actuarial models were used.

For each age and gender cohort, PROST enforces consistency between the projected number of people retiring in this cohort and the cohort's contribution history (accrued pension rights). Thus the projected number of old-age pensioners later in the simulation period is influenced by the number of employees in earlier years. Length of service at retirement is based on actual data for each pension scheme and is assumed to remain the same over time.[25]

Across the pension systems analyzed, with a few exceptions, reserves are likely to be depleted within the next 10 to 20 years. In Bahrain, the reserves of both the Pension Fund Commission (which covers the military and civil servants, but only civil servants are included in the calculations) and the GOSI are likely to disappear around 2020–5. At that point in time, the government will need to intervene either to finance pension payments directly or to default on part of these. In the Islamic Republic of Iran, the CSRO is already in deficit. The SSO is likely to display a primary surplus within the next 20 years, but reserves will be depleted by 2030. In Jordan, expenditures are expected to surpass revenues around 2012–4. Reserves could be depleted as early as 2024. In Morocco, the CMR will be in deficit by 2008, running out of reserves around 2013. For the CNSS, the break-even point will be in 2010, and reserves could disappear by 2021. The RCAR, in contrast, is in a remarkably solid financial position. It has close to a 100 percent level of capitalization and is not expected to run out of reserves within the next 50 to 60 years. In Tunisia, the scheme for civil servants is already in deficit, and the RSNA will see expenditures surpass revenues in 2008. Reserves will be depleted in 2007 and 2014, respectively. Djibouti is the only country where the scheme for private sector workers is expected to remain in surplus for the next 40 years as a result of recent parametric reforms. The scheme for civil servants, however, is already in deficit and has no reserves.

Although 10–20 years might seem like a long time, the impacts of a reform program take time to bear fruit. Waiting to intervene can be costly. First, the implicit debt of the schemes will continue to grow, threatening the credibility of fiscal policy. Second, population aging will aggravate financial problems in the future, requiring more severe adjustments and possibly precluding a gradual approach to reform. Third, delaying reforms will imply putting the bulk of the adjustment costs on future generations. To the contrary, early interventions, when demographic conditions are still favorable, would allow for a more gradual and equitable adjustment.

The numbers reported also reflect the fiscal challenges that countries wanting to move to funded schemes will face. Chapter 2 shows that the fiscal situation in most countries is still frail. With accrued-to-date pension liabilities as a share of GDP in the 50–100 percent range, higher levels of funding can only be achieved gradually.

Conclusions

This chapter discusses issues concerning the institutional organization of pension systems in the region, the size and shape of their mandates, problems related to incentives, problems related to equity within and across genders, financial sustainability, and fiscal impacts. The main conclusions are summarized as follows.

- *Pension systems in the region are quite fragmented.* When transparent and efficient rules to transfer rights across funds are not in place, the mobility of the labor force is restricted, thus precluding an efficient allocation of resources. Fragmentation also increases administrative costs and is a source of inequities, as some segments of the labor force receive preferential treatment from the public pension system.
- *Coverage rates are modest, on average.* Differences in coverage across countries are explained mainly by the structure of the labor market and institutional arrangements for different categories of workers. There are no signs that coverage will expand substantially over the medium term. The implication is that a significant part of the labor force might not be accumulating the necessary savings for retirement.
- *In general, pension systems in the region have onerous mandates with regard to income replacement.* Gross and net replacement rates for full-career workers are high by international standards. While the patterns of income replacement vary widely across countries, in the majority of cases these are flat, reflecting the absence of ceilings on the covered wage or the use of high ceilings. Basic pension guarantees are also high relative to average earnings and can discourage work. The large mandates regarding income replacement are likely to be unaffordable. Moreover, these preclude the diversification of the sources of savings for retirement and therefore the efficient management of risks.

- *With few exceptions, benefit formulas and eligibility conditions distort incentives and make the system vulnerable to adverse distributional transfers.* Individuals are encouraged to manipulate wages, evade or game the system, and retire early. Indeed, rates of return on contributions respond to enrollment and retirement strategies as well as wage histories. Moreover, the systems discriminate as a function of age and gender and penalize blue-collar workers, who tend to have flat earnings during their career.

- *While the various pension laws have attempted to favor women by providing more flexible retirement options and facilitating access to survivor benefits, some also have discriminated against women by restricting the transfer of their pensions to dependents.* In general, women are more vulnerable than men to reform policies, such as the increase in or equalization of the retirement age and the rationalization of benefits.

- *The majority of pension systems in the region are financially unsustainable, reflecting high implicit rates of return on contributions.* High implicit rates of return on contributions result from a misalignment of retirement ages, benefits, and contribution rates. Hence, even with favorable demographics, the pension systems eventually will run into trouble.

- *Pension systems are accumulating large implicit pension debts that threaten the credibility of fiscal policy.* The level of this debt often surpasses 50 percent of current GDP and can be higher than the explicit public debt. These unfunded liabilities are the source of a major intergenerational transfer.

- *While several of the pension schemes, particularly those for private sector workers, still are running surpluses and reserves are unlikely to be depleted before the next decade, delaying action can be costly.* Implementing reforms over the short term will provide more flexibility in the design of reform options and allow for a more gradual adjustment of current systems.

Notes

1. The target populations of the various schemes, along with the parameters defining benefit formulas and eligibility conditions, are described in appendix C. Information on contributors, beneficiaries, revenues, and expenditures is presented in appendix F.
2. Except for special categories (for example, diplomats and parliamentarians).
3. Egypt also has a special scheme for workers in enterprises with more than 1,000 workers, but it is closed to new entrants.
4. See Colina, Lucas, and Tomasi (2002) for a rigorous empirical analysis of the determinants of coverage rates in Argentina, and Disney (2004).

5. This percentage is high relative to the average of median low-income countries, which is closer to 35 percent of the employed population.

6. Two other important assumptions driving the results of the simulations relate to the evolution of wages and pensions. All wages are assumed to grow 2 percent a year, in real terms (the model ignores inflation). Thus individual incomes relative to the average wage are constant in the simulation period. As far as pensions are concerned, while indexation policies are ad hoc in the majority of countries, for consistency and transparency in comparisons across countries, in the simulations it is assumed that all pensions are indexed to inflation. Thus they remain constant in real terms.

7. This refers to the current pension law in Iraq, although it ceased to be applied after the war. See Robalino, Sluchynskyy, and Bogomolova. (2005).

8. See appendix D for a description of the tax treatment of wages and pensions.

9. Calculations of IRR for other countries and behaviors are available on request from the authors.

10. See chapter 4 for a discussion of actuarially fair adjustments.

11. This issue is not only relevant in schemes for private sector workers. In schemes for civil servants, the government, which sponsors the plan, controls wage histories and enrollment strategies, but in some cases salaries are inflated on retirement or a final promotion is given with the intention of boosting a defined-benefit final-salary pension.

12. See appendix E for a demonstration of this result.

13. Pension wealth is the present value of pensions received while alive relative to the individual's earnings. Pension wealth is a better measure of equity than the replacement rate, which has been used in other studies (see James, Cox-Edwards, and Wong 2003).

14. These results include the value of the survivor benefit in the calculation of the internal rate of return accruing to the member. Other analysts have separated out the flow of benefits going to surviving widows and widowers and ascribed them to the relevant gender.

15. The parallel between government bonds and pay-as-you-go systems has its limits; in the latter, plan members do not enter into the agreement voluntarily, so there is no market to trade their acquired rights and less certainty regarding the stream of future benefits.

16. Over the long run, the growth rate of the wage bill is supposed to converge to the growth rate of the economy. Basically, the share of GDP that is allocated to the payment of wages remains constant.

17. It has been argued that the calculation of implicit rates of return in the schemes for the civil service (or the military) can be misleading. First, by design, some schemes are fully financed by the central budget, which implies an infinite implicit rate of return since there are no contributions. However, in the case of all of the pension schemes for the civil service and the military in the region, there is a legal definition of the contribution rates that need to be paid by the employee and the employer, as part of the remuneration package, to make the systems financially self-sustainable. The calculation of the implicit rate of return

in this case can indicate the magnitude of additional resources that the budget will be forced to transfer to finance the scheme.

18. This issue is discussed in detail in chapter 4 and appendix E.

19. At the international level, pension expenditures are correlated with the share of the elderly population (see Palacios and Pallarès-Miralles 2000). The equation used to compute expected expenditures is:

$$PEXP = 0.4992 \times S65 + 0.015558\ (S65\text{^}2)$$

where PEXP is pension expenditures as a share of GDP; S65 is the share of the population aged 65 or more.

20. In Lebanon, pension expenditures for the military represent 2 percent of GDP (these are not taken into account in this discussion).

21. Data and assumptions play an important role in the calculation of the implicit pension debt. In the context of a cross-country analysis, it is essential to find the right balance between taking into account the idiosyncrasy of a country's pension system, on the one hand, and the comparability of the results, on the other. To be consistent with the estimates of standardized international implicit pension debt presented in Holzmann, Palacios, and Zviniene (2004), identical assumptions are used for (a) macroeconomic variables (GDP growth, inflation, and labor productivity growth); (b) the discount rate for calculating present value; (c) earning profiles by age and gender; (d) future changes in coverage rates; (e) pension indexation rules; and (f) rules for wage valorization in the benefit formula. The main country-specific data and assumptions used in the simulations are (a) population projections, (b) base-year average wages, (c) total number and age or gender distribution of system participants (contributors and beneficiaries), (d) retirement patterns (that is, distribution of new retirees by age), and (e) pension system rules (contribution rate, contribution ceilings, if any, retirement age and early-retirement provisions, minimum vesting period, and the benefit formula for calculating entry pensions). A detailed description of the assumptions and their drawbacks can be found in Robalino and Bogomolova (forthcoming).

22. Using cross-country data, Holzmann, Palacios, and Zviniene (2004) estimate an empirical relationship between pension expenditures expressed as a share of GDP and the value of the implicit pension debt (termination measure), also expressed as a share of GDP. The relationship can be written as PensionLiability = 18.984*PensionExpenditures + 42.908. When this relationship is applied to Algeria, Egypt, Tunisia, and Libya, the implicit pension debt is 105, 109, 69, and 32 percent of GDP, respectively.

23. See Holzmann, Palacios, and Zviniene (2004) for a discussion of the importance of reporting the implicit pension debt.

24. In prefunded schemes, the sustainable rate of return becomes a weighted average of the pay-as-you-go sustainable rate of return and the rate of return on the investments of the funded component, where the weight is the share of the contribution going to each component.

25. The following assumptions regarding future changes in the number of pension system participants were used:

Country, scheme, and indicator	2020	2050	Comments
Djibouti			
CNR			
Number of contributors as a percent of 2002	86	86	The system is downsized between 2002 and 2009, constant number of contributors thereafter
Average annual growth rate, 2002	−0.8	−0.3	
Number of pensioners as a percent of 2002	175	185	
Average annual growth rate, 2002	3.2	1.3	
OPS			
Number of contributors as a percent of 2002	267	606	Age-specific coverage rates as a percent of employed assumed to be constant over time
Average annual growth rate, 2002	5.6	3.8	
Number of pensioners as a percent of 2002	274	757	
Average annual growth rate, 2002	5.8	4.3	
Number of contributors as a percent of 2002	267	606	
Islamic Republic of Iran			
CSRO			
Number of contributors as a percent of 2002	110	129	No growth in the first seven years, 50 percent of population growth thereafter
Average annual growth rate, 2002	0.5	0.5	
Number of pensioners as a percent of 2002	226	336	
Average annual growth rate, 2002	4.6	2.6	
SSO			
Number of contributors as a percent of 2002	206	342	Coverage assumed to increase from 35 percent of the labor force in 2002 to about 45 percent by 2050
Average annual growth rate, 2002	4.1	2.6	
Number of pensioners as a percent of 2002	370	2,075	
Average annual growth rate, 2002	7.5	6.5	
Number of contributors as a percent of 2002	206	342	
Jordan			
SSC			
Number of contributors as a percent of 2002	212	500	Coverage assumed to increase from less than 30 percent of the labor force in 2002 to about 45 percent by 2050
Average annual growth rate, 2002	4.3	3.4	

(Continued)

Country, scheme, and indicator	2020	2050	Comments
Number of pensioners as a percent of 2002	387	2,426	
Average annual growth rate, 2002	7.8	6.9	
Number of contributors as a percent of 2002	212	500	
Lebanon			
Civil servants			
Number of contributors as a percent of 2002	100	100	Steady state (no changes in the total number of employees)
Average annual growth rate, 2002	0.0	0.0	
Number of pensioners as a percent of 2002	262	193	
Average annual growth rate, 2002	5.5	1.4	
Number of contributors as a percent of 2002	100	100	
Military			
Number of contributors as a percent of 2002	100	100	Steady state (no changes in the total number of employees)
Average annual growth rate, 2002	0.0	0.0	
Number of pensioners as a percent of 2002	202	291	
Average annual growth rate, 2002	4.0	2.3	
Number of contributors as a percent of 2002	100	100	
Morocco			
CMR			
Number of contributors as a percent of 2002	73	55	Excluding the military
Average annual growth rate, 2002	−1.7	−1.2	
Number of pensioners as a percent of 2002	345	256	
Average annual growth rate, 2002	7.1	2.0	
Number of contributors as a percent of 2002	73	55	
RCAR			
Number of contributors as a percent of 2002	118	118	Total number of contributors assumed to grow at 1 percent a year between 2002 and 2019 and to remain constant thereafter
Average annual growth rate, 2002	0.9	0.4	
Number of pensioners as a percent of 2002	449	782	
Average annual growth rate, 2002	8.7	4.4	

(Continues on the following page.)

(Continued)

Country, scheme, and indicator	2020	2050	Comments
CNSS			
Number of contributors as a percent of 2002	148	172	Age-specific coverage rates as a percent of the population assumed to be constant over time
Average annual growth rate, 2002	2.2	1.1	
Number of pensioners as a percent of 2002	249	617	
Average annual growth rate, 2002	5.2	3.9	
West Bank and Gaza			
West Bank			
Number of contributors as a percent of 2002	100	100	Steady state (no changes in the total number of employees)
Average annual growth rate, 2002	0.0	0.0	
Number of pensioners as a percent of 2002	328	472	
Average annual growth rate, 2002	6.8	3.3	
Gaza			
Number of contributors as a percent of 2002	100	100	Steady state (no changes in the total number of employees)
Average annual growth rate, 2002	0.0	0.0	
Number of pensioners as a percent of 2002	439	681	
Average annual growth rate, 2002	8.6	4.1	

Source: Authors' calculations.

CHAPTER 4

General Guidelines for a Comprehensive Reform Program

As shown in chapter 2, countries in the region are quite heterogeneous in terms of demographic structure, macroeconomic performance, and the level of financial sector development. Nonetheless, their pension systems share important similarities in institutional design and the types of problems requiring attention. This chapter outlines general issues and questions that all countries will have to address when engaging in a reform program and offers a set of policy guidelines based on recent analytical work and the experiences of countries outside the Middle East and North Africa region. Clearly, future reform programs will have to be country specific, reflecting local economic, social, and political realities.

The chapter is organized in four sections. The first is concerned with the question that all societies need to answer when designing a program of pension reform: What should be the role and mandate of the public pension system? It also discusses, along general lines, major choices in system design to implement this mandate, which are then developed in the remainder of the chapter. The second section presents a series of policy recommendations to improve the functioning of current defined-benefit, pay-as-you-go systems. Indeed, regardless of the structure of reformed pension systems, a defined-benefit, pay-as-you-go component is likely to remain an important pillar in most countries. This section also discusses implications for the design of disability and survivor pensions and gender issues that policy makers will need to take into account when designing a reform program. The third section discusses the costs and benefits of introducing a mandatory funded component as well as the conditions that countries will have to meet. The fourth section addresses the issue of coverage and explores measures that governments can consider to protect vulnerable groups during old age. The final section deals with topics that, although important to a well-functioning pension system, have received less attention in this report as a result of space and data constraints. These include the institutional organization, administration, and regulation of pension funds. The issue of pension fund management is treated separately in chapter 5.

Choosing the Mandate of the Public Pension System and Implementation Mechanisms

Three reasons are usually cited to justify government intervention in the area of pensions. The first reason is *poverty*. Some individuals do not have the means to save enough for retirement, and it is desirable for governments to assist in the financing of a basic pension. The second reason is the *imperfection in financial markets*. Individuals might not have access to proper savings instruments (for example, some banks demand a minimum level of income to open an account or do not have offices in rural areas), available instruments can be too risky (for example, in the case where banks are not regulated properly), or individuals cannot insure against the risk of longevity (for example, annuity markets do not exist). It is good policy, then, to develop long-term savings schemes that pool longevity risks. Presumably, as capital markets develop and good banks and annuity markets emerge, the role of government can diminish, giving more room to individual choice and allowing more diversification of the sources of savings for retirement and therefore better risk management. The third reason is *myopia*. The argument goes that individuals might have trouble planning for the future and save too little when young, only to regret it later. Individual myopia, however, is difficult to correct through "forced savings." The problem is that not all individuals have the same preferences: while the mandate of the public pension system (that is, the contribution rate) might be optimal for some, for others it can be too high and therefore welfare decreasing.

Thus countries considering pension reform ought to differentiate policy discussions at two levels: (a) general principles and the objectives for the pension system regarding income replacement targets and (b) implementation mechanisms. Main issues at these two levels are reviewed in the next two subsections.

Making the Objectives of the Pension Systems Explicit and Redefining Income Replacement Patterns

From our prior discussion, it follows that the primary objective of a public pension system should be to ensure that older people have a decent standard of living at retirement. However, there can be two different interpretations of this primary objective:

- *One interpretation is that the pension system should ensure only a basic living standard.* The main rationale for the existence of the pension system in this case is poverty (measured in relative terms), and the focus is on the "adequacy" of the pension benefit, which can be defined relative to the economywide average earnings.[1]

- *A second interpretation is that the pension system should ensure a reasonable standard of living in retirement relative to that position before retirement.* Under this interpretation, the pension system plays an insurance function in the context of imperfect financial markets and myopic individuals. The focus in this case is on the replacement rate: the value of the pension relative to an individual's earnings when working.

Across countries, there are various degrees of emphasis on "adequacy" and "insurance" objectives. This point is illustrated by looking at the experiences of OECD countries. The implicit focus in countries such as Australia, Canada, Denmark, and the United Kingdom is on "adequacy." These countries provide a basic pension ranging between 30 and 50 percent of average economywide earnings at all levels of income (see the left top panel in figure 4.1). Pension systems in Finland and Luxembourg, in contrast, emphasize the insurance function. These countries guarantee relatively high replacement rates, between 60 and 75 percent of the last salary, even for individuals with incomes above the average (see the right top panel in figure 4.1). Austria imposes a ceiling on the covered wage of close to 1.6 times the average, so that replacement rates decline for individuals with higher earnings. Luxembourg also imposes a ceiling of close to 2.5 times average earnings. In between are countries such as France, Germany, and the United States, which balance adequacy and insurance objectives. These countries guarantee not only a basic pension but also a replacement rate ranging between 25 and 50 percent of the last salary (see the bottom panel in figure 4.1).

Thus Middle East and North African countries need to make explicit choices regarding the level of income replacement that the pension system will target for workers with different levels of earnings. Key parameters that need to be defined are (a) the level of the basic pension, (b) the replacement rate for the average full-career worker, and (c) the ceiling on the covered wage. Choices regarding these parameters necessarily reflect social preferences and cultural factors but, at the same time, need to be affordable. Replacement rates that need to be financed by a 40 percent contribution rate or transfers from the central budget amounting to 5 percent of gross domestic product (GDP) are not affordable. A high level of taxation compromises economic competitiveness and the efficient production of public goods. In fact, several OECD countries are already facing this problem.

What factors should be taken into account when defining the level of the basic pension?[2] There are no formal rules for defining the proper level of the basic pension, but choices need take into account economic factors such as the general standard of living of the population, estimates about minimum consumption needs (for example, the poverty line), level of the minimum wage (the basic pension should be below this minimum

Figure 4.1 "Adequacy" versus "Insurance" Functions in Select Pension Systems around the World

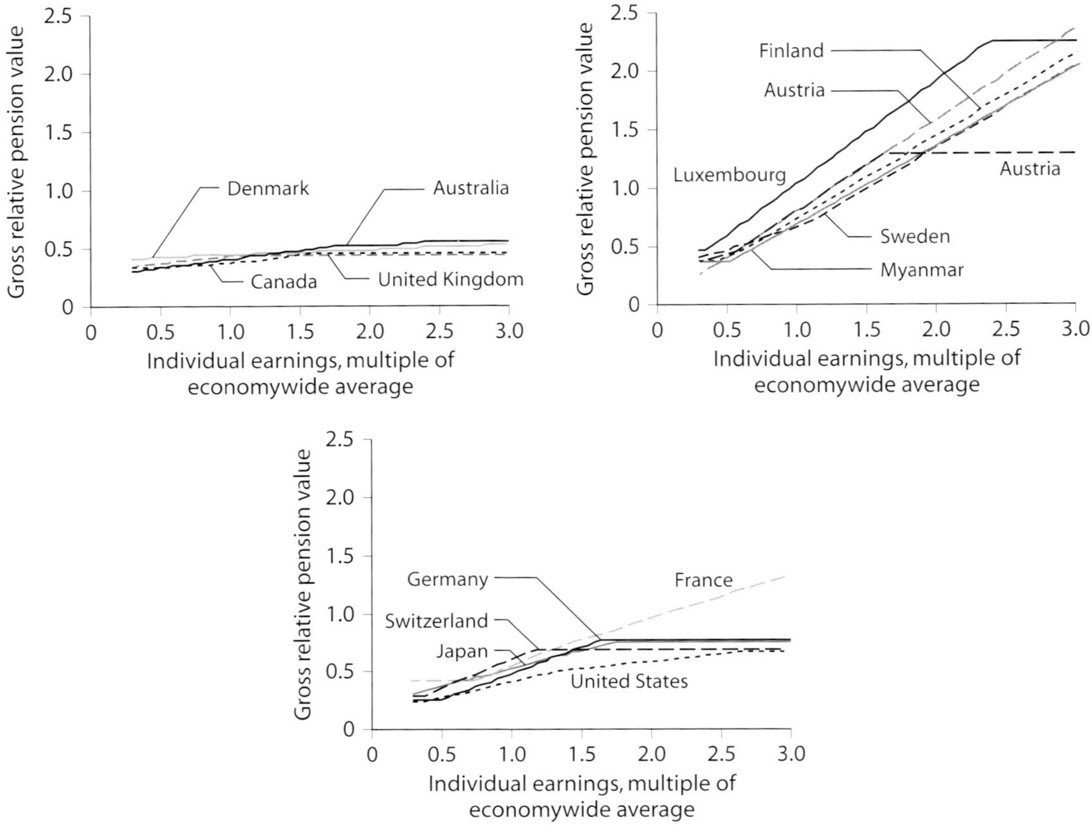

Source: Whitehouse 2004.

wage), the existence of other formal and informal (for example, the family) social assistance, and, of course, the costs. As discussed in chapter 3, today in the Middle East and North African countries, targets for the minimum pension expressed as a share of average earnings are at the high end of the international distribution. Comparing the basic pension with the general poverty line can also inform about its adequacy. In the Middle East and North African countries where information is available, basic pensions are considerably higher than the general poverty line at the national level (see figure 4.2).[3] In Algeria, the minimum pension represents four times the general poverty line. The minimum pension is around 2.5 times the poverty line in the Islamic Republic of Iran and in Jordan and 1.4 times the poverty line in Morocco. Only in Djibouti is the minimum pension below the general poverty line.

What factors should affect the choices regarding replacement rates? Again, there are no precise rules, but issues to consider include the fact

Figure 4.2 Minimum Pension and General Poverty Line in Select Middle East and North African Countries

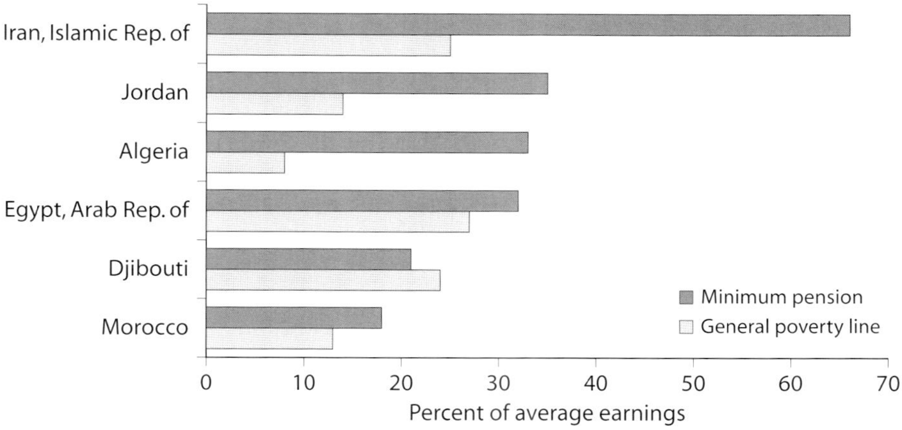

Sources: Authors' calculations based on various poverty reports. See World Bank 2001a, 2003c, 2004d, forthcoming a, and forthcoming b.

that consumption needs at retirement are lower (for example, no work-related costs, no children to support) and taxes are lower (both income taxes and social security contributions). Hence a replacement rate below 100 percent—say, 80 percent—could preserve the standard of living. Now this does not imply that the public pension system should guarantee the totality of the 80 percent. This is particularly true for middle- and high-income individuals, since the capacity of individuals to diversify and manage risks during old age increases with the level of income. Ideally, replacement rates for middle- and high-income workers that are guaranteed by a public pension scheme should be lower than for low-income workers.[4] In general, except for individuals at the bottom of the income distribution, there is no good reason to consider public pensions as the only source of savings for retirement. For middle- and high-income individuals, it would be difficult to justify targeted replacement rates above 50 percent, meaning that individuals should be responsible for financing the remaining 30 percent. Yet chapter 3 shows that, when taxes are taken into account, net replacement rates in Middle East and North African countries can surpass 100 percent, meaning that individuals have more net income in retirement than when working!

Family structures are also important—for both the targeted replacement rate and the basic pension. Although no statistics are available, it is likely, for instance, that the share of the elderly living with their children is considerably higher in the Middle East and North Africa and other middle-income countries than in OECD countries (see figure 4.3). Preliminary calculations for Jordan show, for instance, that 40 percent of those

Figure 4.3 Share of the Elderly Living with Their Children in Select Countries around the World

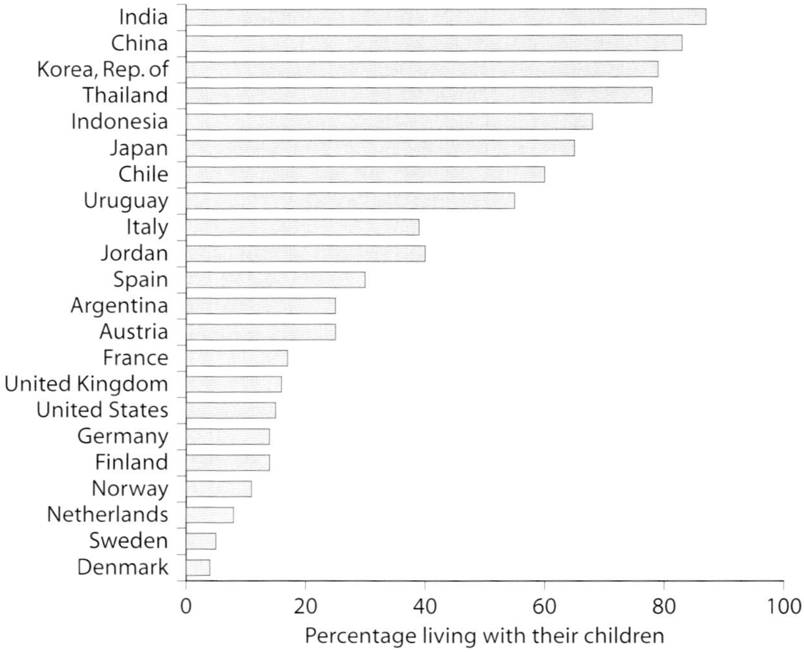

Sources: For OECD countries, Disney and Whitehouse 2001; for Jordan, author's calculations; for other countries, Palacios 2001.

aged 60 or older live with their children. The existence of these informal mechanisms reduces the need for a large mandate of the pension system.

With these considerations, Middle East and North African countries could consider reducing the mandate of their pension systems along the following lines: (a) a basic pension guarantee representing 15–20 percent of average economywide earnings (closer to the poverty line and below the minimum wage), (b) a gross replacement rate for the average full-career worker equal to or below 50 percent, and (c) a ceiling on the covered wage representing two to three times average earnings. The average worker would still have the possibility of replacing 80 percent of his or her income or more, but the additional revenues would need to come from a different source of savings.

It is often argued that, even with currently high replacement rates (often above 80 percent), most retirees do not receive an income that is sufficient to satisfy basic needs. However, average wages and minimum pensions are well above the poverty line. In fact, in most countries the covered population is composed mainly of workers in the formal sector and therefore unlikely to be at the bottom of the income distribution.

Countries where the average level of income is so low as to generate pensions that are below the poverty line with an 80 percent replacement rate—basically where the average wage is equal to or below 1.25 percent of the poverty line—should question whether a contributory system is appropriate. In the Middle East and North Africa region, however, even the poorest countries (Djibouti, the West Bank and Gaza, and the Republic of Yemen) have an average covered wage well above the poverty line.

Regarding the ceiling, the argument that excluding a portion of wages of high-income workers would worsen the financial position of the system does not hold. Indeed, high-income workers contribute higher amounts but also receive higher pensions. Bringing more of them into the system with current implicit rates of return on contributions can actually worsen the long-term financial position of the fund.

Implementing the Mandate

Once the pattern of income replacement has been chosen, a large typology of pension schemes can be designed to achieve the goals. These pension schemes can be classified along three dimensions: (a) how the system is financed (pay-as-you-go, funded schemes, general taxes, or some combination); (b) how the risks are distributed (earnings-related schemes that put most of the risks on plan sponsors or defined-contribution schemes that put most of the risks on plan members, or some combination); and (c) how the system is managed (public versus private, centralized versus decentralized, individual accounts versus a common pool). As shown in table 4.1, there is no universal model for the pension system. Around the globe, choices are dictated by local economic, social, and political conditions.[5]

At the international level, a majority of reforms have been limited to adjusting the parameters of defined-benefit, pay-as-you-go schemes without changing the financing and risk allocation mechanisms or institutional arrangements (Schwarz and Demirgüç-Kunt 1999). As an illustration, between 1993 and 1998, 18 countries increased the retirement age, 57 increased the contribution rate, 28 modified the benefit formula, 10 changed the vesting period, and 14 changed the contributory base or indexation mechanism. Only 21 countries introduced systemic reforms. In the Middle East and North Africa region, an important parametric reform took place in Djibouti in 2002 (see chapter 6). Several other countries also introduced adjustments, but these were often ad hoc and did not always improve the financial situation of the schemes. For instance, in 2000, Jordan's Social Security Corporation increased both its contribution and accrual rates, but the net effect on the finances of the system was negative.

TABLE 4.1

Systemic Reforms in Select Countries in Latin America and Europe

Country	Financing and risk distribution	Size of fully funded scheme (percent of wage)	Management of fully funded scheme	Transition
Latin America				
Argentina	Basic pay-as-you-go (reformed) plus choice of pay-as-you-go or fully funded	7.72	Centralized collection; state-owned managers allowed	Fully funded scheme optional for current plan members
Chile	Fully funded (pay-as-you-go phased out)	10	Decentralized; no state-owned managers allowed	Mandatory for new entrants; optional for current plan members
Colombia	Choice of fully funded or pay-as-you-go (reformed)	10	Decentralized; no state-owned managers allowed	Optional
Costa Rica	First pay-as-you-go and second fully funded	4.25	Centralized collection; state-owned managers allowed	First pillar mandatory for new entrants; fully funded pillar mandatory for all workers
Mexico	Fully funded (pay-as-you-go eliminated)	12.07	Centralized collection[a]; state-owned managers allowed	Mandatory for all workers
Europe				
Bulgaria	First pay-as-you-go (reformed) and second fully funded	2, growing to 5	Centralized collection, state-owned managers allowed	Mandatory for workers less than 42 years of age
Croatia	First pay-as-you-go (points system) and second fully funded	5	Centralized collection; no state-owned managers allowed	Mandatory for workers less than 40 years of age; voluntary for workers 40–50 years of age
Hungary	First pay-as-you-go (reformed) and second fully funded	6	Centralized collection; no state-owned managers allowed	Mandatory for new entrants; optional for current plan members
Latvia	First pay-as-you-go (notional defined-contribution system or virtual accounts system) and second fully funded	2, growing to 9	Centralized collection; state-owned managers allowed	Mandatory for workers less than 30 years of age; voluntary for workers 30–50 years of age
Macedonia	First pay-as-you-go (reformed) and second fully funded	7	Centralized collection; no state-owned managers allowed	Mandatory for new entrants; optional for current plan members
Poland	First pay-as-you-go (notional defined-contribution system or virtual accounts system) and second fully funded	7.2	Centralized collection; no state-owned managers allowed	Mandatory for workers less than 30 years of age; voluntary for workers 30–50 years of age
Sweden	First pay-as-you-go (notional defined-contribution system or virtual accounts system) and second fully funded	2.5	Centralized collection; state-owned managers allowed	Mandatory for workers less than 45 years of age

Sources: Palacios 2003; Gill, Packard, and Yermo 2003; World Bank 2004f.
Note: a. Private ownership by industry.

The second type of reform has been systemic in nature and implied the introduction of a defined-contribution, fully funded component. The majority of these reforms have taken place in Latin America and Eastern Europe, with a large variance in system design and implementation arrangements (table 4.1). Chile, the first country to introduce a defined-contribution, fully funded scheme, closed the "old" defined-benefit, pay-as-you-go system to new entrants and began to phase it out gradually. The new scheme is operated exclusively by private pension fund managers in a highly decentralized fashion. Mexico also introduced a defined-contribution, fully funded scheme but immediately phased out the defined-benefit, pay-as-you-go plan (that is, current plan members joined the new scheme). The collection of contributions remained centralized, with public managers coexisting with private managers. In Colombia, the defined-benefit, pay-as-you-go system was preserved but reformed, and workers were given the choice of enrolling in one or the other. Costa Rica adopted a multipillar approach, with collections remaining centralized; workers simultaneously contribute to the defined-benefit, pay-as-you-go and the defined-contribution, fully funded components. Thus part of the replacement rate targeted by the public pension system comes from a defined-benefit component (which is low risk for individuals) and part comes from a defined-contribution component (which presumably has higher risks but also higher rates of return on contributions). This multipillar arrangement is mandatory for all workers.

Most systemic reforms in Eastern Europe have followed a multipillar approach, combining reformed earnings-related schemes with a defined-contribution, fully funded component. There are differences, however, in the type of earnings-related scheme (standard defined-benefit, points system, or notional accounts),[6] the size of the defined-contribution, fully funded scheme, and the transition mechanism. In most cases, the collection of contributions remains centralized, but investments are outsourced to private sector managers. In Bulgaria, the reformed pay-as-you-go component is a standard defined benefit. The new system is mandatory for individuals younger than 42 years of age. In Poland, the pay-as-you-go component was transformed into a virtual accounts system mandatory for those 30 years of age or younger. A similar scheme was adopted in Latvia and Sweden.

Ultimately, the choice of system design needs to be based on sound economic analysis, and the implementation should follow best practices. By changing the status quo, any reform imposes economic and social costs and benefits, so these should be outlined and quantified to the extent possible (desirably in partnership with civil society), thus maximizing the likelihood that the end program, while not necessarily optimal, is at least welfare increasing. Implementation and management should respond to the needs of the system that is selected. Thus if a country opts to finance part of its pensions on a pay-as-you-go basis, then the parameters of the scheme should respond to the sustainability principles of pay-as-you-go systems. Similarly, if a funded component is implemented, the appropriate regulatory framework should be in place. The necessary conditions for the efficient operation of the various arrangements are discussed in the next two sections.

Bringing Current Defined-Benefit, Pay-As-You-Go Systems up to the Standard

In most countries across the region, defined-benefit schemes are likely to remain at the core of the public pension system. It is, therefore, important to ensure that current benefit formulas and eligibility conditions promote financial sustainability, efficiency, and equity. In a nutshell, this implies having a system that pays an implicit rate of return on contributions that is sustainable, avoids unnecessary variations in this rate of return across individuals to prevent adverse distributional transfers, and corrects distortions in labor supply, savings, and retirement decisions.

This section presents policy recommendations so that, gradually, current earnings-related pay-as-you-go systems start complying with the norms of design that guarantee their proper functioning. It begins by discussing standard defined-benefit schemes, specifically (a) how to set benefit formulas and (b) how to define eligibility conditions. It then addresses the implementation of virtual account systems, which are another type of earnings-related pension scheme (along with points systems), and defines the conditions under which the virtual account system and the standard defined-benefit system are equivalent and the factors that make the virtual account system an attractive option for earnings-related systems financed on a pay-as-you-go basis. Next, it raises the issue of how governments should treat the implicit pension debt of pay-as-you-go schemes. Finally, it discusses necessary reforms in disability and survivor pensions as well as gender issues that need to be taken into account when implementing the various reforms.

Benefit Formulas in Standard Defined-Benefit Schemes

For discussion purposes, it is useful to deconstruct benefit formulas into three components: (a) the measure of income, which is the reference salary used to compute the pensions; (b) the accrual rate, which is the percentage of the income measure that the individual receives for each year of contribution; and (c) the mechanism used to index pensions, which affects the long-term real value of the benefit received on retirement. Recommendations at these three levels are presented next.

Measure of Income Used to Compute the Pension

Countries should consider including all salaries across work history and across income-generating activities in the formula for calculating the pension, but they should be revalorized appropriately. The purpose of this policy is not to reduce the level of the pension—on the contrary, the opposite can occur—but to improve incentives and equity. Indeed, an important part of the variation in the implicit rates of return paid on contributions is due to the fact that still often only the last few salaries count toward determining the pension. Implicit rates of return then become sensitive to changes in wage history. Individuals with a flat wage history (for example, blue-collar workers) receive a lower rate of return than individuals with increasing wages (such as white collar workers). This opens the door to adverse distributional transfers (that is, transfers from low-income to high-income workers). Not using all wages in the calculation of the pension also provides incentives for individuals to manipulate wages, declaring too low wages early in the career and declaring too high wages toward the end.

The increase in the number of salaries included in the calculation should be gradual (that is, a number of additional years of salaries per calendar year) to allow information systems to catch up. There are various choices regarding the index that is used to revalorize past wages and that ultimately determines the implicit rate of return that individuals receive on their contributions and therefore the financial sustainability of the scheme.[7] A technical discussion of the various methods and their strengths and weaknesses can be found in Lindeman, Robalino, and Rutkowski (2003). A good compromise is to use the growth rate of the average covered wage. Making explicit the expected dynamics of this growth rate is important, as it will affect the calibration of the other parameters of the system.

Accrual Rate

The accrual rate should reflect the mandate of the pension system regarding income replacement for the average full-career worker at a given retirement age. For instance, using life expectancies for Morocco, if the targeted replacement rate is set at 50 percent for the individual retiring at age 60 with 40 years of contributions, then the annual accrual rate should be equal to 1.25 percent.

The accrual rate of a well-designed pay-as-you-go system, however, is intrinsically linked to the contribution rate, the retirement age, survival probabilities after retirement, and the index used to revalorize past wages.[8] This rule is represented graphically in figure 4.4. Each line gives

Figure 4.4 Links between Accrual Rates, Retirement Ages, Rates of Return, and Contribution Rates

Source: Authors' calculations.
Note: The survival probabilities used in the calculations correspond to Morocco. The diamonds show the current combinations of accrual rates and contribution rates in various mandatory schemes. In most cases, accrual rates are too high for the current contribution rate and retirement age, even if the real sustainable implicit rate of return that the system can pay on contributions was equal to 5 percent a year.

the possible combinations of the accrual rate and the contribution rate for a given retirement age and a given growth rate for the index used to revalorize wages that ensures financial balance.[9] Figure 4.4 also displays the current combination of the contribution rate (horizontal axis) and the accrual rate (vertical axis) for various pension schemes in the Middle East and North Africa. In most of the cases, the resulting points fall outside the lines. This is the basic source of the current financial problem.

The main message of figure 4.4 is that, from a sustainable pension system, when determining the value of the accrual rate, the normal retirement age, and the contribution rate, policy makers can choose only two of the three. The third has to be computed endogenously. For instance, if the accrual rate is set at 1.25 percent a year and the normal retirement age is set at 60, the contribution rate has to range between 25 and 30 percent, depending on the growth rate of the index used to revalorize past wages. If the retirement age is set at 65 years, then the contribution rate can be lower (between 15 and 20 percent).

What happens with individuals who retire before or after the normal retirement age? In order to guarantee the same rate of return for all individuals, the relationship between the accrual rate and the contribution rate depicted in figure 4.4 needs to hold for *all* retirement ages. This implies that if the contribution rate is the same for all individuals, those who retire *before* the normal retirement age should have a lower accrual rate (that is, individuals would pay an actuarially fair penalty for early retirement). In a similar way, those retiring *after* the normal retirement age should have a higher accrual rate (that is, individuals would receive an actuarially fair compensation for deferred retirement).

Mechanism Used to Index Pensions

Practices vary around the world, but prudence and the aim of preserving a constant rate of return within and across generations suggest that the proper index should be inflation. In most OECD countries, pensions are indexed to prices. In Latvia, the index is an average of the average wage and inflation. In Poland, the growth rate of the wage bill is used. Sweden has the most complicated system, with an index that is a function of the growth rate of the average wage, inflation, and fluctuations of the buffer fund. Indeed, the architects of the system show that simply using the average wage as the index does not guarantee financial sustainability (Swedish Pension System 2003). Again, with the idea of keeping rates of return constant within and across generations, a more conservative index is simply inflation.[10] Labor productivity gains that take place in the economy at large are distributed indirectly to the elderly through better-quality goods and services, a higher minimum pension, and a higher sustainable rate of return that brings higher initial pensions (for simulations of various indexing mechanisms, see Lindeman, Robalino, and Rutkowski 2003).

Eligibility Conditions

To be eligible for a pension, individuals need to meet several conditions: pay a minimum contribution rate, reach a minimum retirement age, and accumulate a minimum number of years of contributions (a vesting period). Here some additional observations are made regarding the choice of each of these parameters as well as the vesting period.

Contribution Rate

Policy makers ought to be careful not to overtax labor, implying that the contribution rate should not be used as the parameter that "closes" the finances of the scheme. Moreover, when assessing the appropriate level of the contribution rate to finance pensions, the payroll taxes financing other benefits (for example, health, family allowances) should be taken into account. In chapter 2, it is argued that payroll taxes can have important effects on the labor market, coverage rates, and individual welfare. High payroll taxes can reduce the level of employment and expand the informal sector: first, because the cost of labor increases relative to other production inputs and, second, because some firms and individuals experience liquidity constraints and cannot afford to pay the high rates. High contribution rates can also reduce individual welfare, even when the expected rates of return on these contributions are high. Indeed, the contribution rate is a form of forced savings for workers. If workers are forced to save well beyond their individual preferences, they are worse off even if they enjoy high pensions when old.

This being the case, the recommendation is to set a contribution rate to finance pensions that is affordable (say, 15 percent, taking into account the total payroll tax) and to keep it constant over time.

Normal Retirement Age

Because there is a limit to how much an economy can afford to pay on contributions and because the accrual rate reflects the mandate of the pension system regarding income replacement (which presumably also should remain constant over the short and medium term), the recommendation is to make the normal retirement age the parameter that adjusts endogenously. Thus for a given contribution rate, the choice of the accrual rate would determine the choice of the retirement age. The higher the accrual rate and the higher the pension individuals receive, the longer they have to work. Clearly, there is also a biological limit to how long individuals can work on average, and this depends on the economic sector. Thus choices regarding the value of the accrual rate are constrained: there is a maximum level that a given economy can afford to pay.

Another implication is that, as life expectancy increases (either at birth or at retirement), the accrual rate and the contribution rate being constant, the normal retirement age will need to be adjusted. Thus the recommendation for a defined-benefit, pay-as-you-go system is to index the retirement age to life expectancy.

Vesting Period

A minimum vesting period, in principle, is not a necessary condition to receive a pension, except for the minimum pension guarantee, as long as the accrual rate is set properly and all salaries are included in the calculation of the pension. Vesting periods traditionally have two functions. One is to mitigate abuses of the system—for instance, individuals contributing for only a few years and then returning to the system when they are close to retirement, thus receiving higher implicit rates of return on contributions. The other one is to mitigate individual myopia by ensuring that the number of years of contributions is sufficient to generate an adequate pension. An extra role that these could play in a badly designed defined-benefit scheme is to force individuals to delay retirement, thus better aligning the accrual rate with the retirement age. It is unclear, however, that vesting periods are effective in addressing these problems with respect to abuses of the system. If incentives are set properly (that is, benefit formulas and eligibility conditions follow the principles outlined in the previous sections), the likelihood that individuals will game the system will be reduced. Moreover, strengthening mechanisms to control compliance among employers and proper information and reporting about the benefits that the system can deliver could be more effective in inducing longer contribution periods. And often short careers reflect adverse conditions in the labor market, (for example, long unemployment periods). Requiring a minimum vesting period will do little to improve the situation. Finally, if the accrual rate is set properly, there is no need to encourage individuals to delay retirement. On the contrary, the introduction of vesting periods becomes another source of variation in rates of return that can deter enrollment. Individuals who join the system late in their life can be penalized, since they are forced to contribute past the normal retirement age without adjustments to their pension. As the accrual rate is realigned with the retirement age and the contribution rate and all salaries are included in the calculation of the pension, vesting periods can be removed gradually. If the accrual rate is set at 1.25 percent, an individual who retires at age 60 and has contributed 20 years instead of 40 will simply receive a lower replacement rate (for example, 25 percent instead of 50 percent). Individuals who have contributed shorter periods will certainly have the incentive to remain in the labor force until they are able to finance an adequate pension or meet the vesting period for the minimum pension guarantee.

Summary

In summary, any well-designed defined-benefit scheme financed on a pay-as-you-go basis should follow the principles outlined above (see also table 4.2). Failing to do so will compromise the financial sustainability of the scheme, economic efficiency, or equity.

It can be argued that mandatory pension schemes do not need to be self-sufficient and that budget transfers to finance part of the pensions are a perfectly defensible policy. This may well be a social choice, but the costs in lost efficiency and the equity implications need to be acknowledged. The resources used to finance the pensions of a few, usually well-off, formal sector workers are necessarily removed from the production of public goods, which brings higher social and economic benefits, while affecting a larger share of the population (for example, education, health, and well-targeted assistance programs).

TABLE 4.2

Best Practices in the Design of a Defined-Benefit, Pay-As-You-Go System

Parameter	Best practice
Benefit formula	
Sustainable rate of return	Over the long run, use the growth rate of the covered wage bill; over the short run, use the growth rate of the average wage or a moving average of the growth rate of the wage bill In general, avoid paying real implicit rates of return on contributions in excess of 3 percent a year
Income measure	Include all salaries in the calculation of the pension indexed by the sustainable rate of return of the system
Accrual rate	Set the accrual rate in relation to the replacement rate for a full-career worker retiring at the normal retirement age Adjust it downward for individuals retiring before the normal retirement age and upward for individuals retiring after the normal age
Index for pensions	Index to inflation
Eligibility condition	
Normal retirement age and basic contribution rate	Given the targeted accrual rate, the sustainable rate of return of the system, and life expectancy, recognize that the choice of one of these parameters implies the level of the other If both are too high given workers' preferences and what the economy can support, revise the accrual rate downward Fix the contribution rate Determine the normal retirement age by the choice of accrual rate Index normal retirement age to life expectancy so that the system can keep its mandate constant over time
Vesting period	Do not set a vesting period if the accrual rate is set properly

Source: Authors' design.

Some of the measures outlined, particularly the reduction in the accrual rate, are difficult to implement politically. To ease resistance, reforms could respect acquired rights, meaning that policy changes would apply only to the new contributions. However, current plans members, not only new entrants, need to be affected. Moreover, this gradual implementation of reforms is only possible if these are not delayed. Waiting to intervene will lead not only to drastic adjustments in the future but also to inequity, as most of the cost of the adjustment will be imposed on future generations.

The Special Case of Virtual Accounts

In recent years, the so-called notional defined contribution or virtual account system has been introduced as a paradigm for reforming earnings-related schemes. In essence, the virtual account system enforces the standards and best practices of the traditional earnings-related pay-as-you-go systems discussed in the two previous subsections. However, the benefit formula is operationalized differently.[11]

In the virtual account scheme, contributions are registered in individual accounts as a "virtual" capital. It is only a registration on "book" because, contrary to funded schemes, individuals do not have real funds accumulated in their account. The contributions are indexed by the sustainable rate of return of the system, again a function of the system's average wage and the covered population. When the individual retires, the pension is computed as an annuity of the sum of revalorized contributions (the "virtual" capital). This is done by dividing the total contributions by a so-called G factor, which is simply the sum of the survival probabilities at various ages after retirement, discounted at a given rate.

The virtual account system has three advantages over the standard defined-benefit system, assuming that it is well designed: (a) precision in the calculation of sustainable pension benefits, (b) a more transparent link between contributions and benefits, which, among other things, can facilitate the tracking of the implicit pension debt of the system, and (c) a change in the paradigm, which can facilitate implementation of the reforms discussed in the previous two sections.

The virtual account formula and the standard defined-benefit formula generate identical outcomes if the latter meets two conditions: (a) all wages are included in the calculation of the pension and (b) the accrual rate is computed *at the time of retirement* and respects the links among the retirement age, the contribution rate, and survival probabilities. However, when the accrual rate is announced ex ante (that is, when the individual joins the system), its calculation needs to be based on expectations about survival probabilities at retirement and the growth rate of the average covered wage or the covered wage bill. If these expectations do not materialize, the accrual rate could be too high (compromising the financial sustainability of the system) or too low (penalizing plan members). In the virtual account system, the pension is calculated using the latest information regarding survival probabilities and the growth rate of the covered wage bill (or the average wage). Clearly, in a defined-benefit scheme the accrual rate can be computed at the time of retirement. In this case, however, the main benefit of the scheme, which is to guarantee plan members a given replacement rate at retirement, is lost. That being the case, one might as well move directly to the virtual account formula, which could create a more transparent link between contributions and benefits.

In the standard defined-benefit scheme, from the perspective of plan members, the link between the absolute value of contributions and the pension is blurred. On the contrary, by not relying on the concept of an accrual rate but simply guaranteeing a rate of return on contributions to its members (a concept similar to a bank account), the virtual account system can improve transparency, promote ownership, and therefore improve incentives to enroll in the system (provided that the rate of return offered by the scheme is credible).[12] The virtual account scheme can also facilitate the transfer of acquired rights between funds (even across countries) in fragmented schemes.[13] Finally, it can facilitate the implementation of policies that make explicit the pension debt of the scheme.

Another potential benefit of introducing a virtual account system is that the change in paradigm can facilitate the implementation of best practices in the design of earnings-related schemes with pay-as-you-go financing. Indeed, some of the necessary reforms might be difficult to pursue using the language of traditional defined-benefit schemes.

The virtual account system is also subject to criticisms that policy makers should take into account. Three stand out: (a) the scheme might be more complicated to administer, particularly regarding record keeping; (b) policy makers lose control over the contribution rate as an instrument to stabilize the finances of the system in the presence of unexpected shocks; and (c) the scheme generates more uncertainty among plan members regarding the final replacement rate. The third point is a fact. Higher variance in replacement rates is the price to pay for improved financial sustainability (that is, more precision in calculating the sustainable level of benefits). Policy makers need to resolve this trade-off. The other two criticisms are less valid.

The administration of a well-designed defined-benefit scheme should meet the same standards as the administration of a virtual account system. An important policy recommendation for all Middle East and North African countries is to move to benefit formulas that include all wages in the calculation of the pension. This requires proper record-keeping procedures and information systems that are able to track past wages for each plan member. Several countries already have the necessary capabilities. Others should implement this measure gradually to allow administrative capacity and information systems to catch up. The implementation of a virtual account system in these countries could also be gradual—for instance, it could apply only to new workers.

Increases in the contribution rate to stabilize the finances of the pension system in the presence of unexpected shocks can be considered an implicit tax on plan members. Indeed, the apparent attraction of a defined-benefit design is that an increase in the contribution rate does not imply an increase in the value of the pension, as in a virtual account system. But this is the same as saying that plan members must contribute an extra amount that does not accrue rights, which is a form of taxation. The same type of tax can be envisioned in a virtual account system. The difference is that, in the latter, the tax is explicit. This being said, a more efficient approach to deal with unexpected macroeconomic or demographic shocks is to build a buffer fund: basically, a minimum level of reserves that can be used during a crisis.

In conclusion, when thinking about reform of an earnings-related scheme that meets the best practices in design, virtual account systems deserve serious consideration.

Making the Implicit Pension Debt Explicit

Whether financially sustainable or not, at any point in time, earnings-related schemes have an implicit pension debt. This implicit debt is the present value of pension promises to current retirees plus the pension rights accrued to date by contributors. As shown in chapter 3, the implicit pension debt for many countries in the region is several times higher than the current level of reserves—probably the only exception is Egypt—and on the same order of magnitude as the explicit public debt.

Unfortunately, this implicit pension debt is seldom taken into account when assessing the sustainability of the fiscal and macro frameworks. This is unfortunate because, ultimately, it is the government that guarantees pension promises. Hence the analysis of the sustainability of the public debt—and resulting policies regarding revenues and levels of spending—can be severely biased.

In the case of a well-designed earnings-related scheme, one way around this problem is to transform the implicit pension debt into explicit government debt, by investing all of the contributions in special government bonds. These bonds would have to pay the same rate of return, or a close proxy, as the implicit rate of return paid by the pension fund on contributions. Initially, implementation of this arrangement simply entails having a "line" on the liability side of the government balance sheet that grows as a function of (a) the index selected to revalorize contributions, (b) the new flow of contributions, and (c) the liquidation of accumulated contributions or pension payments. Another arrangement would be, in effect, to issue bonds with different levels of maturity, which are set to ensure that the liquidity needs of the pension funds are met. Over time, these bonds could become tradable, thus allowing pension funds to diversify away from public debt. Effectively, this implies converging to a defined-contribution, fully funded type of scheme (see Valdés-Prieto 2004).

The advantage of the proposed arrangement is that at any point in time the implicit debt of the pension fund (that is, the sum of the capital accumulated in the virtual accounts) is equal to the explicit pension debt of the government. This is even easier to understand and calculate in the case of a virtual account system.

When individuals retire, two scenarios can be considered. In one, the general budget transfers the totality of the accumulated contributions plus interest for each of the plan members retiring, who then "purchase" an annuity from the pension fund (continuing with the figure of the virtual account system). The pension fund then would have to create a mathematical reserve that is used to pool the longevity risks of the population of retirees. This, however, raises the issue of the management and investment of the mathematical reserve. The second alternative is to continue paying pensions on a pay-as-you-go basis, with the general budget transferring only the funds necessary to cover expenditures in a given period. This is equivalent to reinvesting the mathematical reserve in government bonds. In both cases, longevity risks are managed through sharing.

Egypt is one of the countries that should consider this approach: indeed, a large part of the implicit pension debt is already in the form of explicit government debt and is being serviced. The arrangement presented in this section would ensure that the implicit debt associated with new contributions remains explicit. Moreover, there is room today to change the maturity of the current pension debt of the government (essentially debt with the National Investment Bank) without affecting the need for liquidity of the pension funds and thus reducing financing costs.

Implications for the Provision and Financing of Disability and Survivor Pensions

Given data constraints, the discussion in chapter 3 focuses on old-age pensions and leaves aside consideration of disability and survivor pensions. Yet all schemes in the region combine the three types of pensions. Common issues that require attention over the short term include: (a) reviewing benefit formulas to improve financial sustainability; (b) reviewing the certification and recertification processes for disability benefits to reduce abuse; (c) rationalizing the transfer of survivor pensions to control costs, while at the same time ensuring that divorced spouses are not penalized, that children are protected in the event of the death of the surviving spouse, and that the system does not discourage work among individuals who have the capacity to work; and (d) ensuring that rules apply equally to men and women.

This short subsection focuses on the financing of disability and survivor pensions. Although the financing of disability and survivor pensions should be separate from the financing of old-age pensions from an accounting perspective, in all but a few schemes in the Middle East and North Africa region, permanent disability and survivor pensions are financed jointly with old-age pensions.[14] The subsection starts by looking at old-age survivor benefits and is followed by a discussion of young-age survivor and disability benefits.

Old-Age Survivor Benefits

One possibility, although not likely to be applicable in the region, is not to integrate survivor pensions with old-age pensions, as is the case in the Swedish system. This individual-only option avoids complicated rules about the inheritance of benefits or the rights of divorced spouses and holds down total costs and contribution rates, enhancing individual welfare and incentives. By the same token, it forces households to do more of their own survivor planning and saving in their later working and early retirement years. The individual-only approach, however, is feasible in countries, such as Sweden, with high rates of female labor force participation and substantial access to private life insurance and annuity markets.[15] Middle East and North African countries might find it difficult to implement this approach.

More realistically, survivor benefits for widows and widowers need to be integrated with old-age benefits. In the case of a defined-benefit system, the calculation of the accrual rate would need to be modified to include the survival probabilities of the spouse (or partner). This policy, however, is likely to be difficult to implement. Alternatively, at least a separate contribution rate would need to be set up to internalize the costs of having to pay a pension for a longer period of time. If the earnings-related scheme is managed through virtual accounts, a common provision is a husband and wife sharing their entitlements in retirement in the form of joint-and-survivor annuities. This notion can be extended to other individuals with an "insurable interest." Such relationships might include related siblings living together and so on. Country customs dictate when the joint annuity is mandatory versus elective, which relationships are recognized for elective purposes, and what happens in the event of divorce (this is also an issue to consider in the standard defined-benefit scheme). Thus handling survivor pensions in the context of a virtual account system can be more transparent.

Young-Age Survivor Benefits

Young-age survivor benefits belong in the realm of insurance and not forced savings. Ideally, these benefits could be outsourced to life insurance companies. If this cannot be done, then young-age survivor benefits should be managed in a separate fund, financed by a dedicated contribution rate.

If the earnings-related scheme is managed through virtual accounts, one approach is to offset (reduce) the earnings-related survivor pension by the annuity value of the virtual account. This is similar to what is done in Latin American countries when mandatory funded accounts are coupled with early death and disability insurance coverage. The second approach is to hold the virtual account aside as deferred annuities, with no interaction with early death benefits. This approach is more likely in countries concerned with elderly widows who depend heavily on their husband's pension rights. It also keeps the social insurance accounting more transparent.

Disability Benefits

Disability benefits pose similar design challenges and belong in the realm of insurance and not forced savings. When the benefit cannot be outsourced, it should be covered through a separate fund financed by a separate contribution rate. Morocco is already outsourcing to insurance companies disability due to work accidents.

When the earnings-related scheme is managed through virtual accounts, three options can be considered. One option is to compare the defined-benefit disability insurance amount to the virtual account annuity based on accumulations up to the time of disability; individuals receive the higher of the two. Except for older workers, the disability benefit typically exceeds the virtual account annuity. The disability benefit can also be regarded as a permanent top-up of an underlying virtual account annuity. Finally, the disability benefit can be a completely independent benefit that lasts only to retirement. In this case, imputations to the virtual account are necessary to fill in the disability years. In Sweden, the imputation treats the disability benefit as if it were earned income.

Gender Issues

Chapter 3 shows that in several countries pension laws have tried to provide special treatment for women, albeit with a biased view regarding their role in society. Women are often allowed to retire earlier than men, and because they live longer on average, other things being equal, they extract higher implicit rates of return on their contributions.

The recommendations to reform current defined-benefit, pay-as-you-go systems, through either parametric changes or the introduction of virtual accounts, call for treating women and men equally at all levels of the pension law, including the right to transfer pensions to their dependents. Moreover, the proposed mechanism for computing the accrual rate implies taking into account higher life expectancies for women. The implication is that accrual rates will be lower for women and, other things being equal, so will replacement rates and pensions. The reform would, therefore, tend to impose higher costs on women than on men.

Policy makers ought to consider policies to mitigate the adverse impact of pension reform on women. These policies include the following:

- *Apply a lower pace of adjustment of benefit formulas and eligibility conditions for women.* As an illustration, if in a country the normal retirement age is 55 for women and 60 for men, and the new normal retirement age is set at 65, women should be allowed to reach the target in twice as many years as men. So if the retirement age for men increases from 60 to 65 during a period of 10 years, the retirement age for women should reach 65 in a period of 20 years.
- *Use unisex mortality tables.* By using the same mortality tables, the accrual rate for women will not be reduced relative to the accrual rate for men as a result of longer life expectancies. Implicitly, this involves a subsidy or transfer from men to women.
- *Finance and provide adequate maternity benefits.* Countries should have schemes that provide income support during periods of maternity leave so that, among others, contributions to the pension system are not interrupted. These programs can be financed either by employers, through payroll taxes to the social security system, or through budget subsidies. In all cases, however, the costs should be explicit and the programs affordable.
- *Require additional savings for men with multiple wives.* Men with multiple wives create two types of problems. First, they impose higher costs on the system since the old-age survivor pension has a higher chance of being paid for a longer period of time. Second, wives are poorly insured against the risk of death of their spouse, either as an active worker or while in retirement. The recommendation is, first, to include all potential survivors in the calculation of the accrual rate or the virtual account annuity. This would imply a lower accrual rate for men with multiple wives to keep costs under control. Second, plan members with multiple wives should be mandated to pay a few percentage points in additional contributions for each wife. This would allow the system to pay a higher accrual rate and therefore a higher pension, which is then divided among the survivor spouses.[16] This is a transparent mechanism to internalize the extra costs to the system and to make individuals accountable for the financial implications of their decisions regarding marriage.
- *Establish adequate protection and more flexible rules for divorced women.* Divorced women who do not remarry and do not work should be protected during old age. It is desirable for these women to have rights over part of the pension of their former husband on his death.

Basically, women should have access to a fair share of the pension rights accrued by the husband up to the time of divorce. As seen in chapter 3, some countries do give divorced women rights over the pension of their former husband. Rules, however, can be restrictive.

- *Provisions in the law whereby "free" years of contributions are credited for periods during which women stop working to raise their young children.* Sweden has devised such a provision. This policy, however, generates an implicit nontransparent subsidy within the pension system. Moreover, it is expensive and likely to be unaffordable. When such programs are considered, their costs should be made explicit and financed either through dedicated payroll taxes or from general revenues.

Benefits and Costs of Higher Funding

There are several ways to increase the level of funding of a pension system: (a) increase the funding ratio of earnings-related plans;[17] (b) switch (completely or partially) from a pay-as-you-go to a fully funded system (as was done in Chile and other countries), in which all or part of the targeted replacement rate is financed on a capitalization basis; and (c) reduce the mandate of an earnings-related system with pay-as-you-go financing and promote the development of voluntary complementary funded pensions, for instance, through tax incentives.

In all cases, the operation involves benefits and costs. This section discusses the potential benefits of increasing levels of funding in Middle East and North African countries as well as the main costs and constraints.

Potential Benefits of Higher Funding

International experience suggests that the benefits of higher funding are related to higher rates of return on contributions and a better diversification of risks, implying higher pensions for the same contribution rate; potentially higher national savings; the development of securities markets; the reduction in financial risks confronting firms; and a more stable and efficient banking sector. Each of these is analyzed below in the context of Middle East and North African countries.

Higher Rates of Return on Savings for Old Age and More Efficient Diversification of Risks

Chapter 3 shows that current implicit rates of return on contributions in most pension schemes are too high to be sustainable. Sustainable rates would be closer to the long-term growth rate of the economy (for example, 3 percent a year). Contributions that are invested in financial instruments, as opposed to "human capital," as in a pay-as-you-go scheme, *can* receive higher rates of return, at least over the long run. Given that the rate of return on contributions ultimately determines the level of the pension (that is, the affordable replacement rate), increasing the level of funding of the pension scheme can be a mechanism for offering higher pensions. Clearly, higher rates of return are also associated with higher risks. A well-diversified portfolio of investments, however, needs to include assets with various levels of risk. Higher funding can thus encourage better diversification of the sources of savings for retirement.

National Savings

The impact that higher funding in mandatory systems has on national savings depends, in part, on the government's strategy to finance the transition (for a discussion, see also Bailliu and Reisen 2000 and Bosworth and Burtless 2003). If current unfunded liabilities are financed through debt, the short-run impact will be neutral, as the implicit debt of the pay-as-you-go system is simply transformed into an explicit liability. If, however, this transitional cost is financed via adjustments in the budget for items other than pensions, through either increases in taxation or reductions in other expenditures, national savings may increase. In particular, in the presence of credit constraints, or if current savings are motivated by precautionary rather than life-cycle reasons, agents will be unwilling to reduce their savings in response to a transition tax.

In the case of voluntary complementary pensions, the effects are more uncertain. Simply replacing one form of voluntary savings with another is unlikely to affect aggregate savings. Even if pension funds offer greater (long-term) returns than other savings instruments, it is well known that the effect of a higher real return on savings is ambiguous, as the income effect might offset the substitution effect. Furthermore, if the government decides to encourage voluntary contractual savings plans through income tax incentives, the impact on national savings would depend primarily on the government's fiscal stance. A positive effect on aggregate savings would require that the reduction in income tax revenue be compensated through either higher taxes or lower expenditures.

The most recent empirical studies regarding the impacts of mandatory funded systems on national savings suggest a positive relationship, on average (for a cross-country empirical assessment, see López-Murphy and Musalem 2004). Within a given country, however, institutional factors ultimately can stimulate or preclude a positive effect on national savings rates (for a discussion, see Bosworth and Burtless 2003). In Middle East and North African countries, due to their frail fiscal position, a higher level of funding is unlikely to be associated with higher national savings, at least over the short term. By reducing the long-term implicit debt of the government, however, higher levels of funding today could positively affect national savings over the medium term.

Development of Securities Markets

There is a rapidly expanding literature on the role of funding in promoting the development of financial markets. Funded pension plans affect securities markets through different channels. First, funded pensions (and life insurance) can increase the demand for long-term financial assets, thus stimulating the development of the securities market. Indeed, these funds are more willing than individual investors to hold long-term securities and require lower risk and liquidity premiums. This is, in part, because of transaction costs in capital markets, their ability to diversify risk, and the long-term nature of their commitments. Moreover, funded schemes, because of their size, have the potential to enhance market discipline and promote the interests of minority shareholders in the firms where they invest.[18]

The development of securities markets can also be stimulated if the additional demand of funded schemes is matched by an additional supply of government debt. Indeed, funded schemes create demand for long-term public debt that is matched by the issuance of bonds. This provides a benchmark for setting interest rates and eventually helps to build the yield curve. Of course, the issuance of public debt may come at the expense of the equity and corporate bond markets. Nonetheless, in Middle East and North African countries, where securities markets and the appropriate regulatory framework are still in the making, more reliance on bonds is desirable.

Funded schemes also can contribute indirectly to the development of small and medium enterprises. In Middle East and North African countries, and in developing countries generally, small and medium enterprises have either restricted or no access to bank credit and other financial services due to poor legal and accounting standards, less supportive judiciary systems, and higher transaction and monitoring costs. As a result, small and medium enterprises are often financed by the corporate sector. This is particularly true in industrial structures where large corporations operate in collaboration with a large number of small and medium enterprises, involving the supply of inputs, purchase of output, control of quality, transfer of technology, and financing. Because funded schemes have the potential to shift financial intermediation from banks to capital markets, positive spillovers to small and medium enterprises can be expected (see Musalem and Tressel 2003).

Clearly, not all Middle East and North African countries are ready to capitalize on these benefits. As discussed in chapter 2, stock exchanges have yet to emerge in Djibouti, Syria, and the Republic of Yemen. In the others, with the exception of Jordan, financing through the stock exchange still plays a minor role relative to bank lending. The number of listed companies remains low despite government incentives, and firms are reluctant to dilute ownership, particularly state-owned enterprises. Nonetheless, Egypt, Jordan, Morocco, and Tunisia are reviewing their capital market laws and regulations and have strengthened their supervisory authorities significantly. In these countries, funded pensions could contribute to the development of securities markets and, through this channel, to economic growth.

Mitigation of Firms' Financial Risks

Empirical results suggest that the development of funded pension (and life insurance) schemes influence the financing decisions of firms (for other discussions and empirical evidence, see Impavido, Musalem, and Tressel 2001, 2002, 2003). This is important, particularly in the recent context of currency and financial crises associated with asset-liability mismatches in the balance sheets of banks and firms and an excessive reliance on short-term debt denominated in foreign currency. As seen in chapter 2, this is an issue in Middle East and North African countries: even in countries moving forward with banking reform, loan maturities are generally very short. The same is true of corporate debt.

To the extent that funded pension systems increase the availability of long-term funds to financial intermediaries, these, in turn, are able to allocate a higher proportion of their loan portfolio in long-term credit to the enterprise sector, without the intermediaries themselves undertaking excessive term-transformation risks. Thus longer maturity of debt is likely to induce a shift in resources from low-return, short-term projects to high-return, long-term projects, thus fostering growth.

In the Middle East and North Africa region, these potential benefits are dampened in the presence of business environments that tend to discourage private investments and often constrain the allocation of domestic credit to the private sector. As seen in chapter 2, the majority of countries are struggling to unleash private sector investments by reducing the costs of doing business. In Algeria, the Islamic Republic of Iran, Libya, and Syria, the allocation of domestic credit is influenced largely by the financing needs of the public sector. Nonetheless, in Jordan, Morocco, and Tunisia, with larger shares of domestic credit going to the private sector, the development of funded pensions could be associated with an increase in leverage and the maturity of debt among firms.

Increased maturity of corporate sector liabilities should increase resilience to various shocks.[19]

Bank Stability and Efficiency

The development of funded schemes can also increase the stability of the banking system by reducing systemic risks that can potentially lead to a banking crisis (see Impavido, Musalem, and Tressel 2001). First, credit risk may be reduced if funded pensions promote the development of public information on capital markets and thus improve bank monitoring of borrowers. Second, funded pensions provide resources to the banking system (in the form of loans, deposits, or the purchase of securities issued by banks), making them less vulnerable to liquidity risks for a given level of long-term assets. Banks would therefore be able to avoid losses caused either by unexpected increases in short-term interest rates or by sudden withdrawals.

In countries moving to private ownership of the banking system, funded schemes can also promote efficiency through increased competition. Indeed, these funds compete on the savings side by capturing savings from households, particularly in the case of complementary pension schemes or life insurance, and on the lending side by increasing the demand for long-term securities. This competition can affect prices. As alternative sources of financing become available, banks have incentives to reduce net interest margins, in part because higher liquidity in the capital market reduces issuance costs. Increased competition, however, is not relevant for countries where the ownership of banks is largely public (for example, Algeria, Egypt, and the Islamic Republic of Iran) or where interest rates are capped (for example, Libya and Syria).

Costs of and Constraints on Higher Funding

While there are benefits to increasing the level of funding of pension plans, there are also welfare costs related to sourcing the funds and the risk of capital loss. This is true even for voluntary complementary pensions, which usually involve the setup of tax-incentive policies. In general, the welfare cost is a result of the need to raise additional funds by introducing distorting taxes (including higher contribution rates) or cutting other expenditures (including lower plan benefits). Costs could be exacerbated in the presence of an unstable macroeconomic environment, weak banking system, volatile capital markets, or high risks of capital losses in the funded system as a result of weak institutional capacity to manage investments and inappropriate governance structures and regulations.

In several countries, higher funding in mandatory schemes is constrained by the frail fiscal position (for a discussion of fiscal conditions for introducing funded systems and the implications for the fiscal stance, see Holzmann 1998 and MacKenzie et al. 2001). As some of the contributions are diverted to funded accounts, governments will have to intervene to finance current pensions (that is, current reserves will be depleted sooner). Payments to the current generation of pensioners as a share of GDP are already in the 1–3 percent range. In most countries, the central budget continues to generate primary deficits above 5 percent of GDP and to have a large share of incompressible expenditures (see chapter 2). The most worrisome cases are Jordan, Lebanon, and Morocco. A stronger fiscal stance is observed in Algeria and Tunisia, the former mainly due to high oil revenues. Egypt also has a large fiscal deficit (7 percent of GDP), but the implicit debt of the pension fund is backed almost fully by explicit government debt that the general budget is already servicing. Although no analyses have been conducted to assess the fiscal impacts of alternative transition strategies toward higher levels of funding, it is likely that only a very gradual approach could be considered in most cases.[20]

In some circumstances, a weak fiscal position could be considered an argument in favor of the implementation of a defined-contribution, fully funded scheme. Lebanon provides an illustration. The country still has not implemented a pension fund for private sector workers—they only have access to an end-of-service indemnity. With public debt above 170 percent of GDP, the government is concerned that the introduction of a defined-benefit, pay-as-you-go system could make things worse. Indeed, the system is prone to political manipulation and, if badly managed, would add implicit debt to the high explicit debt of the government, further threatening macroeconomic stability. By doing so, it would increase the risk premium demanded by investors, thus raising the cost of domestic credit, with obvious consequences for economic growth and the cost of servicing the explicit debt. Hence a defined-contribution, fully funded scheme is considered preferable in the Lebanese case.

A more important challenge to higher levels of funding, or the implementation of a mandatory defined-contribution, fully funded scheme, is the presence of weak governance structures and the lack of institutional capacity. As discussed in chapter 5, in the majority of countries, governance structures are not conducive to managing pension funds in the best interests of plan members. Most funds are managed by tripartite boards lacking the necessary expertise; responsibilities are blurred; there are no clear objectives or benchmarks for investment policies, which are poorly shielded from political influence; and no system of incentives ensures proper accountability to plan members. Hence in

Algeria, Djibouti, Tunisia, and the Republic of Yemen, most of the reserves of the pension funds are in the form of government arrears and informal loans. In the Islamic Republic of Iran, two pension funds are involved in the management of a large number of companies, some of which are nonperforming companies transferred by the government to cover part of its debt with the funds. In Libya, the pension fund is also an important entrepreneur mostly involved in the tourism sector. Only in a few cases (for example, Jordan and Morocco) have governments attempted to give more independence to pension funds, staff the investment units or committees with professionals in the field (for example, Jordan and Morocco), and rationalize the investment process by defining clear objectives and benchmarks (see chapter 5). Weak governance structures, accountability, and investment policies also affect the management of reserves in earnings-related schemes.

Incomplete financial markets can also act as a barrier to higher funding in some cases. Chapter 2 shows that only some countries verify the minimum conditions for the implementation of funded pillars, which include having a core of sound banks and insurance companies. In the large majority, investment opportunities remain limited and more risky. Shallow capital markets and an underdeveloped insurance sector also imply less private sector capacity and expertise in the area of fund management. This limits the implementation of outsourcing policies to improve the management of pension funds.

While recent reforms suggest that inappropriate governance structures and weak institutional capacity in the public sector, along with incomplete financial markets, do not necessarily preclude the movement to mandatory funded schemes, these are still being implemented, and it is premature to derive lessons. As discussed in more detail in chapter 6, the West Bank and Gaza, where the various problems discussed in this section are pervasive, is transforming the current defined-benefit system for civil servants into a defined-contribution, fully funded scheme. Policy makers considered this less risky under the current circumstances than preserving a defined-benefit system that would continue to be subject to political manipulation, thus constituting an important contingent liability. To ensure the proper functioning of the new scheme, the West Bank and Gaza is launching an ambitious plan to strengthen institutional capacity. More important, it plans to outsource the management of funds and allocate the majority to foreign assets.

To conclude, countries can be grouped in two broad categories: countries that are better placed to increase funding and countries where the benefits of higher funding are less evident and the risks and constraints more severe.

Countries that are better placed to increase funding—for instance, by implementing a defined-contribution scheme or developing voluntary private funded pensions—include Egypt, Jordan, Lebanon, Morocco, and probably Tunisia. These countries have a core of sound banks, are engaged in reforms of the financial sector, and have a nascent insurance industry with know-how in the management of funds that could serve as the basis for the development of private voluntary pensions. In Egypt and Jordan, particularly in the former, current occupational plans could also serve as the basis for the take-off of voluntary pension plans (the main constraints are still the large mandates of the public sector and the average level of income of the population). In these countries, the main risk regarding a higher level of funding in the mandatory system is related to weak governance and institutional capacity. Morocco is an exception, given that the Régime Collectif d'Assurance et de Retraite (RCAR) is already managing a funded scheme. In all cases, it is important to promote outsourcing policies for the management and even the administration of funds. Given a frail fiscal stance, the transition to higher levels of funding will need to be gradual.

Regarding the management of funds, there is mounting evidence that centralized systems are less costly from an administrative point of view. The model that generates the lowest management cost is a centralized structure such as the Swedish second pillar or the Thrift Savings Plan for Federal Employees in the United States. These provide limited portfolio options to plan members and outsource fund management to mutual funds. Countries where the benefits of higher funding are less evident and the risks and constraints more severe include Algeria, Djibouti, the Islamic Republic of Iran, Iraq, Libya, and the Republic of Yemen. The West Bank and Gaza also belongs in this category. A priority for this group is to bring the defined-benefit, pay-as-you-go system up to standards by modifying benefit formulas and eligibility conditions, improving administration, developing management and information systems, and, to the extent possible, improving investment policies. In parallel, governments need to continue with structural reforms for private sector development, including the financial sector. These countries could then create the conditions for voluntary private pensions. The constraint in this case is given by lower levels of income per capita and therefore less savings capacity. A more important role for voluntary schemes would also imply reviewing the mandate of the mandatory system, at least in the case of middle- and high-income workers.

Expanding Coverage to the Vulnerable and Poor: A Role for Social Pensions?

It has been argued that the coverage of the mandatory pension system is constrained mainly by the structure of the labor market and institutional arrangements, with administrative capacity and incentives probably playing a secondary role. Individuals employed in small enterprises (many of which are short lived) and subsistence agriculture or as self-employed and seasonal workers constitute a considerable share of the labor force in the region. They create a challenge for the authorities in facilitating and enforcing collection of pension contributions. In addition, for many of them, including the long-term poor, current contribution rates are simply unaffordable. The implication is that, even with better administrative capacity, lower transaction costs, expanded geographic distribution of banks, postal offices, or pension branches, and a credible reform program that creates stronger links between contributions and benefits, important segments of the labor force are likely to remain outside the contributory system. Here we discuss two general groups: (a) poor individuals with no savings capacity and (b) vulnerable, low-income self-employed or seasonal workers with *some* savings capacity, but for whom current contribution rates are not affordable or who are excluded from the contributory system.

Noncontributory pensions (also called social or basic pensions) *could* be a mechanism for expanding the coverage of the pension system in order to guarantee a minimum level of retirement income to all. Contrary to earnings-related or defined-contribution pensions, social pensions are flat payments to individuals that depend primarily on age, residency, and, in some cases, means-testing provisions. Policy choices have important implications for costs and incentives. There is also the question of whether social pensions are needed when other assistance programs are in place. These issues are discussed next with reference to international experience.

Choosing the Level of Benefit

There are no stringent rules to define the level of the basic pension, and choices at the international level vary considerably (see chapter 3). The basic pension is equal to 25 percent of average earnings in Australia, 24 percent in Brazil, 18 percent in Kosovo, 19 percent in Mauritius, and 40 percent in New Zealand (see table 4.3). Policy makers, however, need to pay careful attention to the financial and fiscal implications and incentive effects. High benefits—for instance, a minimum pension set at the same level as the minimum wage—can discourage work, particularly in old age, and be financially unsustainable. The goal should be to set a benefit that is adequate and affordable. A possible reference could be the poverty line. Ideally, the level of the basic pension for individuals outside the contributory system should be the same as the minimum pension guarantee provided by the contributory scheme (see chapter 3).

TABLE 4.3

Social Pensions in Select Countries around the World

Country	Program	Benefit type	Reduction in benefit	Retirement coverage (percent)	Eligible age[a]	Maximum individual benefit (US$)[b]	Percent of average national wage	Program expenditure as a percent of GDP
High-income countries								
Australia	Social security	Flat pension	Means testing	66	65 (men); 62.5 (women)	479	25	2.3
Denmark	People's pension	Flat pension	Earnings testing; prorating for residency less than 40 years	Almost 100	65	525	14	—
	Universal pension supplement	Flat supplement	Income testing	—	65	528	14	—
New Zealand	Superannuation	Flat pension	Subject to taxation	Almost 100	65	554	40	4.1
Sweden	Guaranteed pension	Flat pension	Prorating for residency of less than 40 years	—	65	632	31	—
United Kingdom	Basic state retirement pension	Flat pension	Prorating for shorter employment history	—	65 (men); 60 (women)	420	16	—
	Old person's pension	Flat supplement	Pension income testing	—	80+	252	9	—
Low- and middle-income countries								
Botswana	Old-age pension	Flat pension	None	167	65	28	9	0.4
Brazil[c]	Rural old-age pension	Flat pension	None	140	60 (men); 55 (women)	81	24	1.0
	Old-age assistance	Flat supplement	Means testing	8	65			
Estonia	Social insurance old-age pension	Flat-rate component of the old-age pension	None	—	63 (men); 59 (women)	24	7	—
	National pension	Flat pension	Not eligible for social insurance old-age pension	—	63	46	13	—
Kosovo	Basic pension	Flat pension	None	Almost 100	65	40	18	3.1
Mauritius	Universal pension	Flat pension	None	109	60+	59	19	2.0
		Flat pension	None		90+; 100+	221; 252	71; 81	—
South Africa	Old-age pension	Flat pension	Means testing	88	65 (men); 60 (women)	75	10	1.4

Sources: Authors' estimates based on SSA 2002–2004; ILO; Willmore 2001; Barrientos and others 2003; for the Brazil population, Brazil 2000 Census and U.S. Census Bureau International Database Online.

— Not available

Notes: Retirement coverage is the ratio of the number of reported beneficiaries to the number of the age-eligible population.

a. In Australia, Estonia, and United Kingdom, the retirement age for women is being raised gradually. In Brazil, for old-age assistance, the retirement age for women was lowered in 2004 from 67.

b. 2002, except for Botswana, Brazil, Mauritius, and South Africa, where 2003 amounts are shown.

c. For Brazil, the denominator of coverage for the flat pension was the number of senior rural residents, while for the flat supplement, it was total population 65 years of age and over.

TABLE 4.4

Cost of a Flat Pension of 15 percent of National GDP per Capita in Select Middle East and North African Countries, by Eligibility Age, 2004–40

Percent of GDP

	2004		2010		2025		2040	
Country or territory	60	65	60	65	60	65	60	65
Algeria	0.9	0.6	1.0	0.7	1.6	1.0	2.6	1.8
Bahrain	0.6	0.4	0.6	0.4	1.8	1.0	3.7	2.7
Djibouti	0.8	0.5	0.8	0.5	0.7	0.5	0.9	0.5
Egypt, Arab Rep. of	1.0	0.7	1.1	0.7	1.8	1.2	2.4	1.7
Iran, Islamic Rep. of	1.0	0.7	1.0	0.7	1.6	1.0	2.5	1.6
Iraq	0.7	0.5	0.9	0.5	1.2	0.8	1.9	1.3
Jordan	0.8	0.5	0.9	0.6	1.2	0.8	2.3	1.5
Lebanon	1.2	0.9	1.3	0.9	1.9	1.2	3.0	2.2
Libya	0.9	0.6	1.1	0.7	1.6	1.1	2.5	1.7
Morocco	1.0	0.7	1.1	0.7	1.7	1.1	2.5	1.8
Tunisia	1.3	0.9	1.4	1.0	2.1	1.4	3.2	2.3
West Bank and Gaza	0.7	0.5	0.7	0.4	0.8	0.5	1.6	1.1
Yemen, Republic of	0.6	0.4	0.6	0.4	0.7	0.4	1.0	0.6

Source: Authors' calculations.

Choosing the Minimum Eligible Age and Residency Conditions

The eligibility age is another important parameter affecting costs. In Middle East and North African countries, for instance, providing a flat pension equal to 20 percent of GDP per capita to all of the population older than 65 would cost, on average, 0.8 percent of GDP over the short term, increasing to 2.1 percent over the long term. Providing the same benefit to the population older than 60 would cost 1.2 and 3.1 percent over the short and long terms, respectively. Table 4.4 reports projected costs by country for the level of flat benefit of 15 percent of GDP per capita. In general, the minimum age should be set equal to or above the normal retirement age in the contributory system. The benefit can also be adjusted as a function of the length of time that the individual resides in the country prior to retirement. In Sweden, for instance, the full flat benefit is paid to individuals with at least 40 years of residency. For individuals with a shorter period of residency, the flat pension is prorated. Such testing in the Middle East and North Africa region could be complicated, however, by the lack of reliable records.

Means Testing

Means can be defined broadly or narrowly, thus including all income and assets, only income, or only pension income. Countries such as Botswana and Brazil provide universal flat pensions that are not means tested. A similar approach is being proposed in the West Bank and Gaza. This greatly simplifies administration and associated costs. Indeed, means testing can demand a great deal of institutional capacity and data, particularly when based on total income and assets. However, failing to implement means tests increases benefit expenditures. Policy makers need to address a delicate trade-off between the cost associated with targeting and the benefits related to lower pension payments.

An interesting approach that is used in New Zealand is simply to tax the flat pension as other income. Hence, low-income individuals pay lower tax rates than high-income individuals (that is, they receive a higher share of the flat payment). This, however, requires a well-functioning tax system.

Other alternatives involve means testing the basic pension on the basis of earnings-related or defined-contribution pensions, including private pensions. One approach, which is implicitly being used in several contributory schemes in the region, is to provide a top-up to the earnings-related pension. Basically, individuals with an earnings-related pension below a minimum receive a supplement so that this minimum is reached. The problem with this approach is that it reduces the incentives to contribute. Indeed, for low-income individuals, additional years of contributions might not bring the total pension payment above the minimum. In other words, each time the earnings-related pension increases, the top-up is reduced by the same amount (that is, there is a 100 percent implicit marginal tax rate on the top-up). This problem is represented in the left panel of figure 4.5: the total benefit received increases only after several years of contributions.

Figure 4.5 Incentive Effects of Top-Ups and Flat Pensions

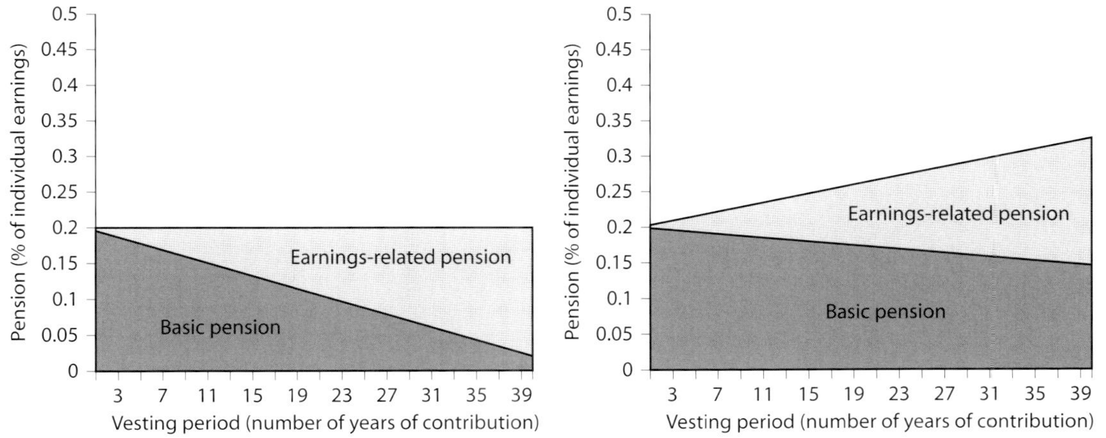

Source: Authors' calculations.

Note: In both figures, the accrual rate is set at 1.5 percent per year. The individual is assumed to earn 30 percent of average earnings. The basic pension is set at 20 percent of average earnings. In the left panel, the reduction factor is 100 percent; in the right panel, 30 percent.

A more efficient approach is to reduce the top-up by only a fraction of the marginal increase in the earnings-related pension. The right panel of figure 4.5 represents this alternative. In the example, the complementary pension or top-up is reduced by 30 percent of the earnings-related pension, and thus the total benefit received increases with the number of years of contributions. This preserves the incentives to work and contribute. For this same reason, there is less need for a minimum vesting period in this type of arrangement. The approach provides a good compromise for controlling the cost of the basic pension without dramatically increasing the costs of administration.

Links to Current Contributory Systems

While designing the noncontributory scheme, it is important to ensure that individuals with savings capacity have incentives to enroll in the contributory pension scheme. This is the case, for instance, for workers in small enterprises and a portion of the self-employed. To this end, several reforms in the contributory scheme can be considered.

The first recommendation is to allow workers in small and medium enterprises, part-time or temporary workers in the agricultural sector, or the self-employed to enroll voluntarily in the contributory scheme and to offer the possibility of paying a lower contribution rate linked to a notional covered wage, thus addressing the issue that, for several of these groups of individuals, it is not possible to measure wage levels. However, lower contribution rates should also be associated with lower accrual rates for a given retirement age. In this way, there are no implicit subsidies within the contributory scheme. Redistribution takes place in a transparent manner through payment of the basic pension.

For this to work, it is necessary to change the current mechanism used to provide the basic pension guarantee in the contributory system. The top-up approach does not introduce incentives to contribute at low levels of income and it needs to be replaced by a flat pension that can be reduced or not as a function of the earnings-related pension (see the previous section).

In general, countries should be discouraged from creating special pension funds or schemes for certain categories of workers, yet several countries in the region have been following this strategy. Algeria, for instance, has a separate scheme for the self-employed, where contribution rates and benefits are lower. Tunisia has a special arrangement for workers in the agricultural sector. Egypt has a quasi-noncontributory scheme for casual workers and schemes for the self-employed and workers abroad. All these systems are financially unsustainable (in part because of a narrower base of contributions), demand nontransparent subsidies from the other regimes or the government budget, discourage enrollment in the main scheme, and fragment the labor market. The Islamic Republic of Iran has an integrated scheme in which the self-employed are allowed to join the system at a lower contribution rate. But because benefits (that is, accrual rates) are the same, this creates an implicit nontransparent subsidy within the contributory system.

Financing

There are two mechanisms for financing the basic pension: contributions (basically a tax on labor) and general revenues. When the basic pension is limited to individuals within the contributory scheme, it is argued that the tax on labor is a superior option for equity reasons. Basically, using general revenues to finance the basic pension of a minority of the labor force is regressive. A counterargument, however, is that the tax on labor introduces distortions in labor markets and, in particular, can reduce wages for workers in agriculture and in the informal sector: neither category of worker usually is enrolled in the contributory system. There is a consensus, however, that when the basic pension is universal and offered to individuals outside the contributory scheme, it should be financed out of the general revenue.

Links to Core Social Assistance Programs

Social pensions can be redundant given the existence of safety nets, which already target poor households. In fact, there is little evidence that the elderly are poorer than the rest of the population in the region (see table 4.5). At the same time, there is limited information about family structure (for example, what proportion of the elderly live with their children?) and no information regarding the distribution of income within households. Hence it is difficult to assess the impact that current safety nets have on the well-being of the elderly and, conversely, that social pensions would have on the well-being of other members of the household. This issue deserves more research and analysis. Under ideal conditions, social pensions and safety nets do not need to be duplicative. As an illustration, an individual participating in a public works program that allows for self-targeting already would have discounted other sources of household income, including the pension of the elderly. The design of conditional cash transfers, in contrast, should not be affected because the focus is on promoting changes in behavior by increasing household income at the margin. Other types of cash and in-kind transfers would be targeted, taking into account the effect of social pensions, either implicitly (as in the case of geographic targeting on the basis of poverty rates) or explicitly (as in the case of means tests). Under this

TABLE 4.5

Age and Poverty in Select Middle East and North African Countries

Percent of total population in age group

Country and age group	Poor	Nonpoor
Yemen, Republic of		
0–25	38.0	62.0
26–64	42.0	58.0
65+	39.0	61.0
Jordan		
0–14	13.5	86.5
15–24	14.7	85.3
25–53	14.1	85.9
54+	12.7	87.3
Iran, Islamic Rep. of		
0–29	9.9	90.1
30–49	59.3	40.7
50–64	23.6	76.4
65+	7.2	92.8

Sources: World Bank 2003e, and forthcoming b; International Bank for Reconstruction and Development (IBRD) 2002.

Note: For Jordan, data refer to 2002; for the Islamic Republic of Iran, data refer to urban households for 1998; for the Republic of Yemen, data refer to 1998. The age refers to the head of household.

approach, social pensions could become a transparent, and relatively easy to administer, mechanism for redistributing income toward poor households, while other safety nets are used to fill in the gaps.

Improving the Institutional Configuration, Administration, and Regulation of Pension Systems

Several areas are not discussed extensively in the section on diagnostics and yet are critical for the proper functioning of the pension system: (a) institutional organization, meaning the types of programs in place and the institutions in charge of managing them; (b) the way in which the administration is designed and implemented; and (c) the way in which pension funds are regulated. This last section raises a series of policy questions and recommendations in these three areas that countries ought to consider when designing an integrated pension reform program.

Institutional Organization of the Public Pension System

Ideally, the reform of pension systems in the Middle East and North Africa region should aim at full integration. Countries would basically converge to a unique pension system covering all categories of workers, although there could be differentiated contribution rates to facilitate the enrollment of vulnerable groups on a voluntary basis.[21] Countries like the Islamic Republic of Iran would also need to seek the integration of occupational plans, which currently operate as substitutes to the main scheme (the SSO). These plans could continue to operate, under appropriate supervision and regulation but would become complements to the SSO. Morocco has recent experience in this area, having integrated the occupational plans of public enterprises into the scheme for contractual workers in the public sector.

The main benefits of integrating the pension system include a more mobile labor force, economies of scale in management and administration, a larger base of contributors in the case of pay-as-you-go systems, and a more equitable pension system. The integration can be conducted in one of two ways: (a) only new entrants are affected or (b) new entrants and also part or all of current plan members are affected.[22] The two approaches are discussed below.

Only New Entrants Are Affected

This approach can be illustrated in the Jordanian case. Jordan had three main mandatory schemes: a mandatory scheme for private sector workers, a scheme for civil servants, and a scheme for the military. Both the civil service and military pension schemes were in a deplorable financial situation. Hence, in 1995, the civil service pension fund was closed to new entrants, and the Social Security Corporation (SSC) was opened to all new civil servants (except for special categories of high-ranking officers). Similarly, in 2003, the regime for the military was closed to new entrants, who began joining the SSC.[23] The closed funds will continue operating until the last of the current contributors retires and dies (around 2060), possibly with some adjustment to benefit formulas. Afterward, Jordan will have a fully integrated public pension system. This approach is attractive because it reduces political resistance from current plan members, who would face a reduction in benefits. Also, because more individuals continue contributing to the old system, transition costs for the government are lower (that is, the share of pension expenditures that need to be financed through the general budget is lower). The drawback is that it takes a long time for the old system to be phased out (that is, for new benefit formulas to sink in) and thus increases the present value of pension expenditures.

Current Plan Members Are Also Affected

The second approach is to mandate, or give the choice to, some or all of current contributors to transfer to the integrating system, which is assumed to be a reformed system. As in the Jordanian case, those who stay in the current systems still might face some adjustments to their benefit formula and eligibility conditions. Most countries in Latin America and Eastern Europe adopted this approach. Two issues are important in this case: (a) to recognize the acquired pension rights of those who transfer to the new system and (b) to ensure that the reformed integrated scheme does not assume the implicit pension debt of the old systems.

To recognize accrued rights, the basic approach, albeit with several variations, is to estimate pension payments at retirement, under the assumption that the individual will continue to contribute and accrue benefits under the current rules, and to prorate these as a function of the time that the individual has been in the system when the transfer takes place. The present value of future pension payments estimated in this way is then transferred to the integrating fund, for instance, in the form of a bond that matures when the individual retires. On retirement, the individual's pension will have two components: the pension under the old rules, which is linked to contributions in the old system, and the pension under the new rules, which is linked to contributions in the new system.[24] There are two problems with this approach: the potential resistance of current plan members, at least when the transfer is mandatory, and the fact that a higher share (or maybe the totality) of the pension for current retirees needs to be paid out of the general budget. The benefit of the approach is its transparency, as the implicit debt is made explicit. The cost of the transition, of course, is higher.

In the case of earnings-related schemes, the contributions in the new system could still be used to pay the pensions of plan members, but through a transparent financial transaction in which the old system—the government—issues debt (that is, bonds) that is appropriately remunerated. This retains the pension debt of the old system as explicit debt. Countries should also consider the possibility of keeping the implicit pension debt of the new system as explicit government debt, by investing the contributions in government bonds that are indexed by a proxy of the implicit rate of return that the system pays on contributions.

If full integration is politically difficult, a compromise in the case of countries with multiple systems is to reduce the number of mandatory earnings-related schemes to two: one for public sector workers and one for private sector workers. This implies integrating workers who are in occupational plans. The occupational plans can continue to exist, if properly regulated, but as complements to the mandatory schemes, not as substitutes. Under this dual-system approach, benefits need to be harmonized to the extent possible between the funds, following the best practices discussed earlier. Clearly, because both systems have a different base of contributors, the parameters cannot be identical. Under either of the two approaches, bilateral agreements (bridges) to facilitate labor mobility need to be put in place.

Improving Administration

The success of any policy initiative aiming to reform the national pension program will depend heavily on administrative capacity and planning. Analysis of the existing systems, procedures, and institutions should be part of any comprehensive reform effort. The focus is on the division of responsibilities among the various public agencies involved in the process, on expenses associated with administering the system, on the administrative burden on employers and employees, and on issues related to the (a) administration of collection, (b) identification of plan members, (c) procedures for paying contributions, (d) process for paying benefits, and (e) information technology infrastructure. To date, this area has received little systematic research and policy advice. This subsection raises a few questions that countries will need to answer when designing and implementing pension reform.

Administration of Collection

Generally the integrated collection of taxes and pension contributions is associated with significant systemic cost savings (for both the government and employers). In all countries of the region, however, pension funds have a separate collection system. This might have the advantage of shortening the circuit between the pension agency and the employer, particularly when the tax administration is institutionally weak. Nonetheless, in Egypt, Morocco, and Tunisia, the autonomous operation of multiple funds suggests the existence of costly duplication.

Identification of Plan Members

In all countries in the region, there are several parallel systems for identifying individuals and businesses (for example, social security, tax administration, national identification). The duplication of identification systems is costly and complicates cross-checks of information. A sound registration system should be able to ensure the uniqueness of identification numbers, appropriate verification mechanisms, and quality of the registration process. If an agency, such as the tax administration or the institution in charge of the civil register, does a good job of managing registrations, there is little rationale for favoring an alternative identification system for pensions.

Procedures for Paying Contributions

The key objective of this system should be to ensure accurate and secure transfers of information and funds, while minimizing transaction costs for employers. In most Middle East and North African countries, employers can pay contributions through the banking system. Paying contributions directly to pension fund agencies is another option, although inferior given the lack of specialized financial services. In some cases (for example, Egypt), simplified payment procedures also exist to attract small businesses and the self-employed. The variety of payment procedures usually reflects an effort to expand coverage and promote compliance, but keeping a delicate balance with administrative costs is an important objective. The challenge in most countries is related to the capacity of the pension fund to verify the accuracy of the data and to track payments efficiently. Usually, payments are made in lump sums and then supplemented with a detailed reconciliation report that presents individualized data on employee contributions. Little is known, however, about reconciliation procedures. Weak capacity to define, manage, and enforce procedures that outline what to do with the unreconciled balances, erroneous overpayments, mistakes in reports, unidentified individual records, and so forth will always lead to a poor quality of pension records.

Procedures for Paying Benefits

Key issues to consider include (a) how to reduce the time needed to process benefit applications, (b) how to verify the information regarding beneficiaries, (c) how to track deceased retirees, (d) how to reduce the effect of fragmentation in pension administration on entitlement to full benefits, (e) and how to make payments in an efficient and secure way. The existence of underdeveloped or decentralized information systems makes processing benefit applications a lengthy procedure in most countries. Furthermore, verification of the applicant's age may be a complex task when the national registration systems are weak (for example, in Djibouti and the West Bank and Gaza).

Tracking deceased beneficiaries is a challenge in most cases. In Egypt, the problem has been addressed by collaborating with the banks in exchanging information on the individual's accounts and by requiring beneficiaries to appear regularly in person to confirm eligibility.

Finally, regarding payment mechanisms, several countries make good use of bank deposits (for example, Egypt, Jordan, and Morocco). In rural or remote areas, various other delivery methods (for example, direct cash delivery, post offices, or pension fund agencies) could be normally used. In Djibouti, however, payments are made only through the pension branch in the capital. Eventually, the mechanism selected should be cost-effective and provide for quality services. Generally, the banking system, if sufficiently developed, should be a preferred method of delivery.

Information Technology Infrastructure

In the majority of countries in the region, information systems are outdated or underdeveloped, and access to modern information technology is limited. Exceptions include Bahrain, Egypt, Jordan, Morocco, and Tunisia. In all the other cases, records regarding contributors and beneficiaries are out of date. Countries such as Djibouti and the Republic of Yemen are investing in information technology infrastructure, but there are concerns regarding the cost-effectiveness of the proposed designs. A good-quality information technology system should provide for efficient management of the process, integration of multiple business operations, effective monitoring, and easy processing of and access to data. It is very important for the design of information technology systems to follow, not precede, the design of the pension system.

Administrative Costs

The level and structure of expenditures associated with administering national pension plans in the region require further analysis, but they should clearly be of concern to managers and policy makers. Inefficiencies in administration and overstaffing, poor infrastructure, and fragmented pension provisions result in higher operational costs. In Djibouti, administrative expenditures of the Organisme de Protection Sociale (OPS) reach 29 percent of program expenditures; in the Republic of Yemen, the cost of administering the Private Pension Fund (GCSS) represents 10 percent of contributions (see table 4.6). For comparison, the average administrative expenditures for public pension agencies in Central and Eastern Europe is under 3 percent. In part, high expense ratios in Middle East and North African countries reflect low coverage of the system so that economies of scale cannot be used fully.

TABLE 4.6

Administrative Expenditures for Select Middle East and North African Countries

Percent

Country	Scheme	Year	Share of total expenditures	Share of total contributions
Bahrain	GOSI	2001	9.5	6.8
Djibouti[a]	OPS	2002	29.0	33.0
Egypt, Arab Rep. of	PPEEPF	1997	3.9	4.0
Iran, Islamic Rep. of	SSO	2000	6.8	6.3
Libya	SSF	2003	2.7	3.1
Morocco	CNSS	2002	5.6	5.0
Yemen, Republic of	GCSS	2003	50.0	9.8

Source: Authors' calculations on the basis of various operational reports.
Notes: Total expenditures include benefits and operational expenses.
a. Unusually high administrative expenses were reported in 2002.

General Issues on Regulation

Another area where work is required concerns the regulation of mandatory and voluntary pension plans. In general, public pension funds are not formally regulated. Morocco can be considered an exception, since the regulator of the insurance industry also "monitors" the mandatory pension plans. Regulation is lacking also in the case of occupational pension plans, for instance, in the Islamic Republic of Iran and in Jordan. In most cases, there are defined-benefit schemes or defined-contribution schemes on "book." Little is known about their financial sustainability, and their investment policies are not transparent. This raises a problem not only for plan members but also for governments, since occupational plans often are part of public companies and thus add to the government's contingent liabilities. Egypt and Morocco regulate voluntary plans. The Islamic Republic of Iran and Jordan are working on regulations to allow these plans to operate through insurance industries. In the other countries, little progress has been made.

The general recommendation is that countries where voluntary plans have the potential to develop should set the necessary regulatory and supervisory framework from the beginning; it is desirable that mandatory defined-benefit schemes and occupational plans also be covered by this framework. Regulation is needed at the following levels: (a) appropriate licensing and capital requirements for providers; (b) full asset segregation among pension assets, sponsors, management firm, and custodian and the use of external custodian banks; (c) asset diversification and the rules of asset management (the qualifications and licensing of internal or external managers); (d) asset valuation rules (mark-to-market) and rate-of-return calculations (the mutual fund instead of the savings account model); (e) periodic actuarial reviews and financial audits; (f) transparency and information disclosure; and (g) effective supervision. For occupational plans, regulations should also deal with funding, investment, and portability rules. As markets develop, however, the approach of requiring legal investment limits should be relaxed gradually so that, in the long run, it converges to the prudent main principle.

Countries wishing to develop voluntary schemes should also review taxation rules. The tax treatment of pension plans, either mandatory or voluntary and independent of the provider, should be the same: either exempt-exempt-tax or tax-exempt-exempt treatment.[25] This is to preserve neutrality in the mobilization of savings. To this end, governments need to consider providing tax exemptions for the investment income of pension funds and the reserves of life insurance plans.

Notes

1. In low-income countries where national statistical systems are not well developed, and therefore estimates of average earnings are either not available or not reliable, a better reference could be income per capita.

2. When implementing a basic pension guarantee, there are key issues to consider with regard to the financing mechanism and eligibility conditions.

3. Countries report various poverty lines. The most common are the *food poverty* line and the *general poverty* line. Usually, these are reported separately for urban and rural areas and at the national level. The general poverty line is always higher than the food poverty line. Rural poverty lines in all the countries reviewed are lower than urban poverty lines.

4. This is achieved by introducing a ceiling on the covered wage. See chapter 3 for a review of choices at the international level.

5. For surveys of international experience with pension reform, see Bonnerjee (2002); Lindeman, Rutkowski, and Sluchynskyy (2001); and Schwarz and Demirgüç-Kunt (1999). Useful international comparisons can be found in Palacios and Pallarès-Miralles (2000). For a discussion on new perspectives on pension reform, see Holzmann et al. (2005).

6. The various systems are discussed in appendix E.

7. See appendix E for further discussion.

8. See appendix E for a derivation of this result.

9. The obvious technical problem is that, in a standard defined-benefit system, the accrual rate is calculated ex ante—that is, when individuals join the system as opposed to when they retire. Therefore, the calculation needs to be based on expectations regarding (a) survival probabilities at retirement and (b) the value of the growth rate of the average covered wage or the covered wage bill. This can reduce the precision of the calculation and compromise the financial sustainability of the scheme. Alternatives around this problem are discussed in the section on virtual account systems.

10. See appendix E for a discussion of the determinants of rates of return of defined-benefit schemes.

11. See appendix E for a description of the virtual account formula and its equivalence to the traditional defined-benefit formula. See also Disney (1999) for a critical review of the scheme, Gorá and Palmer (2003), and Holzmann and Palmer (2005).

12. Although appealing, this idea still needs to receive empirical support.

13. See appendix F for a discussion of transfer formulas.

14. One exception is the Caisse Marocaine de Retraite (CMR) in Morocco, where disability benefits are financed directly from the central budget. Another exception is the RCAR, also in Morocco, where there is a special account for disability pensions, but where survivor pensions are financed through individual accounts and the general fund.

15. A loss under the individual-only approach is that the market prices for private life insurance and annuities are higher to filter high risks (adverse

selection). However, it is not clear if the welfare gains from reducing adverse selection through mandatory pooling exceed the losses for those who are pulled into the pool on an involuntary basis. Pooling also achieves cross-subsidies between genders, but these also can be achieved by using unisex mortality tables.

16. This policy of making husbands accountable for their decisions should be extended to disability and young-age survivor pensions. One mechanism is to require these individuals to purchase additional policies through private companies.

17. This operation does not necessarily imply increasing the level of reserves, because higher funding, for instance, can be achieved by cutting benefits and therefore reducing the implicit pension debt. Here we are more interested in the case where higher reserves are allowed to accumulate, either because contributions increase or because the government assumes part of the implicit debt of the system.

18. Pension funds hold productive policy dialogues with regulators and successfully monitor corporate performance, which improves regulations and corporate governance to the benefit of minority shareholders.

19. In market-based economies, an increase in the proportion of shares in the portfolio of pension funds is associated with a decrease in the leverage of firms. This makes firms more robust to economic cycles and changes in interest rates (see Impavido, Musalem, and Tressel 2001).

20. However, this type of operation does improve the long-term fiscal position of the government by making explicit part of the implicit debt of the pay-as-you-go system, while avoiding its buildup. Hence, government borrowing is justified.

21. In defined-benefit schemes, a different contribution rate also implies a different accrual rate.

22. The discussion here applies to transfers from a fund that is being phased out to the integrating fund. The issue of transfers, however, also emerges in an integrated system that is being reformed—for instance, if a parametric reform is combined with the introduction of a defined-contribution, funded component. Policy makers then need to make decisions regarding which individuals are affected by the reform (that is, who should join the new system).

23. What is problematic in the case of Jordan is that the merger was implemented before the SSC scheme was reformed.

24. If the receiving fund is a defined-contribution, fully funded scheme, the pension can be computed by adding the acquired rights (the value of the recognition bonds at the time of retirement) to the capital accumulated in the individual account and then purchasing an annuity. Depending on the market interest rate, the resulting benefit can be higher or lower than if part of the pension is computed as a defined benefit (that is, on the basis of the replacement rate accumulated at the time of the transfer).

25. See appendix D for a review of tax regulations across the region.

CHAPTER 5

Management of the Public Pension Funds

Although not managed as prefunded schemes,[1] most of the public pension schemes in the Middle East and North Africa region have accumulated reserves. Among the countries reviewed, the reserves range from 4.2 percent of GDP in Djibouti to 52.5 percent of GDP in Bahrain. At the aggregate level, the reserves of mandatory pension systems account for 14.4 percent of regional GDP. This is among the highest levels in the world, second only to South Asia (see figure 5.1).

Recently, the issue of pension fund management has attracted considerable attention by policy makers, practitioners, and development agencies. One of the main motivations is that, in general, public pension funds have been mismanaged and performance, as measured by most reasonable standards, has been poor (Iglesias and Palacios 2000). Around the world, reserves in partially funded public schemes have been used to subsidize housing, state enterprises, and various types of economically targeted investments. They have been used to prop up stock markets and as a captive source of credit, and they probably have allowed governments to run larger deficits than they would have otherwise. Investment decisions typically occur in a regulatory vacuum, with little public accountability, limited access to information, and obscure management processes.

International experience suggests that progress toward improving the management of public pension funds relies on the presence of good governance, meaning the systems and processes that a company or the government uses to manage its affairs. The main components of good governance include transparency, systems for conflict resolution, and accountability for each function and role.

This chapter compares the management practices of pension funds in Middle East and North African countries with best practices at the international level and identifies realistic options for reform. The chapter starts by outlining core principles for better governance, accountability, and investment policy. It then benchmarks current practices along these three dimensions in Middle East and North African countries and

Figure 5.1 Pension Assets as a Percentage of GDP in Middle East and North African Countries and World Regions

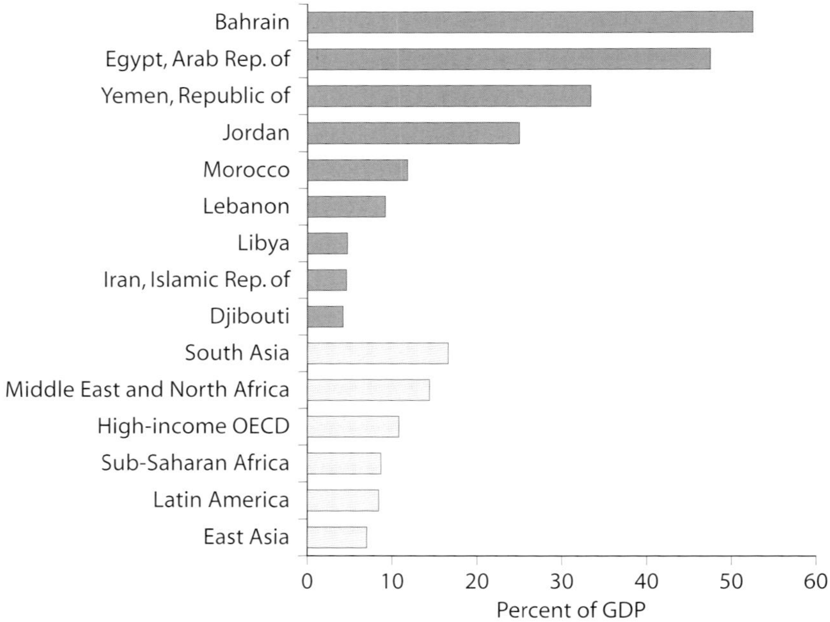

Sources: For East Asia, Latin America, OECD, South Asia, and Sub-Saharan Africa, see Palacios (2003); for the Middle East and North Africa region, authors' calculations based on information provided by the various pension funds.
Note: Calculations are based only on the available data. The regional data cover 45 percent of the countries for high-income OECD countries, 44 percent for Latin America, 47 percent for Sub-Saharan Africa, 56 percent for East Asia, 90 percent for South Asia, and 33 percent for the Middle East and North Africa.

identifies major weaknesses. The final section discusses the constraints on introducing structural reforms in the region and proposes a set of practical guidelines to improve management in the short and medium terms.

Lessons from International Experience in Pension Fund Management

A recent comprehensive review of international best practices identifies core principles for good governance, accountability, and investment policies.[2] These are summarized in this section and presented as a benchmark to assess the current challenges that countries in the region face.

General Principles of Good Governance

The governance provisions of public pension schemes should aim to establish good business practices and avoid corruption, mismanagement, and abuses by the government itself. According to recent evaluations of international experience, the following principles and guidelines should improve the governance of publicly managed pension schemes.

Mandate of the Governing Body

Within the pension fund, roles and responsibilities should be clearly defined. An example can be found in the Canadian pension reforms carried out between 1995 and 1998. Under the Canadian Pension Plan (CPP) Investment Board Act of 1998, the board has a clear fiduciary duty to (a) manage CPP funds in the best interests of contributors and beneficiaries and (b) invest its assets to achieve the maximum rate of return, without incurring undue risks and while taking into account the factors that may affect the funding and ability of the CPP to meet its financial obligations.

Selecting the Governing Body and Shielding Funds from Political Interference

The law establishing the management agency should provide unambiguous conditions under which members of the governing body of the agency can be appointed and removed. For example, in Canada, the finance minister, in consultation with provincial governments, appoints the 12 members of the CPP board. The appointment process involves a nominating committee that recommends qualified candidates to the federal and provincial governments. The board and the appointment process are subjected to close public scrutiny, and candidates for the board, in addition to having suitable qualifications, must meet demanding skill and character requirements.

The managing agency should be free from inappropriate interference from the government in pursuing its objectives and meeting its responsibilities. Ideally, the government should remain at arm's length from the investment decisions of the fund manager. New Zealand has chosen the route of full disclosure. Under New Zealand law, the minister has explicit power to direct the governing board of the public pension fund. However, directions must be submitted in writing, presented to Parliament, and published in the official gazette. Ireland takes a slightly different approach, explicitly prohibiting investments in Irish government securities and thus restricting one avenue by which the government could misuse the fund for its own purposes.

Minimizing Corruption and Fraud

The management agency should be required by law to establish internal governance structures and processes aimed at minimizing corruption, mismanagement, and fraud. Governance procedures should include

(a) the mandatory establishment of a risk management and audit committee; (b) a code of conduct for staff and senior executives; (c) a detailed description of the roles and responsibilities of different groups within the agency; and (d) a process of quality control and rigorous documentation, review, and audit requirements for investment decisions and information technology support systems.

Supervision

The government should require the management agency to be regulated and supervised by the same agency responsible for regulating private pension providers and, where feasible, to meet the same standards imposed on private providers. Canada has not placed its public fund under the jurisdiction of any of its private sector financial regulators, but it has imposed a similar set of standards for governance and investments as those required of the private sector. In contrast, Indonesia is proposing to place the public pension fund under the same regulator as private pension funds. This is already the case in Costa Rica, Kenya, and Morocco.

General Principles of Accountability

Structures that provide managers with incentives to comply with their mandate and run the pension fund in the best interests of plan members are central to the achievement of good governance. To this end, two basic elements need to be considered: transparency and reward structures. Regarding transparency, the objective is to fully disclose information (for example, the financial situation of the scheme, the composition of the portfolio, investment decisions, and performance). Regarding reward structures, the goal is to ensure that those making decisions are held accountable. Good judgment and good performance should be rewarded, while poor judgment and bad results should be penalized.

Disclosure of Governance Structures and Responsibilities

There should be full and open disclosure of the governance structure of the scheme and the managing agency, including rules for selecting members of the governing body and managers. Accountability requires that details about the governance structure be made public. In particular, there should be adequate disclosure of the arrangements put in place to detect and prevent fraud. As part of its disclosure of governance arrangements, the managing agency should be required to publish its formal delegations of powers and responsibilities. Once the agency has formalized its structure of delegations, it should make these available to all stakeholders.

Disclosure of Policy Making, Performance, and Financial Situation

The management agency should be required to report comprehensively on its decisions and performance. This is arguably the key accountability issue. Full disclosure of performance in both absolute and relative terms is fundamental to protecting the interests of plan members. Funding shortfalls should be identified and disclosed, along with the government's proposed remedial actions. The process for assessing and dealing with a funding shortfall should be transparent and preferably contained in law. Where the government has an explicit policy of partial funding, the extent of the underfunding should be assessed and reported in the government's accounts. Both Canada and Ireland use publicly disclosed benchmarks for comparing performance. Canada uses the benchmark of fund performance in the private sector, while Ireland uses a predetermined set of benchmark indexes. In addition, Canadian fund managers are required to hold public meetings in each province at least every two years to discuss performance. Since instituting this type of public reporting, administrative costs have fallen more than 60 percent.

The management agency should be subject to regular governance and performance audits. This practice is common in many countries. In Canada, in addition to the annual financial audit, the CPP is required to initiate a special examination of management practices at least once every six years.

Incentives, Rewards, and Sanctions

To the greatest extent possible, incentives and rewards for performance should be linked to delegated responsibilities and should be risk based. Those who make delegated decisions should be rewarded or sanctioned according to the way in which they exercise their delegations. Managers should be required to review periodically the exercise of delegations they have made. Compliance should be rewarded, and breaches of guidelines, either for governance or for investment, should be penalized, even where the returns are higher than expected.

General Principles of Investment Policy

Public pension fund managers have the responsibility to select an investment strategy that balances risks and returns appropriately for plan members. The investment policy comprises three main components: setting long-term performance targets, defining an acceptable level of risk tolerance, and setting parameters for short-term asset allocation. These need to be set out clearly in an investment policy statement.

The primary focus of investment policies for private investment funds is to balance market risks and returns. Three types of risks need to be managed: (a) the risk of loss due to counterparty default, (b) the risk of loss due to movements in market prices, and (c) the risk of loss due to operational failure. In addition to these risks, public investment funds need to be concerned about their role in the domestic capital market and their exposure to government debt. In the private sector, the market risk dimension of investment strategies is increasingly expressed as a comprehensive measure of risk, such as *value at risk*. This comprehensive measure of risk automatically signals inadequate diversification. Therefore, funds can be managed effectively in the absence of strict sectoral limitations or target ratios. However, this approach has yet to reach far into the public sector, where investments often are handicapped by limited mandates and restrictions that militate against modern risk management practices. Nevertheless, some principles emerge from international practice to ensure prudent management and improve the efficiency of public funds. These principles are discussed below.

Setting Investment Policy

The investment policy should be set by the board of directors or trustees. It should be fully documented and should be available in summary form to members of the scheme. Clearly, for competitive reasons, the publicly disclosed elements of the investment policy should focus only on general strategies and attitudes toward risk. The strategy should be aligned with the objectives of the fund and should be shielded from political influence.

Mandate of the Investment Policy

The investment policy should state that the purpose of accumulating and investing pension reserves is solely for the benefit of members of the pension plan. A policy that is directed solely to the interests of fund members will have few, if any, prohibitions on investments. The interests of fund members will be enhanced by sound diversification of risks. In general, rules that limit or prohibit investments, including investments in foreign securities, reduce the capacity of the fund to diversify and to serve the interests of fund members. The two exceptions to this general rule are loans to related parties—either the government or plan members—and investments in risky derivatives.

Market Power and Corporate Governance

The investment policy statement should identify the potential for the fund to be or to become a dominant force in the domestic market and should specify how the fund would resolve such a situation. The investment policy should be explicit about how the pension fund would exercise its voting rights as a shareholder. The exercise of voice is important but, to avoid a situation in which the government de facto directs private business, it is usually better to delegate this power to the fund managers. One way to minimize the conflicts of interest that may arise from such situations is for the fund to publish, with a lag time, a summary of the way in which it voted in its various shareholder capacities. Fearing the potential for pressure on the public fund to influence corporate governance for purposes other than those in the interests of the fund itself, some countries have imposed concentration limits or delegated voting rights to fund managers; others, such as Sweden, have put a cap on the effective voting power of the fund. In all cases, however, a policy for shareholder voice should be explicit and documented.

Assessing and Managing Risks

The investment policy should identify all relevant risks and the board's approach to measuring, monitoring, and managing each risk. A particular problem arises from investments in nonmarketable assets. These investments reduce the liquidity of the fund and are more prone to malpractice at the time of acquisition, valuation, or sale. Assets can be purchased above market prices or sold below market prices to benefit fund managers. Even in the absence of corrupt practices, valuation problems can make it difficult to assess whether the asset is generating gains or losses.

In general, the investment policy should seek to minimize investment in illiquid assets. However, in many countries this may not be practicable, especially where funds are prohibited from investing in foreign assets. One way to contain the risks involved with investments in illiquid assets is to limit the amount to a benchmark maximum, set by the board, according to a realistic assessment of the spectrum of investments available. Where such investments are permitted, the board should establish a clear policy for their purchase, disposition, and valuation. The policy could include either mandatory independent assessment of each purchase and sale of illiquid assets or supervision by the audit committee of the board before the transaction occurs. This assessment should evaluate the price set for the transaction, the independence of the parties involved, and the appropriateness of the transaction for the fund, with respect to the targeted rate of return. To reduce the scope for corrupt practices, the prices and details of all transactions in illiquid assets should be disclosed to fund members and the public.

Investment policies should respect exposure limits, too. To diversify risk, funds should not invest more than 5 percent of their reserves in a single asset and should not own more than 5 percent of the liabilities of a given company. Respecting these rules reduces the influence that funds might have on corporate governance and thus reduces the possibility of conflicts of interest.

Pension Fund Management in the Middle East and North Africa Region

None of the surveyed countries in the Middle East and North Africa region complies with the best practices of governance, accountability, and investment policies discussed in the previous section. In general, there are no clear mandates for the governing body of the pension funds, pension funds are not shielded from political pressure, investment policies tend to be opaque and do not respect guidance regarding risk exposure, and disclosure and accountability to plan members is weak.

Current Practices in Governance

Governance covers the mandate of the governing body, the process for selecting the governing body and shielding it from political pressure, mechanisms for minimizing corruption and fraud, and supervision.

Mandate of the Governing Body

Very rarely does the law establish the mandate of managing the fund in the best interests of plan members. Pension funds often have mandates that are not related to their core functions. In Egypt, the Islamic Republic of Iran, Lebanon, and Libya, for instance, the funds are explicitly mandated to finance economic and social development projects. The Conseil National de Sécurité Sociale (CNSS-Djibouti) in Djibouti and the Social Security Investment Unit (SSIU) in Jordan are the only institutions within the sample that endow governing bodies with the unique mandate of collecting contributions, paying benefits, and managing the funds in the best interests of plan members.

Selecting the Governing Body and Shielding It from Political Pressure

All of the pension funds under review have tripartite governing bodies that are poorly shielded from political pressure. While the number of governors varies, the composition in all cases includes representatives from the government, plan members, and employers. None of the countries has specific criteria regarding the profile of members of the governing body. As a result, selected members often lack the credentials and experience to manage the fund in the best interests of plan members.

Governments have a dominant representation, mainly through staff from the Ministry of Finance, Ministry of Labor and Social Affairs, or the central bank.

The chairman of the board is usually a representative of the head of one of these institutions. The fact that the chairman of the governing body and the director general are political appointees also creates high turnover in the governing body and the management team. This is particularly problematic in the region, where cabinets are subject to frequent reshuffling. These reshuffles are especially prevalent in Jordan and Lebanon.

In the majority of cases, the director general of the pension fund is appointed and removed by a high-level government official. In Djibouti, the appointment and removal of the director general are made jointly by the minister of labor and the minister of finance, although the president can overrule them. In Libya, the director general of the Social Security Fund is appointed by the prime minister without consultation. In the Islamic Republic of Iran, the heads of the two pension funds are appointed by the equivalent of the minister of planning, who is also the chairman of the governing bodies of the two institutions.

The main consequence of this type of arrangement is the emergence of conflicts of interest between the government and plan members, which impede effective control of corruption and fraud. There are many examples of such conflicts. In the Islamic Republic of Iran, the Civil Servants Retirement Organisation (CSRO) and the Social Security Organization (SSO) have recently signed an agreement accepting public companies—often with dubious financial situations—as payment for part of the government debt with the fund. Both funds plan to keep some of these companies and sell others after restructuring and recapitalization. De facto, both funds have been transformed into government agencies to restructure and privatize public enterprises. In the case of the SSO, the transferred companies represent roughly 40 percent of reserves. This policy benefits the government, but it is unlikely to benefit plan members.

Minimizing Corruption and Fraud

In general, responsibilities of the members of the governing body are loose. Very rarely does the law establish the mandate of managing the fund in the best interests of plan members. With the exception of the SSIU in Jordan and the Caisse Marocaine de Retraite (CMR) in Morocco, none of the laws creating the funds or the associated regulations clearly specifies the responsibilities of board members. Only the SSIU defines in general terms a code of conduct for staff and senior executives.

However, supervisory committees, investment committees, and audit committees are common, but their structure is likely to reduce their effectiveness. In the Islamic Republic of Iran, both the CSRO and the SSO have investment and audit committees, but these are formed mainly by representatives of the government, managers of key companies owned by the funds, and senior members of the management team of the funds. The CMR in Morocco has an investment committee that determines internal rules, a placement committee that implements investment policies, and a supervisory committee that assesses performance, ensures that the implementation of the investments conforms to strategy, and ensures compliance with prudential rules. The supervisory committee, however, reports mainly to the minister of finance and includes three members from that institution. Moreover, the Ministry of Finance mandates the CMR to keep close to 90 percent of its reserves in government debt.

Weak governance also reflects weak administrative capacity. All funds define the organic structure of the agency and the functions of the different departments, but they do not evaluate the performance of the various units and their staff or implement quality control processes. With a few exceptions (for example, Bahrain, Jordan, Lebanon, and Morocco), information technology support systems are underdeveloped. In the Islamic Republic of Iran, even senior management has difficulty obtaining an integrated view of the allocation of assets and their performance.

Supervision

There is no explicit framework for regulation and supervision in any of the countries surveyed. Pension funds usually fall under the umbrella of the Ministry of Labor and Social Affairs or the Ministry of Finance (this is always the case in schemes for the military and civil servants). These ministries have representatives on the boards of the pension funds. Only in Morocco is the regulator for the insurance industry, which is within the Ministry of Finance, also in charge of monitoring all mandatory schemes.

Current Practices in Accountability

Accountability covers the disclosure of governance structures and responsibilities, the disclosure of policy making and performance, and the creation of incentives, rewards, and sanctions.

Disclosing Governance Structures and Responsibilities

All pension funds in the region make public the information regarding the structure of the governing body, which is part of the law. However, the rules for nominating members, other than government representatives, as well as their specific responsibilities to the board are not transparent.

Disclosing Policy Making and Performance

Little information is made available to the public regarding the decision-making process within the governing bodies. For instance, none of the funds reports making public the minutes of the meetings of the governing body.

The main weakness, however, relates to reporting procedures and investment policies. All funds publish annual reports describing their financial situation, but these often are subject to significant delays, and the information tends to be neither relevant nor sufficient. For instance, with the exception of Bahrain, none of the reports reviewed contains sufficient information about investment strategies and outcomes.[3] In the Islamic Republic of Iran, the annual reports are prepared for the governing body and other government institutions; the public does not have access to them. The publications that are targeted to the public take more the form of an advertising brochure listing the various activities in which the pension funds are involved.

Benchmarking of performance and independent auditing are insufficient, and the results are not properly disclosed. Overall, no clear criteria for benchmarking the operations and performance of pension funds have been defined yet.

In all cases, periodic audits and evaluations of investments are required, but these often are not executed by independent agencies. With the exception of Algeria, all pension funds conduct periodic actuarial valuations, either internal or external, but the results often are kept confidential. Only in Bahrain, Jordan, and Morocco do the pension funds report making use of external auditors who disclose the results of these valuations automatically. In the other countries, the auditors are government agencies or specialized departments within the institutions that administer the funds. Even in Jordan, where efforts have been made to improve transparency, the results of the actuarial valuations are not published or made publicly available. This situation impedes good governance and creates an additional avenue for the emergence of conflicts of interest.

This lack of transparency is likely to be amplified by, in general, limited understanding of plan members regarding the finances and functioning of the pension fund. In this context, information asymmetries are exacerbated, and the main stakeholders (contributors and beneficiaries) have limited ability to safeguard their interests. This reduces the incentives of managers to make policy decisions in the best interests of plan members.

Creating Incentives, Rewards, and Sanctions

The incentives of fund managers are not aligned with the interests of plan members in any of the countries surveyed. The delineation of responsibilities between the governing body and the management team is often blurred. This is evident in the Islamic Republic of Iran, Jordan, and Libya, where the managing director is also the chair of the governing body, which also includes other senior managers. In none of the cases does the governing body have the power to elect and remove the managing director, who is appointed directly by the government. Remuneration policies are not set by the governing bodies and are not linked to the performance of the management team. Mechanisms for rewarding good performance and penalizing bad judgment are lacking. The fact that the governing body does not appoint and remove the general manager of the fund also reduces incentives to respond to board policies.

Current Practices in Investment Policy

In the large majority of cases, investment policy is set on an ad hoc basis. Few funds attempt to define a coherent strategy that sets targets for acceptable levels of risk, expected rates of return, and asset allocations that match the maturity of liabilities. With few exceptions, there are no explicit mechanisms to assess and manage risks, and exposure limits in investments are not respected. The resulting investment policies are risky, with many funds overexposed to explicit and implicit public debt as well as direct investment in companies, which interferes with corporate governance. Lending to plan members and investments in real estate (and management of real estate property) are also widespread. Clearly, nonexistent or shallow and narrow capital markets constrain investment choices over the medium term (see chapter 2). Still, with the exception of the Caisse Interprofessionnelle Marocaine de Retraite (CIMR) and the Caisse de Dépôt et de Gestion (CDG) in Morocco, which outsource the management of reserves, the majority of funds remain large players in these markets, which can discourage private investors. Some of these issues are illustrated next by reviewing investment policies in Egypt, the Islamic Republic of Iran, Jordan, Lebanon, Libya, and Morocco.

In *Egypt*, all surpluses of the pension funds are invested in the National Investment Bank (NIB). Today, 63 percent of the NIB's liabilities are with the pension funds (see table 5.1). By law, the NIB finances the government's capital expenditures. In fact, the government is mandated to borrow from the NIB at a predetermined interest rate, which is currently above market levels (see figure 5.2). Interest paid on this debt accounts for 40 percent of revenues of the pension funds (see World Bank 2005c). When employer contributions and other transfers are

TABLE 5.1

Balance Sheet of the National Investment Bank in Egypt, 2002–4
Percent

Item	2002	2003	2004
Assets			
Government	46.8	45.1	43.6
Economic authorities	19.4	18.2	17.5
Other investments	10.1	10.3	13.8
Soft loans	2.5	2.3	2.1
Public companies	6.5	7.0	7.4
Joint venture companies	0.7	0.6	3.8
Other investments	0.4	0.5	0.4
Bank deposits	1.2	3.2	1.3
Other	22.5	23.2	23.8
Liabilities			
Social security funds	63.6	63.6	63.7
Investment certificates	23.2	22.5	21.7
Development bonds (US$)	0.5	0.6	0.6
Post office savings	7.0	8.1	9.0
Other	0.5	0.7	0.7
Other debt	5.1	4.5	4.3

Source: National Investment Bank (NIB).

Figure 5.2 NIB and Market Interest Rates in Egypt, 1979–2000

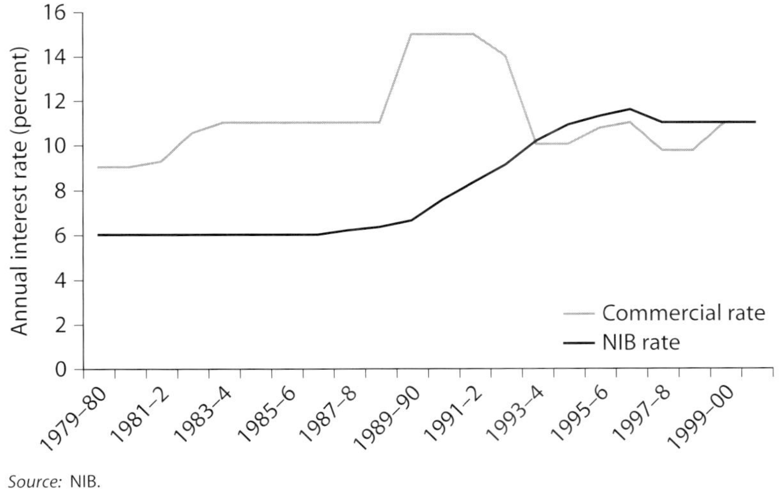

Source: NIB.

included, the government is basically providing 80 percent of the revenues of the funds, which are generating a surplus of 6 percent of GDP. This surplus is deposited back into the NIB. This practice is contrary to the more common case, where governments consider pension funds to be a low-cost source of funding. In Egypt, the current arrangement increases financing costs. In principle, this situation could be considered ideal for the pension fund, but it is unlikely to be sustainable in the long run. Close to 70 percent of the portfolio of the NIB is made of public debt (table 5.1). Ultimately, the liabilities of the NIB are a direct responsibility of the government. Given these circumstances, it might be more appropriate to consider the NIB not as an entity with an autonomous balance sheet but rather as a liability line in the general budget. At the same time, any reform program of the Egyptian pension system should aim at keeping the implicit debt of the scheme in the form of explicit government debt (see the discussion in chapter 4).

In the *Islamic Republic of Iran*, investment policies for both the SSO and the CSRO are highly complex and risky. The SSO has become a large industrial conglomerate with considerable market power in several economic sectors, which can impede private sector development and interfere with corporate governance. Up to 1976, the SSO invested its cash reserve fund in the Worker's Welfare Bank in the form of fixed deposits. After creation of the Social Security Fund in 1976, the SSO started to diversify its investment activities, but by 1989 close to 80 percent of the portfolio was still composed of long-term deposits. By 2000, however, the share of deposits had dropped to 10 percent, while the share of indirect and direct investment had increased to 27 and 43 percent, respectively, or 70 percent of the total portfolio. The companies owned by the SSO (directly and through its investment company, Shasta) produce 43 percent of pharmaceutical and hygienic products, 36 percent of cement, 35 percent of televisions, 25 percent of fireproofing products, 31 percent of refrigerators and freezers, and 35 percent of rubber. The SSO is one of the most active investors in the stock exchange, with 11.3 percent of market capitalization in 2001. In addition, the SSO invests in government securities, provides financial support for public construction projects, accords liquidity to the banking system, and gives financial assistance to pensioners and contributors (for example, housing loans, marriage aid) at subsidized interest rates (see figure 5.3).

Clearly, the SSO has expanded its mandate too far, rendering it difficult for managers to assess the performance of investment policies and to implement corrective measures when necessary. Beyond problems of governance and disclosure, it is unclear whether the SSO has the resources (human and physical) to monitor effectively the operations of the large number of companies it owns directly or indirectly through Shasta. Since the managing directors of the companies know the limitations of the monitoring system, they are more willing to take risks. Some SSO staff have observed, for instance, that the managing directors of the companies often present unrealistic cost-benefit analyses to justify additional investments. During implementation, results usually diverge

Figure 5.3 Structure of the Portfolio of Investments of the SSO in the Islamic Republic of Iran, 1989–2000

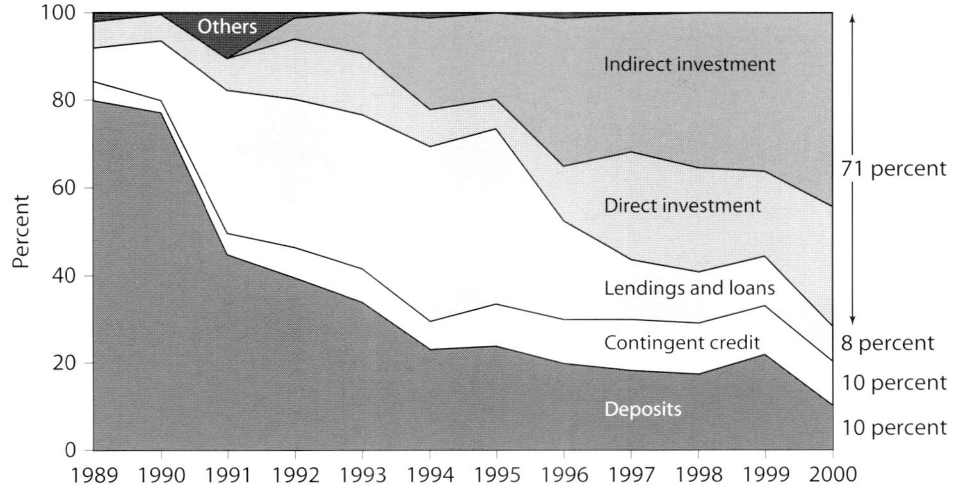

Source: Data provided by SSO Economic and Investment Affairs Department.
Note: Indirect investment refers to investments through the investment company Shasta. *Direct investment* refers to investments in companies directly owned by the SSO.

dramatically from predictions and yet are approved during the meetings of the General Assembly. Another problem with the direct management of several corporations is that considerable resources need to be allocated to deal with administrative problems.

Other SSO activities, such as housing projects, lending to the corporate sector (including its own companies), and subsidized lending to beneficiaries, also incur administrative problems that divert the attention of the board and create conflicts of interest. A pension fund that concentrates on collecting contributions, paying benefits, and allocating investments does not need to consume resources for other activities. The Department of Economic, Investment, and Planning Affairs is currently proposing to break Shasta into smaller holdings that are more specialized but that would respond to the same governance structure. This is unlikely to bring sizable improvements in management, since incentives would remain unchanged.

The CSRO pursues two types of investment activities: direct investments, which are executed by the Department of Investments and Economic Affairs of the CSRO, and indirect investments, which are executed by the newly created investment company. Direct investments refer to investments in companies (that is, equity positions) that do not take place through the stock market. The level of CSRO ownership in these companies varies from 100 percent of assets, as in the case of a

TABLE 5.2

Structure of Reserves of the CSRO in the Islamic Republic of Iran, 2001

Category	Amount (millions of US$)	Percent
Companies transferred by the government	500	19.60
Investment company	125	4.90
Construction company	37	1.45
Long-term deposits	25	0.98
Government bonds	63	2.45
Loans	1	0.04
Government arrears, including interest and penalties	1,800	70.57
Total	2,551	
Share of GDP		3.29

Source: Authors' calculations based on interview with the head of the Investment Department.

construction company, to less than 13 percent. Companies where CSRO ownership exceeds 50 percent of assets are managed directly. In companies where the CSRO owns between 13 and 50 percent of the assets, CSRO has representatives on the board of directors, and in companies where ownership is below 13 percent, the CSRO has no representation. Direct investment activities have intensified with the recent transfer of public companies to cover part of the government debt with the fund. Looking forward, however, the strategy is to prioritize indirect investment activities through the investment company, which was created to manage investments in the stock market. It currently has assets equivalent to 5 percent of total reserves (see table 5.2). In practice, fund managers have a very narrow margin of maneuver in which to reallocate assets and improve rates of return. To give the company some degree of autonomy from the CSRO, the investment company was created with its own "supreme council." However, its supreme council is composed of the same members as the supreme council of the CSRO. There is no information about company-specific investment policies or strategies, except that investments cannot be above 15 percent of the capital of a given company (to avoid involvement in decision making) and that, above a given threshold, approval is required from the board of directors.

In *Jordan*, important reforms have recently taken place with the creation of the SSIU. The SSIU was established as an entity with its own board of directors, which has a classic tripartite structure (that is, representatives of government, employees, and the private sector). Three of the seven members are representatives of the Social Security Corporation (SSC), including the director general. The design of the SSIU's organizational structure has been completed, and the majority of personnel have been hired. The hiring process has been conducted on the basis of detailed descriptions of functions, skills, and required qualifications for each of the positions. Candidates were selected through a highly competitive process. Personnel were not transferred automatically to the SSIU from the former investment unit within the SSC.

The SSIU has prepared a statement of investment policy that follows internationally accepted principles and practices regarding investments. The statement emphasizes two principles of investing: (a) long-term investment and (b) diversification. It states that investment policies will be conducted with the main objective of benefiting plan members. Although SSIU investments could contribute to the development of the financial sector in Jordan, this is considered a by-product of investment policies. The statement also emphasizes adherence to a strict code of ethics, which forbids SSIU staff from taking advantage of information gained in the execution of their function for their personal benefit. It also forbids speculative investments and investment practices such as short sales, complex derivatives, use of leverage, or speculation in foreign currencies. It calls for periodic evaluation and benchmarking of performance. Finally, it emphasizes the importance of research and education: in particular, continuous training for staff and the systematic evaluation of the various investment strategies that are implemented to identify those that work, those that do not, and why.

After the reforms, which took place in 2001, the SSC portfolio moved more aggressively into equities, while the share of real estate and of loans and bonds was reduced considerably (see figure 5.4). Bank deposits,

Figure 5.4 Composition of the Portfolio of the SSC in Jordan, 1980–2002

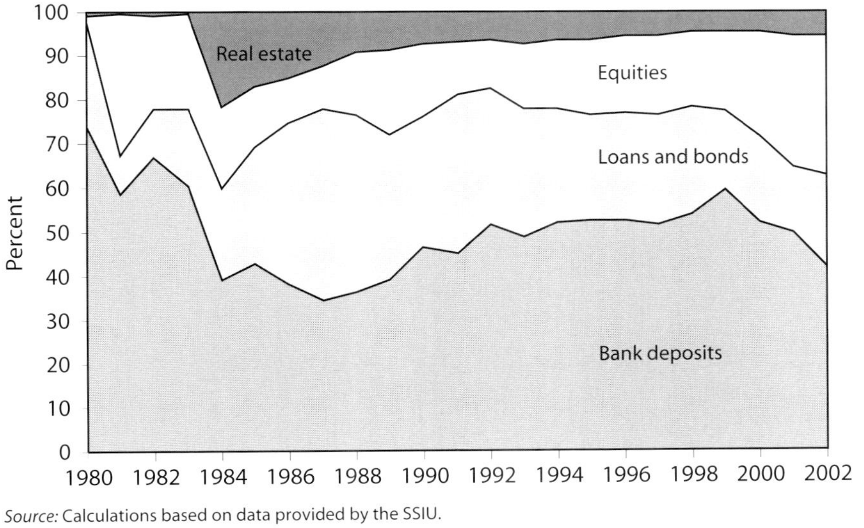

Source: Calculations based on data provided by the SSIU.

however, continue to capture more than 40 percent of reserves. This can be risky, as all deposits are treated as a single account and thus insured at only JD 10,000. The main challenge is to develop and implement adequate outsourcing policies. Currently, the SSC remains a large player in a shallow capital market (see chapter 2). This can interfere with corporate governance and discourage the participation of other investors.

In *Lebanon*, the institution that runs the End-of-Service-Indemnity Program for Private Sector Workers (NSSF) has a tripartite board and an investment committee. The board is nominated for a period of four years. The investment committee is chaired by the general director of the NSSF and has as members a general manager from the Ministry of Finance, the general manager of accounting in the NSSF, and 11 members of the tripartite board. The chair of the investment committee is a political appointee, so there is little continuity, with frequent changes in government. The responsibilities of the investment committee of the NSSF are very limited. The present rule is that pension assets have to be invested 50 percent in bank deposits and 50 percent in government bonds. The Accounting Department of the NSSF makes decisions regarding the allocation of these assets among the different maturities. Investments in other types of instruments are prohibited according to the current rules. Table 5.3 provides details regarding the maturity of instruments in the two categories of investments and the average nominal interest rate earned. This investment strategy precludes the efficient diversification of risk, in particular through investment in long-term instruments.

In *Libya* today, no governing body is in place. The chairman of the Social Security Fund is nominated by the prime minister and his cabinet and has discretion in setting investment policies. In practice, the

TABLE 5.3

Distribution of NSSF Assets in Lebanon, 2002, 2003

Percent

Type of investment and maturity	Total portfolio	Allocation	Average nominal interest earned
Bank deposits, 2003	50		
3 months		25.0	8.52
6 months		39.6	8.66
12 months		35.5	8.86
Government bonds, 2002	50		
3 months		0	
6 months		0	
12 months		0	
24 months		100.0	14.14
36 months		0	

Source: NSSF.

TABLE 5.4

Distribution of Reserves of the Social Security Fund in Libya, 2002

Category	Assets (LD)	Total share (percent)
Hotels and resorts	268,055,302	9.1
Administration and maintenance companies	12,225,000	0.4
Factories and sport garment	3,000,000	0.1
Medical services	3,000,000	0.1
Maintenance company	500,000	0.0
Hotels and resorts	3,000,000	0.1
Administration, east region	2,000,000	0.1
Administration, Hotel Almahari	725,000	0.0
Real estate	350,000,000	11.9
Investment in companies	57,486,624	1.9
Other machinery and factories	12,459,000	0.4
Bank deposits	214,100,000	7.3
Government debt	1,601,329,395	54.2
Military pensions	424,349,470	14.4
Total	2,952,229,791	100.0

Source: Social Security Fund.

decisions are subject to approval by the Ministry of Finance. The result is that the largest share of reserves, around 64 percent, is allocated to government debt, which is often not explicit (see table 5.4). For instance, 26 percent of this debt is related to arrears in the payment of military pensions, which are supposed to be financed directly by the government. No interest is recognized on this debt. Other sources of investments are hotels, resorts, and real estate, which capture 25 percent of reserves. The hotels and resorts are managed by administrative companies also owned by the SSF. Finally, the SSF has full ownership of companies operating in the sport garment, pharmaceuticals, and maintenance sectors. The managers report that the company in the sport garment business is not operating but that employee continue to be paid. Nonetheless, these companies represent less than 3 percent of total assets.

In *Morocco*, the public pension fund managers have a reasonable institutional capacity, but performance is compromised by the lack of independence from the government. The funds of the CMR are managed through an internal investment unit. This unit has three committees: (a) the *investment committee*, which provides the investment strategy based on the planned financial needs and market conditions, fixes the short-term investment objectives, and assesses performance; (b) the *placement committee*, which proposes the placement policy to the investment committee, implements the investment strategy, taking into consideration market conditions, and reports on performance; and (c) the *supervisory committee*, which assesses performance, controls the conformity of the implementation of investments with the strategy, ensures compliance with prudential rules, and sends proposals on investment policy and strategy to the Ministry of Finance, if necessary. The unit has competent personnel, but intervention on the part of the Ministry of Finance has placed excessive restrictions on investments, including the use of these funds as a quasi-captive source of financing for the public sector. Indeed, the minimum requirement for investments in government securities recently was increased from 80 to 88 percent of the portfolio; the remainder can be invested in securities listed on authorized exchanges and in real estate. Ineligible assets, among others, are foreign assets, mortgages, bonds, and investment funds. The CMR uses acceptable exposure limits, which are 10 percent per issue or issuer.

The CDG manages the funds of the scheme for private sector workers (CNSS-Morocco) and the scheme for contractual workers (RCAR). The CDG has built an impressive structure, with highly qualified staff; however, it is not fully independent from the government, and its governance, accountability, and investment policy do not meet modern good practices. The CDG does not charge management fees on market-based investments (the RCAR and the CNSS-Morocco mutual funds). In the case of the deposit account with the CNSS-Morocco, which earns a fixed interest rate, it charges 0.7 percentage point. The CDG implements the investment policy of each fund through its own investment management unit. In 2002, it outsourced only DH 3 billion out of DH 30 billion in funds to two fund managers. It is not allowed to invest abroad and has one investment committee per portfolio. It uses its own fund managers and does not seek the advice of external experts or investors. The CDG participates in the shareholder general assemblies of the corporations in which it has invested. In addition, it is a dominant player in the securities market, which has the ability to discourage the participation of other institutional investors. The CDG holds about 25 percent of government bonds, 20 percent of corporate bonds, and 30 percent of mortgage bonds and represents only 5 percent of stock market capitalization (see table 5.5). This high concentration on the demand side could create

TABLE 5.5

Portfolio Allocation of CDG Assets in Morocco, 2003

Percent

Type of investment	Portfolio allocation
Government bonds	25
Corporate bonds	20
Mortgage bonds	30

Source: CDG.

uncertainties in market behavior and discourage the participation of private investors. Further uncertainties could result from the fact that the CDG is both the market maker for public debt and a fund manager.

Improving the Management of Public Pension Funds: Constraints and Opportunities

This section starts by examining some of the constraints that limit the ability of Middle East and North African countries to adopt the set of good practice principles for pension fund management outlined in this chapter. It then highlights areas where even marginal changes could lead to better governance and management. The chapter closes with specific recommendations regarding investment opportunities.

Limitations on Better Governance and Better Management

In order to make realistic recommendations to improve governance and management in the Middle East and North African countries, it is important to understand local institutional and economic constraints. These constraints come from four main sources: (a) a legal framework that makes the application of best-practice models difficult, (b) governance problems at the macro level, (c) limited administrative and institutional capacity, and (d) the level of development of financial markets. These are discussed below.

A first observation is that the best-practice models and principles for improved management and governance have limited applicability in Middle East and North African countries because they were constructed based on the experience of developed countries founded on a legal system of English common trust law. The principles discussed in the previous sections are based on practices observed in countries like Australia, Canada, Ireland, New Zealand, the United Kingdom, and the United States, where the implicit responsibilities of the trustees for supervision and good conduct stem from the very nature of English trust law (see Clark 2004). The actions of the trustees and their ability to take on responsibilities with discretion are crucial to the efficient provision of pension benefits. Because code law traditions prevail among Middle East and North African countries, the behavior and responsibilities of trustees have to be codified. This process is inefficient and hinders improvement of accountability and other governance processes.

A second observation is that progress on pension fund governance needs to build on the level of governance in the whole economy, which remains weak for the region. Most of the principles of good governance, accountability, and investment policy involve clear, high-quality rules and regulations to enforce good behavior, control corruption, limit government interference, and ensure proper accountability.

Since the management of pension funds in Middle East and North African countries is heavily linked to management in the public sector, applying these principles successfully depends to a great extent on political stability, accountability, effective government, regulatory quality, control of corruption, and enforcement of the rule of law throughout the economy. These factors are considered to be the main indicators of good governance for the economy as a whole (see Kaufmann and others 2003). Evidence suggests that many Middle East and North African countries are located on the lower end of the international distribution on most indicators (see figure 5.5). Therefore, rapid progress toward better governance in pension fund management is limited in the context of political instability, low accountability, and poor regulatory quality.

Figure 5.5 Governance Indicators in Middle East and North African Countries: Voice, Accountability, and Regulatory Quality, 2002

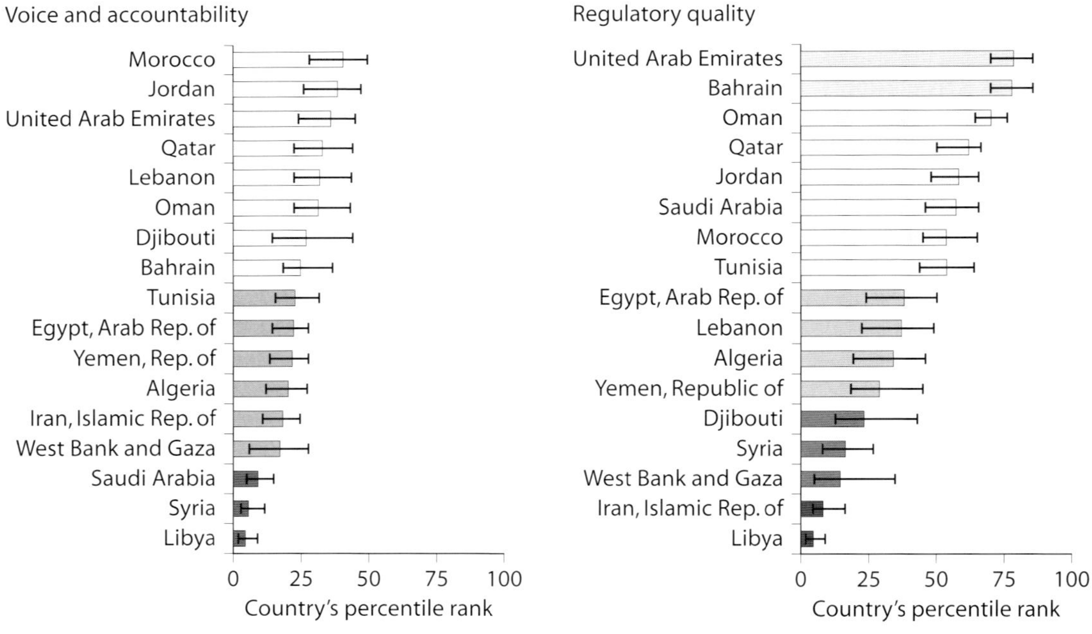

Source: Kaufmann and others 2003.

Note: The governance indicators presented here reflect the statistical compilation of responses on the quality of governance given by a large number of enterprise, citizen, and expert survey respondents in industrial and developing countries, as reported by a number of survey institutes, think tanks, nongovernmental organizations, and international organizations. Countries' relative positions on these indicators are subject to margins of error that are clearly indicated. Consequently, precise country rankings should not be inferred from these data.

Finally, there are economic constraints, the level of development of financial markets being a critical one. As pointed out in chapter 2, debt instruments and publicly traded equity instruments are available in most Middle East and North African countries, but the supply is limited. Stock exchanges exist in most countries reviewed in this report, but financing through the stock exchange is marginal, and the number of listed companies is very small. The insurance industry, and in particular the life segment, remains small in most countries.

These incomplete or shallow financial markets pose an additional constraint on good governance because they limit the availability of appropriate structures for outsourcing pension administration functions to independent and qualified third parties. For example, management of pension assets cannot be outsourced to private parties such as specialized securities or equities trading companies because such institutions do not exist or are in an incipient stage of development. Furthermore, experienced trustees and pension professionals are in very short supply even in developed countries, and systemic problems of asymmetrical information and moral hazard work against the efficacy of pension fund governance in all countries (see Clark 2004; Myners 2001).

Opportunities for Better Governance and Better Management

Even in the context of the limitations discussed earlier in this section, there are real opportunities for all the Middle East and North African countries to improve the governance and management of their pension systems. The main argument is that, in the absence of drastic changes to governance structures, reforms over the short term should focus on (a) improving transparency, which involves mandating pension funds to fully disclose their operations; (b) building technical capacity to design investment policies and reducing constraints on investments; and (c) where possible, promoting the outsourcing of fund management. Practical recommendations in each of these areas are offered below.

Transparency

Governance of public pension funds in the region could be improved by increasing transparency of management processes and stakeholder access to information. These objectives could be achieved by combining several measures, as follows.

First, public pension funds should issue formal mission statements to focus the functional mandate of the scheme and explicitly list the categories of actions that would accomplish this mandate, while promoting the best interests of stakeholders. Even if a mission statement does not have immediate practical implications, it would significantly improve transparency because it states explicitly the connection between the interests of stakeholders and the mandate and role of administrators in pursuing them.

Second, it is desirable to review internal regulations or procedures in order to define clear responsibilities and benchmarks for each of the three main functions performed by a pension fund: administration (that is, collection of contributions, custody of assets, and protection of contributions); determination of benefit eligibility; and management of assets. This potentially could be achieved, even in countries where governance bodies are not separated from management bodies, by making use of internal committees, specialized in the main functional activities of the fund. This could significantly improve the accountability and transparency of management processes. An example to that effect is the CMR in Morocco, where operations are managed internally by different committees with specific functional responsibilities, specified in detailed internal regulations. The draft law on public pensions in the West Bank and Gaza is another example of the use of specialized committees as a tool for improving transparency and efficiency of the management processes for public pension assets. The draft law mandates the establishment of an audit committee and an investment committee, with detailed responsibilities and reporting requirements (see box 5.1).

Third, transparency and stakeholder access to information could be improved by setting up a routine of standardized reporting to all stakeholders and to the supervisory and regulatory entities. Basic reporting requirements within the pension fund include annual financial reports prepared by the management entity for the board of directors of the pension fund;[4] internal audit reports of accounting and asset valuation procedures, giving preference to market or mark-to-market procedures; audit reports prepared by external, independent auditors for the managing entity; and investment reports prepared by the investment entity for the managing entity. Disclosure of information to members is also very important. In the Middle East and North Africa region, there is much room for improvement in this area, since mandatory reporting is scarce.

Finally, transparency and governance would improve if countries would put management processes under mandatory supervision by a third-party entity. Best-practice examples delegate authority for supervision either to specialized entities or to financial market supervisors, such as the central bank, insurance supervisor, or security market supervisor. Delegating supervisory authority to the financial market supervisor would be most advisable for Middle East and North African countries because it would draw on existing technical capacity in these institutions

BOX 5.1

Provisions of the Draft Law on the Public Pension Scheme in the West Bank and Gaza

The West Bank and Gaza has an ambitious draft law for the public pension scheme that dedicates an entire chapter to governance and management of pensions. The provisions proposed by this draft law are in line with international best practices in pension fund governance and management. According to the draft law, the pension fund will have a multipartite board of directors that is nominated by the prime minister, at the recommendation of an independent nomination committee that is multipartite as well. There are clear provisions regarding the obligations and responsibilities of the members of the board of directors, including the obligation to adopt an investment policy. Management of the pension fund will be undertaken by a general manager, who will oversee implementation and management of individual accounts for participants, accounting of contributions and benefits, and reporting to participants and the governing board. The draft law states expressly the annual obligation to prepare detailed financial reports for the board and to undertake actuarial valuations every two years. An audit committee and an investment committee will carry out the regulations and functions stipulated by the law.

The main responsibilities of the audit committee are as follows: (a) oversee the selection process for an independent external auditor and recommend an auditor for appointment by the board, (b) order that an audit be performed at the end of each financial year, (c) receive and review the audit report and accompanying financial statements, (d) discuss with the auditor the methodology used and the findings, (e) present a report to the board on the results of the audit and a letter to management, (f) make recommendations to the board for improving weaknesses in accounting and associated internal controls, and (g) review the activities and results of the internal auditor quarterly.

The main responsibilities of the investment committee are as follows: (a) oversee development of investment guidelines for consideration by the board, (b) recommend investment options for consideration by the board, (c) oversee the criteria for selecting a custodian and asset manager and make recommendations regarding their appointments, (d) undertake quarterly reviews of portfolio allocations and investment returns using appropriate indicators of performance, and (e) periodically review the asset management operations of the fund.

The assets of the pension fund are entrusted to an independent custodian that has at least 15 years of experience and is licensed within the jurisdiction of an internationally recognized regulatory authority of well-established and widely acknowledged expertise as a supervisory agent. Investment of assets is done by an asset manager that is subject to similarly strict criteria and has to comply with a full disclosure policy regarding fees and transaction costs. These requirements ensure that the custodian and the asset manager are recognized international institutions with substantial experience in the field.

These new legislative efforts seek to reform weak governance structures that lack internal resources and infrastructure. The success of implementing the draft law remains to be seen, but the effort to devise a solution to improve governance and management is commendable.

and add an additional layer of protection against discretionary interventions of the government. Jordan, Morocco, and Tunisia could make significant progress in this direction since they have the opportunity to capitalize on the positive developments that have taken place in their financial markets with regard to growth of the banking sector and efforts to strengthen the financial regulatory environment (see chapter 2).

Progress toward implementing these measures could be achieved gradually within the existing framework, without a major redesign of the system providing retirement income. If successfully implemented, these measures would improve both internal and external transparency of the management process, therefore improving accountability and stakeholder voice. Such developments would reduce the opportunities for discretionary government interventions, directly addressing the most serious threats to governance for the countries in the Middle East and North Africa region.

Capacity to Design and Implement Investment Policies

Pension fund management could be improved by strengthening the capacity to design and implement investment policies and by defining explicit investment strategies. Investment strategies should be designed and executed by investment committees composed of qualified professionals, with the only objective being to benefit plan members. The SSIU in Jordan is a good example.

Investment committees should be able to assess the investment opportunities available in both domestic and international markets and tailor portfolio allocation to the specific characteristics of the pension fund they are advising. Expectations regarding targeted rates of return and risk exposure should be consistent with the interests of members and beneficiaries.

Pension funds should issue investment statements or policies that, given estimated future liabilities, define investment objectives and, in particular, the risk tolerance of the portfolio and the expected rate of return. Investment policies should include explicit standards and procedures regarding limitations on allowable asset classes, concentration of ownership, issuer, risk, and type of financial instruments. The focus must be on long-term investment and diversification. Investment statements could also prohibit unauthorized use of pension assets to finance budget deficits, lend funds to employees, or invest in various economic or social development projects. It is very important that the statement of investment policies define benchmarks against which the performance of investment policies can be evaluated.

Countries should also pursue opportunities to outsource the management of part of the funds. It is essential to promote outsourcing under contracts with clear investment strategies and benchmarks. Countries where management capacity is limited or not available at the local level (for example, Djibouti, Iraq, Libya, the West Bank and Gaza, and the Republic of Yemen) should consider foreign managers. Outsourcing should be pursued through public bids, and the funds should monitor outsourced fund managers and assess their long-term performance. The outsourced contracts could be terminated in cases where the contractor does not comply with the agreed upon conditions, including performance relative to benchmarks. In order to preserve market competition and transparency, no fund manager, including the in-house operation, should manage resources in excess of 5 percent of the country's total financial resources (the aggregate of money, quasi-money, and bond and stock market capitalization). The funds should delegate the representation on corporate boards, including decisions on voting, to outsourced fund managers.

Investment Opportunities

These vary across countries, depending on the level of development of the financial sector (see chapter 2). In general, given poorly developed stock markets, the main sources of potential investments will continue to be (a) direct investments in companies, (b) loans to plan members, (c) public debt, (d) bank deposits, (e) real estate, and (f) foreign assets. Exceptions are Egypt, Jordan, and Morocco, where listed equities and collective investment schemes could capture between 15 and 30 percent of pension reserves. The main issues to consider when investing in these asset classes are as follows:

- *Direct investments in companies.* Direct investments can be risky, particularly when the funds have majority ownership and are involved directly in management (for example, Bahrain, the Islamic Republic of Iran, and Libya). Countries are encouraged to minimize this type of investment and certainly not to interfere with corporate governance: management of companies is not a function of pension funds.
- *Loans to plan members.* While most pension funds face strong pressure to offer loans to plan members (for instance, loans for housing), such loans entail high administrative costs and excessive risks to the system. Moreover, if public pension funds are to provide adequate income replacement for retirement, they should be exposed to a set of risks that are as different as possible from those that members face

during their working life. Therefore, this type of investment should be discouraged. When it occurs, rules, including selection procedures, should be transparent, and no implicit or explicit subsidies should be involved.

- *Public debt.* Government debt continues to be an important component of the portfolio of most pension funds. This debt is not always explicit; it simply is related to arrears in contributions or loans that have not been documented properly (for example, Algeria, Djibouti, the Islamic Republic of Iran, and Libya). In all countries, the supply of treasury bills and tradable public bonds is low relative to the size of the total explicit government debt, and governments are encouraged to review the structure and maturity of this debt. Over the short term, an effort should be made to make explicit part of the implicit debt with the pension funds and to ensure that this debt is remunerated appropriately. Morocco, where the government recently issued tradable bonds to cover its debt with the scheme for civil servants and the military, is an example to follow. In countries without a core of sound banks (for example, Djibouti and the Republic of Yemen), explicit public debt is likely to be the most promising source of investment over the short and medium terms. In any case, public debt should not be imposed on pension funds. The demand for this asset class should respond to the objectives set in the statement of investment policies.

- *Bank deposits.* In countries with a core of sound banks (for example, Jordan, Lebanon, Morocco, and Tunisia), public debt can play a less prominent role, while long-term bank deposits capture the largest share of the nonequity portfolio. Clearly, in cases where the banking sector is overexposed to government debt, bank deposits will not be a substitute.

- *Investments in real estate.* Real estate investments are likely to remain important for most countries. These should not involve the management of hotels or office buildings but rather should focus on actual real estate. Because investing in illiquid assets creates opportunities for corruption, clear procedures for purchasing and disposing of these assets should be approved by the board. By the same token, independent assessors should value these assets at least once a year.

- *Foreign assets.* To improve risk diversification, pension funds should be allowed to invest part of their portfolio abroad (for example, in treasury bills or indexes). An interesting initiative in this area comes from the West Bank and Gaza, where a significant component of pension assets is expected to be invested abroad.

Conclusions

The region faces a compelling challenge in improving governance and management outcomes for public pension funds. Indeed, the examination of governance structures and management of public pension fund systems in the Middle East and North Africa region reveals a serious gap when compared with best international standards and practices for good governance and sustainable management.

However, structural constraints might continue to hinder progress. These include (a) a legal framework that makes the applicability of best-practice models difficult, (b) governance problems at the macro level, (c) limited administrative and institutional capacity, and (d) the level of financial sector development. Major changes in governance and administrative structures are unlikely to be feasible in the current context.

Nevertheless, there are encouraging stories. Recent progress in Jordan and the West Bank and Gaza in improving governance and management of their pension systems suggest that there are real opportunities to make changes that will have a large positive impact.

Governance overall would benefit significantly from increased transparency of management processes and stakeholder access to information. Feasible actions include mission statements, internal regulations that define management responsibilities, routine standardized reporting to stakeholders and regulators, and independent supervision of public pension funds.

Pension fund management could be improved by strengthening the capacity to design and implement investment policies. Countries need to invest in teams of qualified professionals to manage their pension funds. There should be clear guidelines for investment policies that, given estimated future liabilities, define investment objectives, including the risk tolerance of the portfolio and expected rates of return. Asset allocations should respect clearly defined exposure limits. In particular, pension funds should not be involved in the direct management of companies; in financial, economic, or social development projects; or in lending to plan members. Finally, there should be clearly defined benchmarks to evaluate investment policies.

Finally, countries should actively pursue outsourcing the management of part of the funds. Outsourcing contracts should be based on clear investment strategies and benchmarks. In countries where management capacity is limited or not available at the local level, foreign managers should be considered. Outsourcing should be pursued through a process of public bids. In order to preserve market competition and transparency, no fund manager, including the in-house operation, should manage resources in excess of 5 percent of the country's total financial resources. Funds should delegate the representation on corporate boards, including decisions on voting, to outsourced fund managers.

Notes

1. The only exception is the RCAR in Morocco.
2. All the issues and principles discussed in this section are based on Carmichael and Palacios (2004) and Musalem and Palacios (2003).
3. This is likely to change in Jordan, where the SSIU is reviewing reporting procedures.
4. A complete annual financial report should include the following: a balance sheet, a statement of revenues and expenditures, a statement of change in net assets, and a statement of investments.

CHAPTER 6

Progress to Date and Prospects

This final chapter assesses progress on pension reform across countries in the non-gulf region of the Middle East and North Africa and explores political and economic factors that could explain the observed differences. For discussion purposes, countries are organized into three groups. The first group includes three countries, which are in the very early stages of the reform process: Algeria, Libya, and Syria. The second group involves the Islamic Republic of Iran, Iraq, Tunisia, and the Republic of Yemen, where policy discussions are more advanced but governments still have not arrived at a coherent reform strategy. The third group refers to countries that are leading pension reform and have either (a) developed detailed reform proposals and laws or (b) introduced important structural reforms, even if only in parts of the pension system. These countries are Djibouti, Egypt, Jordan, Lebanon, Morocco, and the West Bank and Gaza. The ensuing discussion is based on the work and experience of various technical teams advising governments throughout the Middle East and North Africa region on social protection and pension reform. The classification of countries is necessarily subject to some degree of discretion on the part of the authors.

Countries in the Early Stages of Reform

In countries at the very early stages of reform, the challenges facing the pension system are poorly understood and are not part of the government's agenda. Discussions of the issue remain enclosed within the pension funds and probably the ministries in charge. These countries have not undertaken an in-depth assessment of the financial situation of the funds. Only Algeria and Libya are discussed here, but Syria, for which scant information is available, also falls in this group.

Algeria

The Algerian government, through the Ministry of Finance and the Ministry of Labor and Social Affairs, acknowledges that the pension system and the social insurance system more generally are facing problems. However, there has been no mandate to conduct an in-depth analysis of the issues facing the pension system and initiate preparation of a reform program. Recently, resources were mobilized to prepare an evaluation of the financial situation of the pension funds. This task had been delayed because poor record keeping made it difficult to generate the data necessary to conduct the analysis.

From discussions with technical staff and managers, there seems to be a tendency to underestimate the magnitude of the problems facing the Caisse Nationale des Retraites (CNR) and the Caisse d'Assurance Sociales des Non-Salariés (CASNOS). The reasons for the lack of widespread interest in pension reform are difficult to discern. Powerful unions dominate labor negotiations and wage-setting policies in Algeria, yet in Morocco, where labor unions are also important, the reform process is considerably more advanced.

In Algeria, the pension system is sometimes perceived as a social assistance program. Within this framework, the use of government transfers to cover the deficits of the pension funds is considered appropriate. The presence of high oil revenues might also reduce the incentives for reform, as future pension payments might appear to be affordable.

Libya

Discussions of pension reform in Libya are still not part of the broad policy debate. This reflects, in part, the lack of information regarding problems facing the fund. As in Algeria, the presence of oil revenues might reduce the incentives to assess and correct the financial situation of the scheme. It is interesting that, even with lax budget constraints, the government has not been complying with its obligations toward the fund. Today, 70 percent of the assets of the Social Security Fund are constituted by public debt, which is often implicit (for example, arrears on contributions).

The newly appointed chairman of the Social Security Fund (SSF) is undertaking a detailed assessment of the institution, including of its medium- and long-term financial situation, and there seems to be a commitment to introducing reforms to improve the management system, information system, and investment policies as well as to controlling the growth of implicit pension debt. The main constraint at this stage is the lack of institutional capacity. Although the management team is highly qualified, technical and support staff lack the necessary experience and qualifications to undertake this type of assessment. Serious problems with record keeping (which is not centralized) further complicate preparation of the data necessary to conduct the analysis.

Countries in Motion

In countries in motion, the main challenges facing the pension system have been diagnosed and various options for reform have been evaluated, but the government does not yet have a strategic, unified vision as to where the pension system is going. This group includes the Islamic Republic of Iran, Iraq, Tunisia, and the Republic of Yemen.

The Islamic Republic of Iran

Pension reform was not an issue of concern in Iran until 2002. In that year, under the leadership of the Management and Planning Organization (MPO), a technical team with representatives from the MPO and the two main pension funds—the CSRO and the SSO—prepared a detailed assessment of the main challenges facing the pension system and explored options for reform.

In the same year, the MPO and the Ministry of Finance organized a seminar to present the results of the assessment to a large audience that included representatives of civil society. The event received broad media coverage. The government also established a commission in charge of preparing a multiyear program on pension reform. The work of this commission provided input to the Fourth Five-Year Development Plan, which now incorporates pensions and social security in general as an important area for reform.

While an integrated reform program has failed to emerge, the policy dialogue continues. Five groups or stakeholders are at play: the MPO, the Ministry of Finance, the SSO, the CSRO, and a commission in charge of social security reform within the Parliament. Both the CSRO and the SSO favor the status quo and mostly seek reforms to improve the financial situation of the funds and investment policies, although the current proposals are not aligned with the recommendations presented in chapter 4.

Recently, a new Ministry of Social Welfare was put in place. This creates new opportunities for reforming the pension system and the social protection system at large. Indeed, the new ministry has the mandate to identify mechanisms to integrate or better coordinate dispersed social programs and to prepare a strategy for pension reform. One of the options under discussion is the gradual merger of the CSRO and the SSO.

Iraq

Iraq is, of course, in a unique position. After the end of major military operations, the Coalition Provisional Authority replaced regular pensions with emergency "flat" payments that are now capturing an estimated 3.5 percent of GDP (estimated 5 percent in 2006). At the same time, the SSW reserves (ID 19 billion, less than half a percentage point of GDP) were frozen in Al Rafaidin Bank (the central bank). Since then, emergency payments have been supported by the state budget and represent a growing expenditure item. This has provided incentives to think about mechanisms to normalize the situation. The transitional government realizes, however, that the Iraqi pension system has an opportunity to be fully redesigned, instead of converging back to the old rules. The strategy's core is to move to an integrated system that is self-sustainable and built on the basis of best international practices. The Ministry of Labor, in coordination with the Ministry of Finance, is working on a draft law. At the same time, the two pension funds have launched an evaluation of their financial situation.

Yet important challenges lie ahead, as the war has disrupted financial and information flows, leaving contribution records outdated and liquidations severely backlogged. There are also significant administrative problems regarding the payment of benefits, particularly in rural areas. In the scheme for private sector workers, the system for tracking contributions is weak, and underdeclaration of wages, evasion of payment, or moratoria are pervasive.

Tunisia

In 2002, the Tunisian government completed a comprehensive and ambitious assessment of the pension system, which outlined various reform options, including mechanisms to cover seasonal workers in the agricultural sector and fishermen. A steering committee was put in place with the task of preparing a reform strategy on the basis of recommendations in the report.

The strategy at this stage is to focus on implementing measures to improve the financial sustainability of the pay-as-you-go system. Structural reforms will require further discussions and negotiations.

The Republic of Yemen

Discussions of pension reform in the Republic of Yemen go back to the late 1990s. Initially, the focus was on integrating the schemes for government employees and for private sector workers, which took place in 2000. The merger implied a transfer of pension liabilities from the civil service scheme, which is more mature and has higher wages, to the private sector scheme. As a result, the merger was ultimately reversed, and today both funds are pursuing reforms independently, without the benefit of an integrated framework.

A recent actuarial valuation of the pension funds for private sector workers presented several recommendations to improve the long-term financial position of the system. There were also recommendations to improve the management of reserves, although investment possibilities remain limited. The fund is preparing a proposal to reform the relevant law, but progress has been slow. The focus instead has been on building institutional capacity and particularly on upgrading information systems.

Similarly, the scheme for government employees is introducing legal amendments to increase retirement ages, the wage base, and the minimum pension. No assessment of the financial situation of the funds has been conducted. There also has been a series of initiatives to improve administration (for instance, by reducing the time necessary to process pensions from six months to one week) and to reduce costs. These include decentralizing various activities to the 22 branches of the fund and implementing an integrated management and information system.

The challenge in the Republic of Yemen is to take an integrated and long-term view of pension reform.

Countries Leading Pension Reform

In addition to solid analysis of the problems facing the schemes and the outline of options for reform, countries in the lead have identified an integrated vision for the pension system, or are close to doing so, and have implemented important reforms. This group includes Djibouti, Egypt, Jordan, Lebanon, and Morocco, in addition to the West Bank and Gaza.

Djibouti

In 2002, the Djibouti Parliament adopted a comprehensive reform program aimed at improving the financial position of the pension system, integrating the CNR with the scheme for private sector workers (OPS), and reviewing governance structures to strengthen investment policies. The reform program included (a) a series of parametric adjustments to reduce the mandate of the public system; (b) creation of the Conseil National de Sécurité Sociale (CNSS-Djibouti) to integrate the OPS and the CNR with a more independent governance structure; and (c) adoption of a statement of investment policies that mandates the use of funds in the sole interests of plan members and limits the types of asset classes in which funds can be invested.

The motivation for reform was the frail financial situation of the schemes, particularly the CNR, the large outlays to finance the pensions of the military and civil servants, and the refusal by the OPS to retire government contractual workers until government contributions were normalized.

The minister of finance and the minister of labor led the design of the reform program in coordination with the pension funds and were in charge of creating consensus at various levels of the government and in Parliament. The Office of the Prime Minister undertook the negotiations with employees and retirees, and the directors of the CNR and the OPS were in charge of the communication campaign through the media. The leadership of the president was crucial in the final stages of parliamentary negotiations.

The challenges that Djibouti now faces are related to implementation of the new laws, particularly with respect to the creation of the CNSS-Djibouti, the implementation of appropriate administrative processes, and the development of the necessary information systems. Current benefit formulas and eligibility conditions, although improved, are still not in line with best practices discussed in chapter 4. Moreover, the pension fund for the military has not been reformed and continues to be open to new entrants. Thus its implicit pension debt continues to grow. Finally, as the mandate of the public pension system is reduced over time, it is necessary for other long-term savings instruments to develop and for the government to prepare the necessary regulations.

Egypt

During the last decade, several assessments of the Egyptian pension system were conducted by international organizations, academics, and private consulting companies. A recent report prepared by the Ministry of Social Insurance summarizes the results of these studies and the recommendations for reform (Egyptian Ministry of Social Insurance 2003).

The minister of social insurance, the minister of finance, and the minister of investments have put pension reform high on their reform agenda. The first two are responsible for the mandatory public component, while the latter is responsible for the voluntary private component (Egypt has around 600 occupational plans).

The government is currently working on the design of a new integrated public health system and the rationalization of voluntary private pensions. The general strategy is under discussion and a final draft is expected by the end of the year.

Jordan

Since 1995 pension reform in Jordan has been an important component of the policy agenda of the government. Early efforts focused on the civil service pension system, given its budgetary implications, and resulted in the system's closure to new entrants in January 1995. Subsequently, new civil servants have enrolled in the Social Security Corporation (SSC), along with employees from the private sector.

In 2002, under the leadership of the minister of finance, a reform program for the military was prepared. The core of the proposal was to close the military pension scheme to new recruits and to enroll them in the SSC, while rationalizing the benefits offered to current military personnel. Because military personnel are unlikely to retire at the same age as other members of the SSC, this measure will be accompanied by the creation of individual accounts to complement the SSC early-retirement pension or to assist in the transition to private sector work. The Council of Ministers adopted the reform program, and implementation started in 2003, although progress has been slow.

The focus of the government is now switching to the SSC, which eventually will become the integrated pension system. So far, important measures have been adopted to strengthen investment policies by creating a more autonomous investment unit, appropriately staffed, with a clear mandate and statement of investment policies. In 2003, a detailed assessment of the SSC was conducted, and several measures to strengthen the system were recommended to the prime minister and his cabinet. In parallel, the Ministry of Planning has been working with the Insurance Commission to prepare the necessary regulatory framework to allow life insurance companies to offer pension products. A draft regulation is now under review by the industry.

An integrated reform program, however, remains elusive. To date, discussions of pension reform have taken place with little or no coordination among the various institutions involved. These include (a) the SSC, (b) the military and civil service pension funds, (c) the occupational plans, and (d) the insurance industry. Policy measures at these four levels are interrelated. For instance, the mandate given to the SSC regarding income replacement will depend on the choices regarding the role of occupational plans and voluntary private pensions as sources of complementary savings for old age. Similarly, the design of individual accounts for military personnel joining the SSC will depend on changes in benefit formulas and eligibility conditions implemented by the SSC.

Hence the government is considering setting up a steering committee supported by a technical unit that would guide the preparation of a multiyear, integrated pension reform program. The steering committee would be composed of representatives from key ministries as well as the SSC and the Insurance Commission. The responsibilities of the steering committee would be to define the principles to guide the reform of the pension system (for example, the roles of the public and private sectors) and create consensus regarding the general strategy. A technical unit, composed of full-time, independent consultants and technical staff from the represented institutions would (a) conduct the technical and analytical work necessary to operationalize the strategic guidelines provided by the steering committee; (b) draft a multiyear reform program for the pension system; (c) draft the necessary regulations to implement the reform program; and (d) contribute to the design of information and awareness campaigns.

Lebanon

After seven years of analytical work and consultations, the Lebanese government submitted to Parliament a draft law closing the current end-of-service indemnity (EOSI) scheme to new entrants and creating a new institution that will manage a fully funded, defined-contribution pension system for private sector workers. Parliament recently approved this law, marking the beginning of the first major systemic reform in the region. Part of the motivation in Lebanon was the realization that the EOSI program did not provide adequate protection for workers during old age and operated poorly as an income protection system for workers. Looking forward, the challenge now is to implement the law, ensuring that the new institution meets the necessary standards of administration, governance, accountability, and investment policy. There are also important questions to answer regarding transition mechanisms and the financing of the fiscal impacts of reform. Indeed, the EOSI is likely to have accumulated a substantial implicit debt that is not backed with sufficient reserves. Moreover, the majority of reserves are invested in government debt. A unique feature of the EOSI is that employers also have an implicit liability toward plan members. Finding the appropriate financing mechanisms of this implicit liability is another issue that will require attention.

Regarding the schemes for civil servants and the military, the government recently finalized an assessment of their financial situation. As reported in chapter 3, the results are worrisome. A draft law that closes these two schemes to new entrants is under consideration. New personnel are expected to join the newly created pension system for private sector workers. If this law is approved, Lebanon, like Jordan, will converge to an integrated pension system.

Morocco

The policy dialogue on pension reform in Morocco is very advanced, with discussions going back at least to 1997. At the time, the prime minister established the Comité de Suivi des Etudes Actuarielles (CSEA) to assess the financial sustainability of the various funds and explore options for reform. Five years later, in February 2002, the CSEA presented a report to the prime minister that emphasized the worrisome financial position of the various schemes and evaluated plausible strategies to redress the situation. The pension funds, too, have conducted independent assessments of their financial situation and have proposed, and in some cases adopted, measures to strengthen their systems, albeit with little or no coordination. The most important reform achieved to date is the integration of various large occupational plans within state-owned enterprises under the Régime Collectif d'Assurance et de Retraite (RCAR).

The special feature of Morocco's political strategy is the transparency of the policy dialogue and the willingness of the government to create consensus for reform with all segments of civil society. On December 16, 2003, the prime minister held a national conference on pension reform that involved various representatives from civil society, including labor unions. More than 200 participants attended, and the conference received broad media coverage. The directors of the various pension funds and the Ministry of Finance presented the main challenges facing the system and outlined options for reform that were openly debated.

As a result of the discussions, two tripartite commissions were established to pilot the reform program. One of the commissions is technical in nature and has the mandate to validate the studies and assessments conducted to date and to evaluate the financial, economic, and social impacts of alternative reforms. The second commission has a political role that consists of providing general strategic guidelines for reform on the basis of the recommendations and proposals of the technical commission. The predominant strategy arising from the discussions seems to be two separate defined-benefit, pay-as-you-go schemes (one for civil servants and one for private sector workers), but one integrated defined-contribution, fully funded system.

The West Bank and Gaza

In the West Bank and Gaza, the Palestinian Authority is well advanced in its effort to reform the public sector pension system. The Palestinian Authority first became aware of potential problems within the existing system as early as 1997, when a report prepared by the Ministry of Finance urged and recommended reforms. At the time, however, the

Palestinian Authority took no action. Work began again in 2001 under a new minister of finance. A more in-depth assessment of the pension schemes was prepared that quantified, for the first time, the full extent of the problem and set out possible scenarios for reform. It was recognized that the large implicit pension debt threatened the fiscal sustainability of the Palestinian government. International donors had been, largely, financing civil service salaries since the start of the intifada, but under the status quo the pension system's cash flow would start showing a negative balance within three to five years. In addition, the hope for progress in reaching a peaceful settlement of the conflict with Israel invoked a sense of urgency to ratify the draft law on pensions for security forces, since the security services, previously not covered by any pension system, would be looking for the means of retiring older staff.

To develop and promote the reform agenda, the Palestinian cabinet established a national pension committee under the chairmanship of the minister of finance, made up of civil and security service officials, representatives of the legislative council, and the judiciary. The draft public sector pension law envisions a multipillar system, with defined-benefit and defined-contribution components, managed by a new independent institution. In addition, the committee is looking to introduce a "citizens pension" to provide a basic level of support for all old-age Palestinians. The Palestinians are also taking particular care to develop a new pension agency to improve the governance and administrative structures and to minimize the risks to pension assets.

If the legislature passes the reform, implementation could begin in 2005. Substantial assistance from the international donor community will be required for financing the technical assistance to introduce the new system and implement the transition from the existing systems.

Conclusions

This short review displays countries in very different stages of the reform process and following very different strategies toward reform. Commonalties across the spectrum, nevertheless, highlight a few patterns:

- *In countries that are leading reform efforts, crises of civil servants' and military pension schemes have been an important motivation.* This is the case of Djibouti and Jordan as well as the West Bank and Gaza. It has also been a push factor in Lebanon, although the lack of a proper pension system for private sector workers has been the main driver of reform. In Egypt, the fact that the implicit pension debt is matched by explicit debt with the National Investment Bank (close to 50 percent of GDP) and that the government is already servicing this debt also create incentives for reform.

- *Good analyses and diagnosis have also played an important role in putting countries into motion.* This is definitely the case in the Islamic Republic of Iran, Jordan (in the case of the SSC), Morocco, and Tunisia. In all these countries, discussions about pension reform within and outside the government followed the publication of reports highlighting the problems of the various pension schemes.
- *In all countries leading pension reforms, a high-level policymaker or institution has been driving the reform process.* Basically, a person or a group of persons understands the issues, takes the initiative to create awareness about the need for change, proposes solutions, and generates consensus for reform within the government.
- *In those countries lagging behind, these three elements are not present.* In Algeria and Libya, the availability of significant oil revenues might be minimizing the magnitude of the financial problems facing the pension system and their threat to fiscal stability.

Differences in the political process surrounding pension reforms are evident in various countries. The Islamic Republic of Iran, Lebanon, and Morocco included the civil society in the policy dialogue from the outset. To this end, multisectoral commissions were put in place. Morocco also took a comprehensive approach to reform, including all pension funds and relevant institutions. On the contrary, in Djibouti, initially the policy dialogue and preparation of the reform strategy took place without consultations outside the government. Plan members were involved only toward the end. No commission was set up to design the reform program. In Jordan, the discussions are taking place within the SSC, with little coordination with the various ministries and other relevant institutions (for example, the Insurance Commission).

With regard to reform strategies, the inclination is to preserve, but rationalize, defined-benefit schemes, while allowing voluntary pensions to develop. There is, however, considerable variation in reform strategies. Djibouti and Jordan have integrated earnings-related schemes, and Jordan is also developing voluntary private pensions. Morocco is considering two earnings-related schemes and one integrated fully funded, defined-contribution scheme. Lebanon is proposing an integrated defined-contribution scheme with a basic pension guarantee. A similar approach is being taken in the West Bank and Gaza.

Challenges for the future are necessarily different in the three groups of countries. Among the countries in the early stages of the reform process, the goal should be to prepare the necessary baseline data to conduct a proper assessment of the financial problems facing the schemes. Without this baseline, it is not possible to initiate discussions about the costs and benefits of alternative reform packages. In the second group of countries, the goal should be to move from strategic guidelines to a detailed reform concept, which will require further analytical work and consensus building. The remaining group needs to consolidate an integrated reform strategy or move toward implementation.

In all cases, it is hoped that this report will raise awareness about the need for prompt interventions, thus allowing governments to take a gradual approach toward reform and avoid drastic adjustments in the future. The report also is intended to provide an analytical framework to guide discussion about options for reform as well as the implementation of new laws. In all Middle East and North African countries, the time for change is now.

Appendices

APPENDIX A

Demographic Indicators

TABLE A.1

Population Size in Middle East and North African Countries and World Regions, 1960–2000

Thousands of persons

Country or region	1960	1965	1970	1975	1980	1985	1990	1995	2000
Algeria	10,800	11,923	13,746	16,018	18,669	21,879	25,022	28,060	30,385
Bahrain	149	182	210	262	334	425	503	577	670
Djibouti	83	114	155	210	300	354	490	580	666
East Asia and the Pacific	9,02,224	9,79,833	11,17,980	12,54,985	13,59,404	14,68,735	15,96,706	17,08,449	18,05,490
Eastern Europe and Central Asia	3,38,476	3,63,357	3,84,878	4,05,704	4,25,820	4,46,889	4,66,230	4,72,724	4,75,029
Egypt, Arab Rep. of	25,922	29,389	33,053	36,289	40,875	46,511	52,442	58,180	63,976
Iran, Islamic Rep. of	21,554	24,661	28,429	33,206	39,124	47,100	54,400	58,954	63,664
Iraq	6,847	7,976	9,356	11,020	13,007	15,317	18,078	20,779	23,224
Jordan	844	1,128	1,508	1,810	2,181	2,644	3,170	4,195	4,887
Kuwait	278	471	744	1,007	1,375	1,712	2,125	1,802	2,190
Latin America and the Caribbean	2,14,531	2,46,349	2,80,557	3,17,317	3,56,417	3,95,468	4,34,236	4,73,143	5,10,040
Lebanon	1,968	2,280	2,617	2,947	3,002	3,275	3,635	4,005	4,328
Libya	1,349	1,623	1,986	2,446	3,043	3,786	4,306	4,751	5,237
Middle East and North Africa	99,655	1,13,639	1,30,344	1,49,389	1,73,682	2,04,025	2,37,132	2,67,005	2,94,431
Morocco	11,626	13,323	15,310	17,305	19,382	21,648	24,043	26,386	28,705
OECD	6,55,391	6,95,041	7,28,851	7,63,232	7,90,438	8,13,997	8,39,918	8,69,368	8,98,541
Oman	558	631	723	847	1,101	1,397	1,627	2,135	2,410
Qatar	45	70	111	171	229	358	485	505	585
Saudi Arabia	4,075	4,793	5,745	7,251	9,372	12,379	15,803	18,205	20,723
South Asia	5,62,319	6,31,809	7,11,828	8,01,344	9,01,258	10,05,209	11,20,422	12,35,272	13,54,192
Sub-Saharan Africa	2,23,765	2,53,802	2,89,427	3,30,967	3,83,247	4,43,109	5,10,406	5,80,401	6,58,296
Syria, Arab Rep.	4,561	5,325	6,257	7,438	8,704	10,397	12,116	14,221	16,189
Tunisia	4,221	4,630	5,127	5,611	6,384	7,260	8,154	8,958	9,564
United Arab Emirates	90	120	220	505	1,043	1,379	1,844	2,341	2,809
West Bank and Gaza							1,970	2,396	2,966
Yemen, Republic of	5,247	5,843	6,332	6,991	8,538	10,078	11,876	15,200	17,507
World average levels	30,20,382	33,11,960	36,75,589	40,58,401	44,30,067	48,21,152	52,52,836	56,57,296	60,51,380

Source: World Bank 2003f.

TABLE A.2

Average Growth Rates, by Region and Period, 1960–2003

Percent

Region	1960–4	1965–9	1970–4	1975–9	1980–4	1985–9	1990–4	1995–9	2000–3
Middle East and North Africa	2.63	2.79	2.74	3.00	3.25	3.01	2.68	2.02	1.91
OECD	1.20	0.98	0.95	0.74	0.62	0.59	0.70	0.67	0.62
Latin America and the Caribbean	2.82	2.67	2.51	2.39	2.15	1.92	1.76	1.56	1.44
East Asia and the Pacific	1.48	2.61	2.50	1.70	1.55	1.67	1.44	1.17	0.92
Sub-Saharan Africa	2.54	2.65	2.69	2.92	2.98	2.87	2.63	2.64	2.30
South Asia	2.35	2.41	2.40	2.39	2.25	2.19	2.01	1.88	1.75
Eastern Europe and Central Asia	1.44	1.24	1.05	1.00	0.96	0.92	0.38	0.11	−0.14
World average levels	1.81	2.10	2.05	1.80	1.72	1.72	1.55	1.39	1.23

Source: Authors' calculations based on World Bank 2003f.

TABLE A.3

Average Population Growth Rates in Middle East and North African Countries, 1960–2003

Percent

Country	1960–4	1965–9	1970–4	1975–9	1980–4	1985–9	1990–4	1995–9	2000–3
Algeria	1.91	2.74	3.05	3.06	3.16	2.80	2.40	1.71	1.49
Bahrain	3.90	3.07	4.07	4.87	4.87	3.67	2.60	3.27	2.07
Djibouti	5.82	6.22	5.89	7.49	3.70	5.16	4.71	2.94	2.08
Egypt, Arab Rep. of	2.46	2.46	1.88	2.28	2.57	2.46	2.15	1.91	1.86
Iran, Islamic Rep. of	2.64	2.80	3.06	3.22	3.62	3.23	1.72	1.57	1.46
Iraq	3.02	3.17	3.26	3.32	3.26	3.34	2.93	2.35	1.95
Jordan	5.52	6.07	3.92	3.66	3.90	3.61	5.69	3.09	2.90
Kuwait	9.59	9.93	6.33	6.27	4.89	4.26	−3.95	4.52	3.32
Lebanon	2.96	2.82	2.46	0.60	1.55	2.09	1.96	1.66	1.30
Libya	3.64	3.99	4.14	4.31	4.49	3.11	1.84	1.95	1.96
Morocco	2.70	2.82	2.51	2.29	2.22	2.13	1.92	1.71	1.62
Oman	2.78	2.64	2.91	4.98	5.09	3.17	5.51	2.46	2.59
Qatar	7.95	9.12	9.20	5.63	8.73	6.98	1.45	2.44	2.55
Saudi Arabia	3.12	3.44	4.49	5.01	5.60	5.06	3.20	2.60	2.68
Syria, Arab Rep.	3.05	3.16	3.47	3.14	3.51	3.11	3.25	2.72	2.43
Tunisia	1.78	2.09	1.76	2.47	2.50	2.45	2.04	1.40	1.13
United Arab Emirates	5.00	10.18	16.17	16.14	6.98	4.81	5.85	3.22	6.02
West Bank and Gaza	—	—	—	—	—	—	3.92	4.20	4.28
Yemen, Republic of	2.18	1.68	1.70	3.81	3.48	3.15	5.12	2.82	2.97

Source: Authors' calculations based on World Bank 2003f.
Note: — = Not available.

TABLE A.4

Labor Force Participation Rate, by Gender, in Middle East and North African Countries and World Regions, 1960–2003

Percent of the population ages 15–64

Country or region and gender	1960–4	1965–9	1970–4	1975–9	1980–4	1985–9	1990–4	1995–9	2000–3
Female									
Algeria	17.1	17.4	17.9	18.7	19.3	19.8	22.2	27.8	32.5
Bahrain	—	—	6.7	13.2	19.6	26.0	30.8	33.0	34.7
East Asia and the Pacific	66.3	67.0	68.1	69.8	71.7	73.8	75.2	75.4	75.2
Eastern Europe and Central Asia	63.4	65.7	67.4	68.4	68.3	66.5	65.6	66.2	66.7
Egypt, Arab Rep. of	26.2	27.0	27.8	28.7	29.8	31.2	33.0	35.6	37.7
Iran, Islamic Rep. of	19.8	19.8	20.0	20.4	21.0	21.7	23.8	27.9	31.5
Iraq	16.4	16.4	16.3	16.3	16.0	15.5	16.0	18.2	19.9
Jordan	13.8	13.9	14.2	14.4	15.3	17.1	20.0	24.9	28.6
Kuwait	6.8	10.0	13.8	18.3	24.6	33.5	39.2	40.8	43.1
Latin America and the Caribbean	24.1	25.7	27.9	31.2	34.8	38.9	42.2	44.1	45.6
Lebanon	13.6	16.5	18.9	20.5	22.4	24.7	27.5	30.7	32.8
Libya	20.4	19.7	20.1	22.1	22.9	22.0	22.3	24.7	26.6
Middle East and North Africa	22.3	22.7	23.4	24.3	25.1	25.8	27.5	30.5	33.0
Morocco	32.9	33.7	35.0	37.0	38.6	39.8	41.1	42.7	44.0
OECD	37.0	40.0	43.7	48.7	53.2	56.7	59.7	61.6	62.6
Oman	4.4	5.3	6.1	7.0	8.6	11.6	14.7	18.0	21.0
Qatar	—	—	—	—	16.7	27.3	34.2	35.9	38.4
Saudi Arabia	3.7	4.5	5.9	8.2	10.8	13.7	16.8	20.2	23.5
South Asia	50.1	49.5	48.9	48.2	47.1	45.1	44.4	45.7	46.8
Sub-Saharan Africa	65.0	64.6	64.1	63.4	62.8	62.4	62.2	62.1	62.1
Syria, Arab Rep.	23.2	23.3	23.4	23.5	23.8	24.2	25.5	28.2	30.5
Tunisia	22.7	24.3	27.1	31.7	34.5	34.6	35.6	38.1	40.1
United Arab Emirates	—	—	8.6	13.2	18.8	25.8	30.9	32.7	33.8
Yemen, Republic of	27.6	27.9	28.2	28.4	28.7	29.1	29.8	30.9	31.7
World average levels	52.8	53.8	55.0	56.5	57.7	58.7	59.6	60.4	60.8
Male									
Algeria	87.6	85.2	83.0	81.4	80.3	79.8	79.5	79.5	79.7
Bahrain	86.7	85.4	85.5	87.7	89.2	89.7	89.0	87.8	88.1
East Asia and the Pacific	93.4	92.5	91.6	90.8	90.0	89.1	88.7	88.7	88.2
Eastern Europe and Central Asia	86.8	85.0	83.9	83.7	83.1	81.7	80.7	80.2	79.8
Egypt, Arab Rep. of	89.4	87.3	85.6	84.3	83.5	83.4	83.2	82.5	82.2
Iran, Islamic Rep. of	91.3	88.6	86.4	84.8	83.5	82.6	81.5	80.4	79.8
Iraq	87.3	85.0	82.9	81.1	79.3	77.5	76.4	76.3	76.2
Jordan	85.4	85.2	83.8	80.7	78.5	78.0	77.9	78.8	79.4
Kuwait	89.7	88.9	88.0	87.0	86.2	85.8	83.5	80.0	79.7
Latin America and the Caribbean	90.6	89.1	88.0	87.2	86.6	86.3	86.0	85.7	85.5
Lebanon	84.2	81.7	79.7	78.5	77.7	77.6	78.4	80.3	81.1
Libya	87.7	86.8	86.1	85.8	85.0	83.5	81.7	79.4	77.8
Middle East and North Africa	89.4	87.3	85.5	84.1	83.0	82.4	81.7	81.1	80.8
Morocco	89.7	87.7	86.2	85.2	84.3	83.5	82.8	82.6	82.6
OECD	89.7	87.9	86.4	85.2	83.9	82.5	81.7	81.5	80.9
Oman	91.1	90.2	89.4	88.7	87.3	84.9	82.6	80.3	78.3
Qatar	88.4	90.7	91.9	91.7	92.0	93.4	93.4	91.6	90.2
Saudi Arabia	92.3	90.6	89.0	87.3	86.3	86.3	85.2	83.0	81.4
South Asia	91.5	90.7	89.9	89.1	88.6	88.2	87.8	87.3	86.8
Sub-Saharan Africa	91.7	91.0	90.3	89.6	88.9	88.4	87.8	87.2	86.7
Syria, Arab Rep.	86.8	85.6	84.4	82.9	81.8	81.1	80.6	80.3	80.3
Tunisia	89.0	86.9	85.4	85.1	84.5	83.6	83.0	83.0	83.2
United Arab Emirates	91.7	91.7	92.4	93.9	94.4	93.1	91.9	90.1	88.2
Yemen, Republic of	89.4	89.2	87.9	84.8	82.9	82.8	83.1	83.9	84.2
World average levels	90.8	89.7	88.7	88.0	87.2	86.5	86.0	85.8	85.4

Source: World Bank 2003f.
Note: — = Not available.

APPENDIX B

Methodology for Demographic and Employment Projections

Survival and fertility rate forecasts are provided by staff of the World Bank's Human Development Network. Survival and fertility rates, the current age distribution of the population, and net migration flows represent the main input of the calculations explained below (see figure B.1).

Life Expectancy, Total Fertility Rate, and Population Projections

Future life expectancy and total fertility rates are calculated using a standard life table methodology. In order to be consistent with the modeling of pension reform options, population projections are generated using a standard linear model. Being μ_t^M and μ_t^F, the male and female age distributions of the population at time t, population dynamics can be described by the following linear model:

$$\mu_{t+1}^M = \Gamma_t^M \mu_t^M + \gamma_t \Phi_t \mu_t^F + \eta_t^M$$
$$\mu_{t+1}^F = \Gamma_t^F \mu_t^F + (1-\gamma_t) \Phi_t \mu_t^F + \eta_t^F,$$

where Γ_t^M and Γ_t^F are the transition matrixes for males and females, which are functions of the age- and sex-specific survival rates prevailing at time t; Φ_t is the fertility matrix, which is a function of the age-specific fertility rates prevailing at time t; γ_t is a coefficient that is a function of the sex ratio at birth prevailing at time t; and η_t^M and η_t^F are the net migration flows for males and females for time t. Finally, the size of the total population is obtained by summing the male and female population: $\mu_t = \mu_t^M + \mu_t^F$. In order to generate population projections, the sex ratio is kept constant and exogenously set to 104, meaning that 104 male babies are born for every 100 female newborns. With σ as the sex ratio, γ is calculated as follows: $\gamma = \frac{\sigma/100}{1+\sigma/100}$. Finally, net migration flows are naively assumed to converge to zero by 2030. The results of the projections are presented in table B.1 and figure B.2.

Figure B.1 Age-Specific Survival Rate Forecasts in Middle East and North African Countries, 2002 and 2030

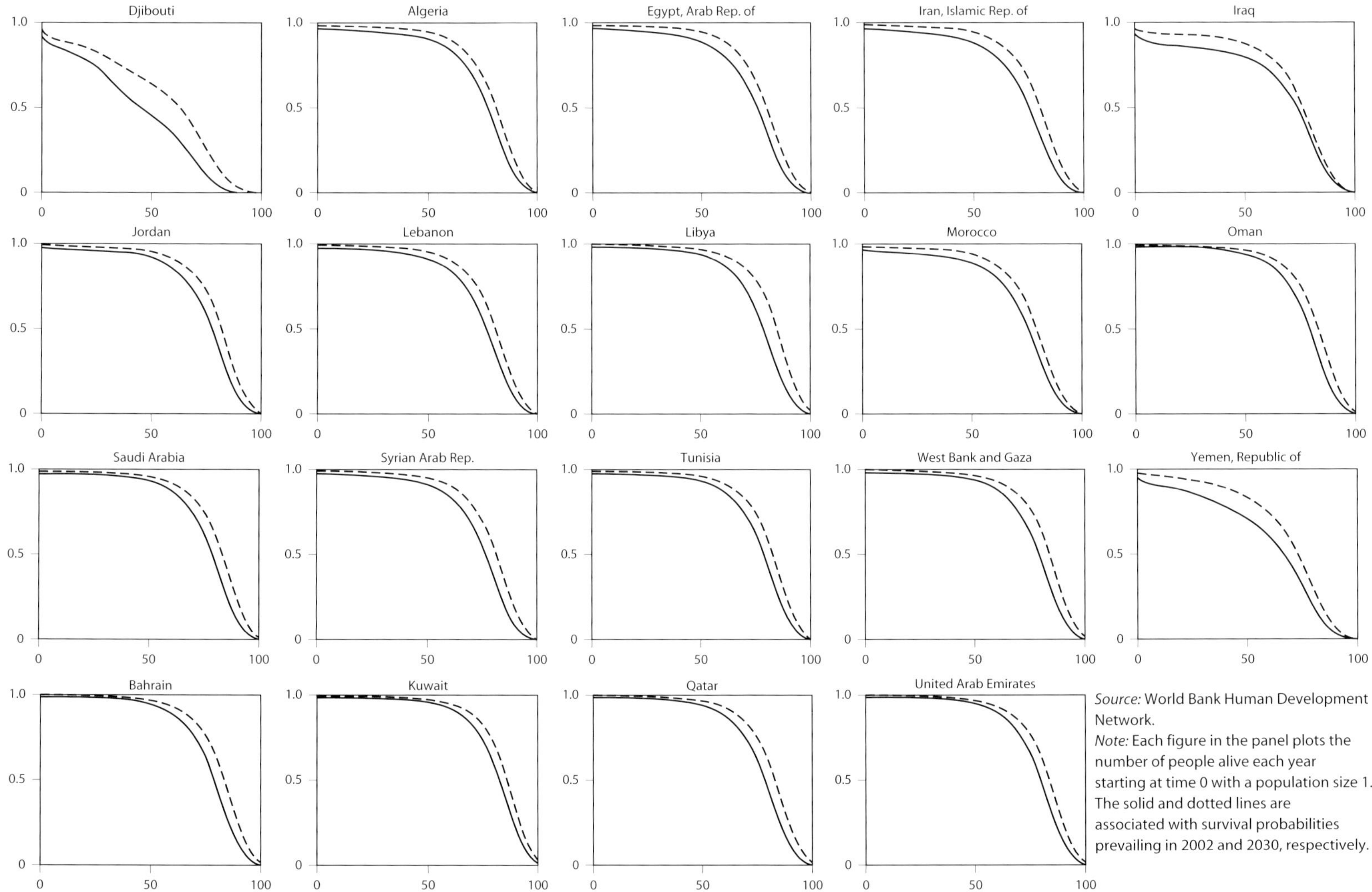

Source: World Bank Human Development Network.

Note: Each figure in the panel plots the number of people alive each year starting at time 0 with a population size 1. The solid and dotted lines are associated with survival probabilities prevailing in 2002 and 2030, respectively.

TABLE B.1

Projected Population Growth Rates, 2003–39

Average by period

Country	2003–4	2005–9	2010–4	2015–9	2020–4	2025–9	2030–4	2035–9
Algeria	1.68	1.64	1.51	1.36	1.25	1.09	0.94	0.80
Bahrain	2.13	1.98	1.70	1.38	1.11	0.91	0.77	0.65
Djibouti	2.05	1.83	1.65	1.59	1.48	1.33	1.21	1.29
Egypt, Arab Rep. of	1.76	1.68	1.48	1.25	1.17	1.05	0.93	0.80
Iran, Islamic Rep. of	1.58	1.67	1.59	1.32	1.13	0.99	0.92	0.84
Iraq	2.17	2.06	1.84	1.60	1.48	1.29	1.10	0.95
Jordan	2.69	2.47	2.05	1.68	1.51	1.36	1.22	1.09
Kuwait	2.58	2.18	1.71	1.32	1.05	0.84	0.64	0.45
Lebanon	1.31	1.24	1.18	1.13	1.03	0.89	0.75	0.63
Libya	2.30	2.15	1.75	1.33	1.22	1.16	1.09	0.96
Middle East and North Africa	1.99	1.94	1.77	1.53	1.38	1.21	1.07	0.97
Morocco	1.56	1.49	1.35	1.20	1.12	0.99	0.86	0.72
Oman	2.33	2.28	2.12	1.89	1.70	1.44	1.22	1.11
Qatar	2.15	1.91	1.53	1.09	0.71	0.41	0.20	0.07
Saudi Arabia	3.25	3.01	2.70	2.43	2.17	1.87	1.60	1.51
Syria, Arab Rep.	2.46	2.30	1.95	1.57	1.46	1.35	1.23	1.08
Tunisia	1.30	1.33	1.28	1.13	0.94	0.79	0.70	0.61
United Arab Emirates	2.35	2.11	1.68	1.18	0.83	0.60	0.47	0.39
West Bank and Gaza	3.63	3.39	3.01	2.60	2.20	1.80	1.49	1.42
Yemen, Republic of	3.02	3.06	2.92	2.62	2.24	1.88	1.63	1.53

Source: Author's calculations.

Labor Force Projections

The labor force is projected using demographic projections as well as current and projected age-specific activity rates for males and females. Regarding activity rate projections, values for the years between 2002 and 2010 are calculated by linearly interpolating current estimated age- and sex-specific activity rates and projected age- and sex-specific activity rates provided by ILO (2003). For the years beyond 2010, values are linearly interpolated assuming that age- and sex-specific activity rates in all Middle East and North African countries will converge to the average levels currently observed in the OECD by 2040. The resulting activity rates are shown in figure B.3. Having generated activity-rate projections, labor force projections are obtained by multiplying each activity rate with the associated projection for the population bracket (see table B.2).

Unemployment Projections

In order to evaluate the potential dynamics of the unemployment rate, a relatively simple accounting framework should be used to ensure consistency among economic aggregates.

Figure B.2 Projected Old-Age and Total-Dependency Ratio in Middle East and North African Countries, 2000–40

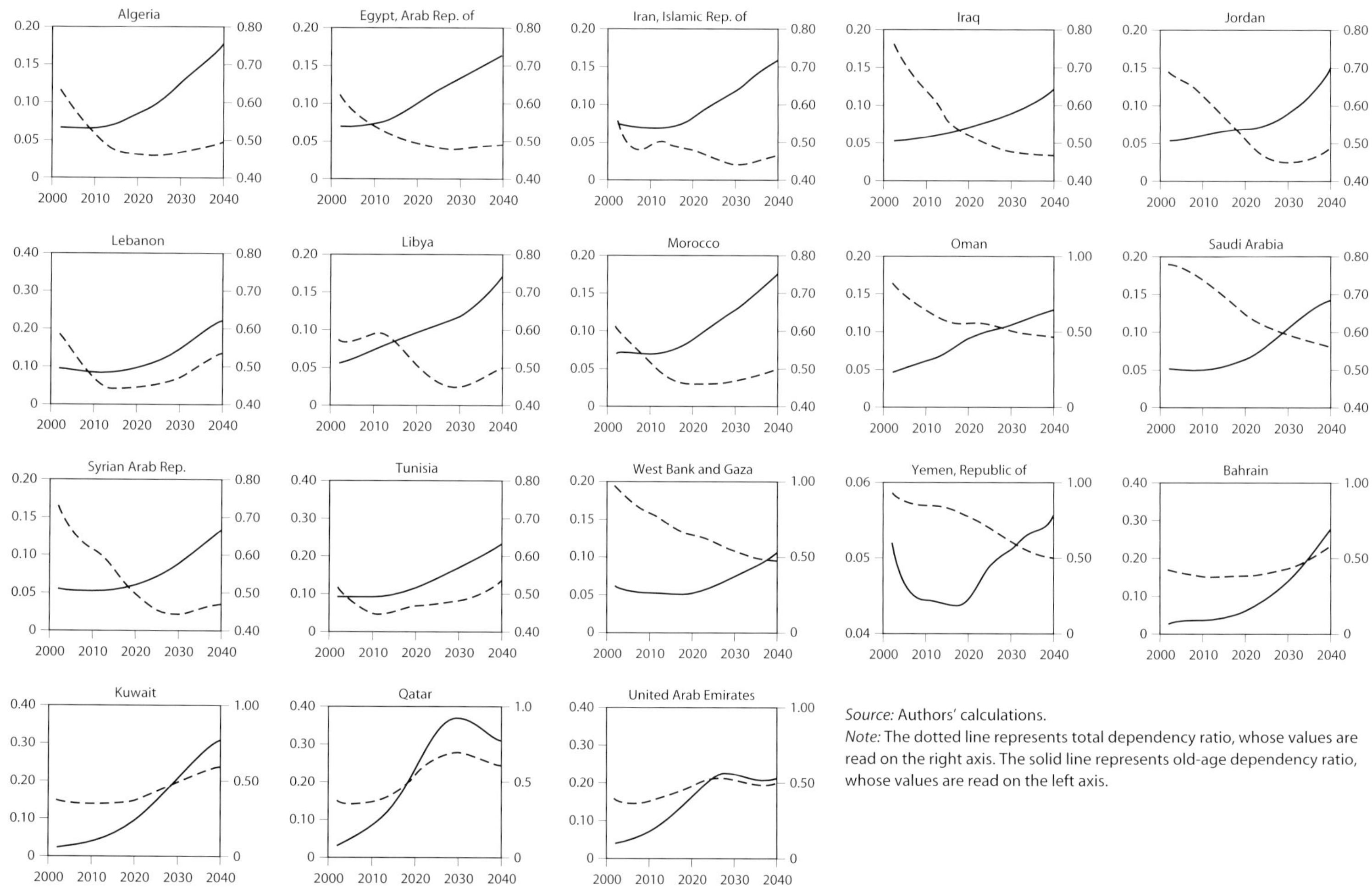

Source: Authors' calculations.
Note: The dotted line represents total dependency ratio, whose values are read on the right axis. The solid line represents old-age dependency ratio, whose values are read on the left axis.

Figure B.3 Projected Female and Male Participation Rates in Middle East and North African Countries, 2000–30

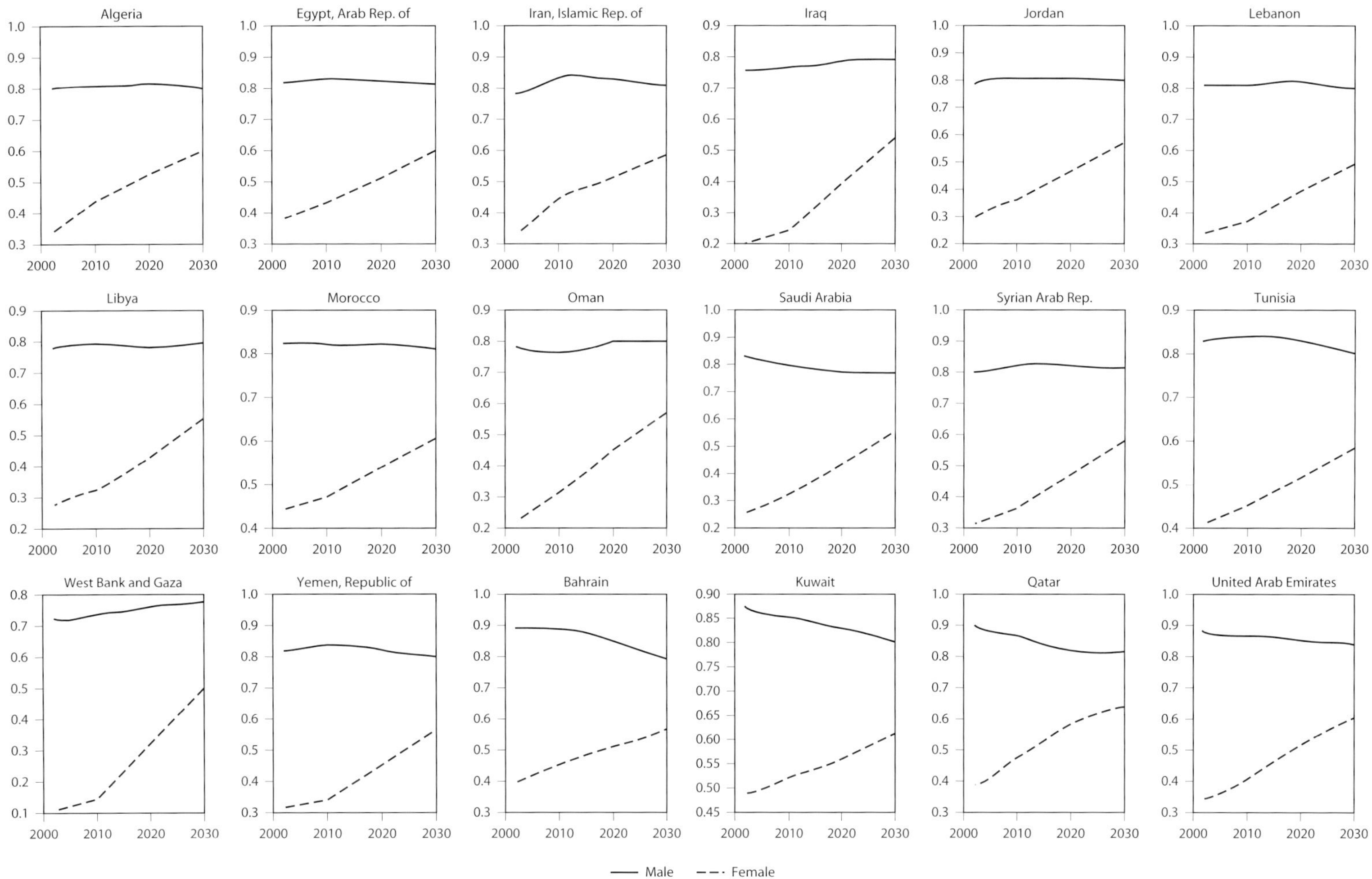

Source: Authors' calculations.

TABLE B.2

Excess Growth Rate of Working-Age Population over Dependent Population, 2003–39
Percent

Country or territory	2003–4	2005–9	2010–4	2015–9	2020–4	2025–9	2030–4	2035–9
Algeria	2.7	2.6	2.0	0.5	0.3	−0.3	−0.5	−0.6
Bahrain	1.3	1.4	0.3	−0.4	−0.7	−1.4	−2.6	−3.2
Djibouti	0.1	0.8	1.0	1.0	1.6	2.1	2.1	1.8
Egypt, Arab Rep. of	2.5	1.6	1.1	0.8	0.5	0.3	−0.3	−0.2
Iran, Islamic Rep. of	4.9	0.7	−0.5	0.7	0.8	0.9	−0.3	−0.7
Iraq	2.9	2.2	2.4	1.7	1.1	0.8	0.4	0.1
Jordan	1.0	1.2	1.8	2.2	2.2	0.9	−0.2	−1.2
Kuwait	1.2	0.7	0.1	−1.0	−2.6	−2.8	−2.8	−1.6
Lebanon	2.6	2.9	1.7	0.0	−0.3	−0.7	−1.4	−1.3
Libya	0.5	−0.7	0.3	2.1	2.1	1.0	−0.8	−1.3
Middle East and North Africa	2.3	1.4	0.8	0.4	0.3	0.3	0.0	−0.2
Morocco	2.2	2.1	1.9	0.8	0.0	−0.2	−0.6	−0.6
Oman	3.7	3.0	2.5	0.7	0.6	1.2	1.1	0.9
Qatar	2.5	−0.3	−2.4	−4.8	−4.4	−1.7	0.9	1.7
Saudi Arabia	0.3	0.8	1.1	1.5	1.1	0.8	0.7	0.6
Syria, Arab Rep.	3.3	1.9	1.6	2.5	2.0	0.7	−0.6	−0.6
Tunisia	2.7	1.7	0.1	−0.7	−0.3	−0.3	−0.7	−1.2
United Arab Emirates	2.5	0.2	−2.2	−2.5	−2.3	−0.1	1.2	0.3
West Bank and Gaza	3.6	2.4	2.3	1.9	1.6	1.8	2.0	1.1
Yemen, Republic of	2.4	0.8	0.3	1.1	2.1	2.8	2.8	1.8

Source: Authors' calculations.

Starting from a Cobb-Douglas production function, such as

$$Y = AK^{\alpha}L^{1-\alpha}, \tag{B.1}$$

where Y is real output, A is the productivity level, K is physical capital, and L is labor supply. Expressing the equation in terms of variable growth rates, it is possible to obtain the following relationship:

$$\dot{y} = \dot{a} + \alpha\dot{k} + (1-\alpha)\dot{l}. \tag{B.2}$$

Economic Effects of the Demographic Transition

Different assumptions about the dynamics of each variable in the equation lead to different approaches in evaluating the economic effects of the demographic transition. In order to understand the differences among them, a brief description of the most common assumptions follows (Dhonte, Bhattacharya, and Yousef 2000 for approaches A and B).

Approach A

By assuming that $\dot{l}$ is equal to the growth rate of the labor force and by specifying a given dynamic for $\dot{k}$ and $\dot{w}$, it is possible to calculate the rate of growth of the productivity that does not increase current levels of unemployment:

(B.3) $$\dot{a} = \dot{w} + \dot{l}(1 - \alpha) - \alpha \dot{k}.$$

Approach B

By assuming an exogenous dynamic for the real wage—that is, $\dot{w} = \dot{y} - \dot{l}$—there is a unique relationship between the growth rates of labor demand, real wages, productivity, and physical capital:

(B.4) $$\dot{l} = \frac{1}{1 - \alpha}(\dot{a} + \alpha \dot{k} - \dot{w}).$$

This approach allows calculating the growth rate of labor demand consistent with given assumptions on the behavior of productivity, capital, and real wages. The difference between the growth rate of labor demand and the growth rate of the labor force represents the growth rate of employment.

Approach C

In order to avoid setting an exogenous dynamic for capital accumulation, it is possible to assume that the ratio of capital per laborer remains constant during the projection horizon. Therefore, since $\dot{k} = \dot{l}$, real wages adjust to changes in productivity ($\dot{w} = \dot{a}$), and the following relationship holds:

(B.5) $$\dot{l} = \dot{y} - \dot{a},$$

which delivers the dynamics of labor demand for a given dynamic of economic output and productivity.

Coverage Rate Projections

Coverage rates measure the number of employed workers who are enrolled in the pension system as a share of the labor force. Two approaches are used here to project coverage rates: an "enrollment" approach, linking coverage to capacity of the system to enroll new workers, and an "income" approach, linking coverage rates to the level of GDP per capita. In the enrollment approach, workers can be enrolled or not enrolled in the national pension system. Once enrolled, workers are assumed not to quit the system, and uncovered workers are assumed not to enter the system in their middle or late career. Both enrolled and uncovered workers can be employed or unemployed. Then projections

Figure B.4 Projected Unemployment Rates in Middle East and North African Countries, 2000–30

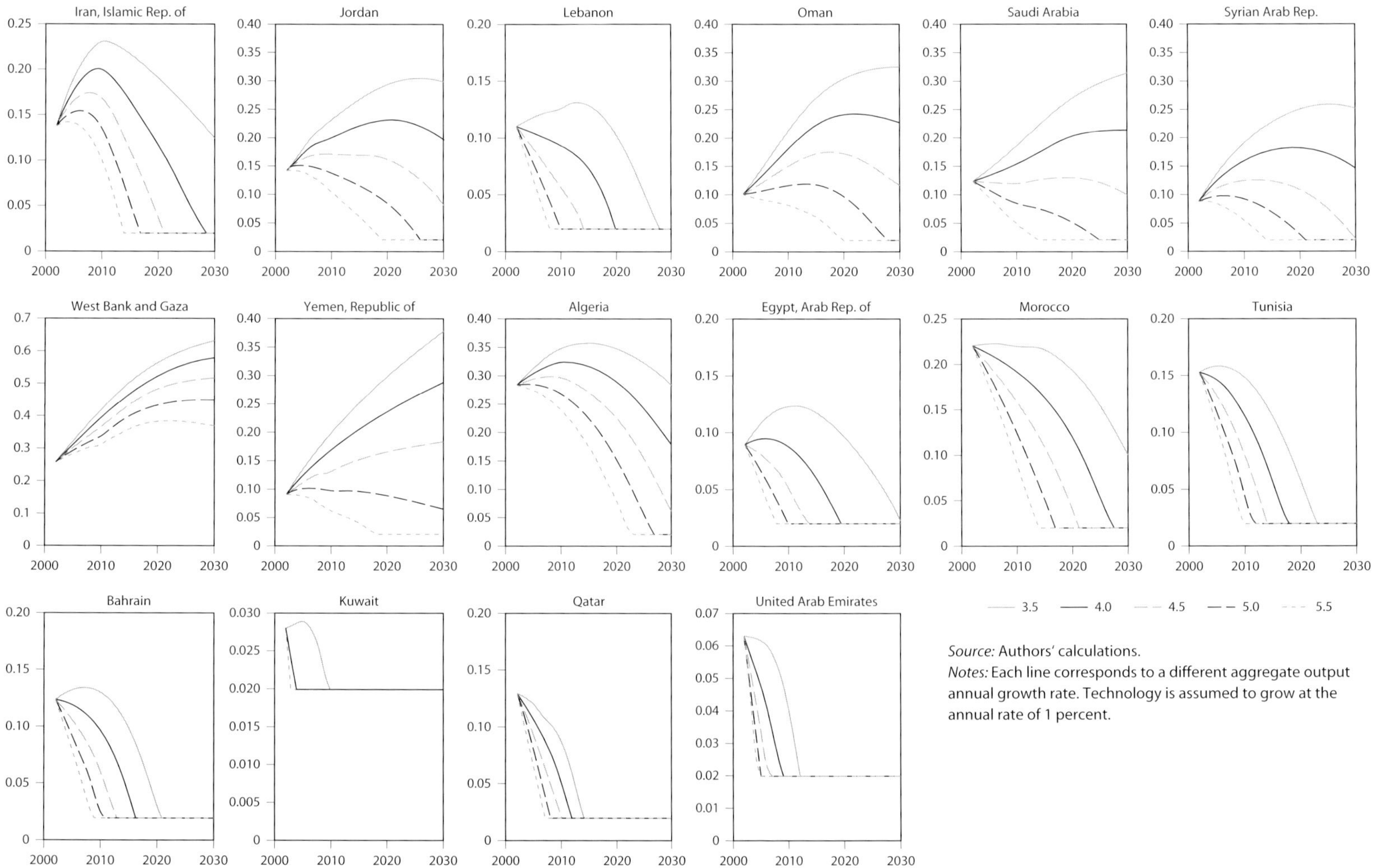

Source: Authors' calculations.

Notes: Each line corresponds to a different aggregate output annual growth rate. Technology is assumed to grow at the annual rate of 1 percent.

for the coverage rate are generated using projections for modeling the labor force and the unemployment rate (see chapter 2) as well as for modeling the enrollment rate for new workers. In the "optimistic" scenario, a gradually increasing share of new workers is enrolled in the system, until 100 percent of the labor force is reached. It is assumed that all the countries take 30 years to obtain a 100 percent rate of enrollment. In the "pessimistic scenario" there is no improvement in the enrollment of new workers. The income approach is based on Palacios and Pallarès-Miralles (2000), who estimate the relationship:

$$c = -0.15y^2 + 7.42y + 0.47, \tag{B.6}$$

where c is the coverage rate and y is GDP per capita (purchasing power parity adjusted). To ensure consistency with the "enrollment" approach, a 1 percent technology growth rate and a constant labor force demand growth rate are assumed. Then a series of GDP per capita is generated using the population projections calculated in chapter 2. The results are presented in figure B.4 and in figure 3.2 in chapter 3.

APPENDIX C

Main Parameters of Pension Schemes in the Middle East and North Africa

TABLE C.1

Characteristics of the CNR and CASNOS in Algeria

Characteristic	CNR	CASNOS
Eligibility conditions		
Age	55 years for women; 60 for men	60 years for women; 65 for men
Vesting period	10 years for women; 15 for men	15 years
Rules for early retirement	45 years for women; 50 for men, with 14 years of employment for women and 20 years for men or 32 years of contributions without minimum age. A 0.5 percent additional contribution is required from both the employer and the employee. The pension is reduced by 1 percent for each year of discrepancy prior to normal retirement age	—
Rules for delayed retirement	—	—
Rules for abandoning the system	Retirement settlement is set at age 65 with five years or 20 quarters of coverage. There is no minimum pension	—
Social security contribution rates	Total: 34.5 percent of gross salary (employer, 25 percent; worker, 9.5 percent). For pensions, 16.5 percent; for unemployment insurance, 4 percent of gross salary; for health insurance, 14 percent of gross salary	Only for pensions, 7.5 percent of gross salary
Accrual rate	2.5 percent	2.5 percent
Income measure	Average five best years of salary (no indexation)	Average 10 best years of salary (no indexation)
Ceiling on covered wage	15 times the minimum wage	Eight times the minimum wage
Maximum replacement rate or maximum pension	80 percent replacement rate and maximum pension of 15 times the minimum wage	80 percent replacement rate and maximum pension of 15 times the minimum wage
Pension indexation	Ad hoc annual indexation	Ad hoc annual indexation
Minimum pension	75 percent of the minimum wage	
Economy-wide minimum wage	DA 10,000 a month	
Economy-wide average wage	DA 23,000 a month	

Sources: CNR and CASNOS.
Notes: CNR covers civil servants and the military and administers retirement, survivor, and disability insurance. CASNOS covers the self-employed.
— = Not available or not offered.

TABLE C.2

Characteristics of the GOSI and PFC in Bahrain

Characteristic	GOSI	PFC (civil servants)	PFC (military)
Eligibility conditions			
Age	55 years for women; 60 for men	60 years for men and women; five years can be added, as in the case of the military	60 years for men and women
Vesting period	10 years for women, 15 for men (at retirement, workers get five extra years to a maximum of 30)	15 years	10 years; at ages 55–59, workers are credited by law with five additional years of contributions provided that the total is less than 60 years
Rules for early retirement	15 years of contributions for women, 20 for men; early-retirement pensions are reduced by 20 percent if the worker is younger than 45 years, by 15 percent if the worker is 45–50, and by 10 percent if the worker is 50–55	10 years of contributions if the position is canceled; otherwise, 25 years of contributions for women and men, with no age restriction, or 15 years of contributions with age 50; the pension is reduced by 5 percent if the worker is younger than 45 years and by 2.5 percent if the worker is 45–50. If service is terminated due to health conditions, the pension is computed as fully paid	20 years of contributions or 15 if the position is canceled; employees can purchase up to five additional years of service if the total is less than 40; the pension is not adjusted
Rules for delayed retirement	—	—	—
Rules for abandoning the system	If individual leaves the system before accruing pension rights, he or she receives a lump sum at age 55 (women) or 60 (men) equal to 15 percent of the last wage times years of contributions	Same as military	Same as GOSI, however, if termination is due to resignation, the lump sum is reduced as follows: by 25 percent with less than five years of contributions; 20 percent with 5–10 years of contributions; 15 percent for 10–15 years of contributions; if termination is due to cancellation of the position, the lump sum is multiplied by 1.5
Social security contribution rates	12 percent of gross wage for old-age and survivor pensions (employer, 7 percent; worker, 5 percent)	15 percent of gross wage (for state government, 10 percent; for worker, 5 percent)	For Bahrainis, 15 percent of gross wage (state government, 10 percent; worker, 5 percent)
Accrual rate	2.2 percent	2 percent	2 percent
Income measure	Average wage for last two years with no indexation	Last month wage	Last month wage
Ceiling on covered wage	No	No	No
Maximum replacement rate or maximum pension	80 percent	80 percent	80 percent
Pension indexation	Ad hoc	Ad hoc	Ad hoc
Minimum pension	BD 1,800 a year	BD 45 a month (plus BD 9 for each dependent)	BD 45 a month (plus BD 9 for each dependent)
Economy-wide minimum wage	—		
Economy-wide average wage	BD 4,285 a year		

Source: World Bank 2003b.
Note: — = Not available or not offered.

TABLE C.3

Characteristics of the OPS and CMR in Djibouti

Characteristic	OPS (after reform, Law 154/AN/02/4L)	CMR (military)
Eligibility conditions		
Age	55 years for women and men	None
Vesting period	For those born after 1951, 25 years; for those born in 1950, 1949, 1948, 1947, 1946, and before, 23, 21, 19, 17, and 15 years, respectively	15 years
Rules for early retirement	Workers can retire at age 55 or after, without having completed the vesting period, but the pension is adjusted downward (government has not issued the regulations yet). Beginning at age 50, workers can also apply for early retirement, but only for medical reasons, and they need to have a vesting period equal to 25 minus the number of years missing to reach the normal retirement age; for ages 50, 51, 52, 53, and 54, the pension is reduced by 50, 60, 70, 80, and 90 percent, respectively	—
Rules for delayed retirement	—	—
Rules for abandoning the system	—	—
Social security contribution rates	19.7 percent (employer, 50 percent; worker, 50 percent); for old-age pension, 8 percent; family allowance, 5.5 percent; health and work accidents, 6.2 percent	20 percent of gross wage (employer, 13 percent; worker, 7 percent)
Accrual rate	2 percent for years contributed until December 2001; 1.8 percent between 2002 and 2006; afterward, 1.5 percent	3 percent
Income measure	Average wage of last 10 years. Article 109 of the law indicates that wages need to be indexed and that the cabinet defines the index (no regulations have been issued to date)	Last month wage
Ceiling on covered wage	No	No
Maximun replacement rate or maximum pension	81 percent	Unknown
Pension indexation	Ad hoc	Ad hoc
Minimum pension	DF 170,000 a year	Unknown
Economy-wide minimum wage	There is no minimum wage	
Economy-wide average wage	DF 800,000 a year	

Sources: OPS and CMR.
Notes: OPS covers private sector workers; CMR covers the military forces.
— = Not available or not offered.

TABLE C.4

Characteristics of CNR in Djibouti after Implementation of Reform Law 155/AN/02/4L

Characteristic	Civil servants	Police	Parliamentarians
Eligibility conditions			
Age	55 years for those born after 1955 (for those born between 1947 and 1954, retirement age is reduced by half a year for each calendar year)	Same as for civil servants	55 years for women and men
Vesting period	25 years	26 years	10 years
Rules for early retirement	Early retirement is possible if for physical or institutional reasons the employee cannot continue to work	Same as for civil servants; maximum 37.5 years of contributions can count to this pension	Same as for civil servants; pension is equal to two-thirds of normal pension
Rules for delayed retirement	—	—	—
Rules for abandoning the system	—	—	—
Social security contribution rates	20 percent of basic wage (employer, 14 percent; worker, 6 percent); covers old-age and survivor benefits	22 percent of gross wage (employer, 15 percent; worker, 7 percent)	36 percent of gross wage (employer, 19 percent; worker, 17 percent)
Accrual rate	Until December 2001, 3 percent for first 15 years; 2 percent thereafter; between January 2002 and January 2007, 1.8 percent; between January 2007 and January 2010, 1.5 percent; after January 2010, 1.3 percent	Until December 2001, 3 percent for first 15 years, then 2 percent; between January 2002 and January 2007, 1.8 percent; between January 2007 and January 2010, 1.5 percent; after January 2010, 1.3 percent	Until December 2001, 4 percent; afterward, 3 percent
Income measure	Last month wage	Last month wage	Last month wage
Ceiling on covered wage	No	No	No
Maximum replacement rate or maximum pension	81 percent	81 percent	75 percent
Pension indexation	—	—	—
Minimum pension	DF 170,000 a year	DF 170,000 a year	DF 170,000 a year
Economy-wide minimum wage	—		
Economy-wide average wage	DF 800,000 a year		

Source: CNR.
Note: — = Not available or not offered.

TABLE C.5

Characteristics of the Government Pension Fund, Public and Private Enterprises Employee Pension Fund, and the Scheme for the Self-Employed in Egypt

Characteristic	Government pension fund and public and private enterprises employee pension fund	Scheme for the self-employed
Eligibility conditions		
Age	60 years for women and men	65 years women and men
Vesting period	10 years	10 years
Rules for early retirement	At any age with 20 years of contributions, subject to penalties: at less than 45 years of age, basic pension is reduced by 15 percent; at 45–50, 10 percent; at 50–55, 5 percent; and before age 60, variable pension is reduced by 5 percent for each year of contributions missing to reach the normal retirement age	20 years of contributions
Rules for delayed retirement	Workers who have contributed for more than 36 years or who have a vesting period greater than that required to attain the maximum pension (whichever is larger) have the right to a lump-sum indemnity at the rate of 15 percent of the last annual wage for each of the years in excess, based on the basic wage	—
Rules for abandoning the system	Individuals not meeting retirement conditions receive, for each year of contributions, a lump sum of 15 percent of the last two-year average monthly wage on which contributions were paid	Unknown
Social security contribution rates	Employer, 15 percent of basic wages and 15 percent of variable wages; worker, 10 percent of basic wages and 10 percent of variable wages; government, 1 percent	15 percent of gross wage, paid by employee
Accrual rate	2.2 percent (2.77 percent of those who served in the armed forces for relevant period). There is also a bonus of 25 percent of the basic pension; the minimum is LE 20 a month, and the maximum is LE 35 a month	2.22 percent
Income measure	One part of the benefits is based on the basic wage, in the amount of LE 8,000 a year; another part is based on variable income (including all bonuses and allowances) and is the amount in excess of the basic wage, up to LE 6,000 a year. For the pension benefit based on the basic wage, the average wage during the last two years is taken, no indexation is applied. For all but civil servants, the average monthly wage for the last two years cannot be greater than the average of five years preceding the averaging period. For the benefit based on the variable wage, remunerations over the entire carrier are taken, whereby the non-indexed full-career average is increased by 2 percent for each year of contributions. The adjusted average has a ceiling of LE 6,000	The base for calculating both contributions and benefits is one of 23 different income classes; all income counts toward the pension; revalorization policies are unknown
Ceiling on covered wage	Effectively LE 8,100 (basic) + LE 6,000 (variable) = LE 14,100 a year	Unknown
Maximum replacement rate or maximum pension	80 percent, yet if less than LE 70 a month, the pension becomes 100 percent of the reference wage; maximum pension is LE 900 a month	Unknown
Pension indexation	Ad hoc	Unknown
Minimum pension	LE 105 a month for civil servants and LE 45 a month for other groups; for those with more than 20 years of contributions, a minimum replacement rate of 50 percent is set	Unknown
Economy-wide minimum wage	60 percent of the average wage	
Economy-wide average wage	LE 8,000 a year	

Sources: Law 79 of 1975; technical staff from the pension funds.
Notes: The Public and Private Enterprises Employee Pension Scheme is governed by Law No. 79 from 1975. The Scheme for the Self-Employed is governed by Law No. 108 from 1976.
— = Not available or not offered.

TABLE C.6

Characteristics of the Scheme for Egyptians Working Abroad and the Casual Employment Sector/Comprehensive Scheme in Egypt

Characteristic	Scheme for Egyptians Working Abroad	Casual Employment Sector/Comprehensive Scheme
Eligibility conditions		
Age	60 years for women and men	65 years for women and men
Vesting period	10 years	10 years
Rules for early retirement	Unknown	At any age with 35 years of contributions
Rules for delayed retirement	Unknown	—
Rules for abandoning the system	Unknown	Unknown
Social security contribution rates	22.5 percent of gross wage, paid by employee	Workers contribute a flat rate of LE 3 a month
Accrual rate	2.22 percent	Flat rate of LE 80 a month
Income measure	All remunerations, revalorization policy is unknown	All remunerations
Ceiling on covered wage	Unknown	Eight times the average monthly wage
Maximum replacement rate or maximum pension	Unknown	—
Pension indexation	Unknown	Ad hoc
Minimum pension	Unknown	LE 80 a month; "Sadat" pension is LE 65 a month
Maximum pension	Unknown	—
Economy-wide minimum wage		—
Economy-wide average wage	60 percent of the average wage	

Source: Public and Private Enterprises Employee Pension Fund

Notes: The Scheme for Egyptians Working Abroad is governed by Law No. 50 from 1978. The Casual Employment Sector/Comprehensive Scheme is governed by Law No.112 from 1980. A secondary act stipulates that the "Sadat" pension is an unfunded benefit provided on a means-tested basis to all poor elderly above 65 years of age.

— = Not available or not offered.

TABLE C.7

Characteristics of the CSRO and the SSO in the Islamic Republic of Iran

Characteristic	CSRO	SSO
Eligibility conditions		
Age	Option 1: 60 years for men and women (no minimum number of years); men can also choose to retire at age 50	55 for women, 60 for men
Vesting period	No vesting or 25 years of service	10 years for both men and women
Rules for early retirement	Women with 20 years and men with 30 years with no minimum age; men can also retire at 50 years of age with 25 years of contributions; in none of the cases do penalties apply	Women can retire at age 42 with 20 years of contributions; men can retire with no minimum age after 30 years of contributions; no penalties apply
Rules for delayed retirement	—	—
Rules for abandoning the system	Individuals not meeting retirement conditions receive a lump sum equal to three months of salary for each year of contributions (in the case of unskilled workers) or 45 days for each year (in the case of skilled workers)	Individuals not meeting retirement conditions do not receive pensions or compensation
Social security contribution rates	Total: 22.5 percent of basic salary, which represents 75 percent of the total (worker, 13.5 percent; employer, 9 percent). Workers with more than 30 years of service do not pay contributions. These funds cover old-age, disability, and survivor benefits, as well as health insurance contributions for retirees	Total: 33 percent of gross wage (employer, 23 percent; worker, 7 percent; government, 3 percent). For unemployment insurance, 3 percent of gross wage; for health insurance, 9 percent of gross wage; for all pensions and cash transfers, 21 percent of gross wage
Accrual rate	3.3 percent	3.3 percent
Income measure	Pensions are calculated on the basis of the basic wage, which on average represents 75 percent of total earnings; the average of the last two years is taken; no revalorization applies	Average last two years; no revalorization applies
Ceiling on covered wage	No	Eight times average wage
Maximum replacement rate or maximum pension	100 percent maximum replacement rate	116 percent of gross wage
Pension indexation	Ad hoc	Ad hoc indexation
Minimum pension	Equal to the minimum wage	Equal to the minimum wage
Economy-wide minimum wage	Rls 850,000 a month (66 percent of average wage)	
Economy-wide average wage	Rls 1,287,879 a month	

Sources: CSRO, SSO, and World Bank 2003d.
Notes: The CSRO covers civil servants only; the SSO covers private sector employees.
— = Not available or not offered.

TABLE C.8

Characteristics of the SEP and SSW in Iraq[a]

Characteristic	SEP	SSW[a]
Eligibility conditions		
Age	60 for men and women	60 for men; 55 for women
Vesting period	15 years	20 years
Rules for early retirement	55 for men with 30 years of service; 50 for women with 25 years of service	At any age with 30 years of contributions; no penalties apply
Rules for delayed retirement	Compulsory retirement at 63	—
Rules for abandoning the system	Individuals not meeting retirement conditions (age and minimum 15 years of service) receive a lump-sum payment equaling one month's pension for each year of contributions	Individuals not meeting retirement conditions receive the average monthly wage of the last three years times the number of years of service
Social security contribution rates	The contribution rate varies with the level of wages. For state-owned enterprises, it ranges between 3 and 30 percent (1 to 10 percent by employee, matched 200 percent by employer); for civil servants, 1 to 10 percent, also matched 200 percent by the employer; for the military, not known	Employer, 12 percent; worker, 5 percent; out of the 17 percent contribution, only 14 percent covers pensions. The equivalent portions of the contribution for pensions are employee, 4.1 percent, and employer, 9.9 percent. There are also exceptions: banks, 10 percent of the annual salary; oil companies, 25 percent of the annual salary
Accrual rate	12/420 = 1/35 = 2.86 percent	12/480 = 1/40 = 2.5 percent
Income measure	Last month wage	Average monthly wage last three years
Ceiling on covered wage	No	No
Maximum replacement rate or maximum pension	75 percent plus 5 percent for each additional dependent up to a maximum of 90 percent	There is a maximum pension of ID 80,000 per month
Pension indexation	Ad hoc	Ad hoc
Minimum pension	The law stipulates a minimum of ID 8 a month, but is now outdated	Before the war, a minimum pension of ID 6,000 a month was approved, but never implemented.
Economy-wide minimum wage	No	
Economy-wide average wage	Unknown	
Monthly average wage	ID 243,400	ID 45,000

Source: Ministry of Finance and SSW.

Notes: The law does not apply after the war, as flat pensions are being paid. Categories of workers excluded from the system include agricultural workers, temporary employees, domestic servants, and family labor.

— = Not available or not offered.

TABLE C.9

Characteristics of the SSC, Civil Service System, and Military Pension System in Jordan

Characteristic	SSC	Civil service system	Military pension system
Eligibility conditions			
Age	55 for women; 60 for men	None	None
Vesting period	15 years	15 years for women; 20 for men	16 years
Rules for early retirement	For men, 45 years of age with 18 years of contributions; for women, 15 years of contributions at any age. There are penalties for early retirement. Early-retirement reduction factors by gender and age are for women, age 45–49, 10 percent; age 50–54, 5 percent; age 55–59, 0 percent; for men age 45–46, 18 percent; age 47, 16 percent; age 48, 14 percent; age 49, 12 percent; age 50, 10 percent; afterward falling by 1 percentage point a year away from normal retirement	Unknown	Unknown
Rules for delayed retirement	—	—	—
Rules for abandoning the system	Individuals not meeting retirement conditions receive lump-sum payments constituting 15 percent of final earnings for each year of contributions of 15–18 years, 12 percent for contributions of 5–15 years, and 10 percent for contributions of 1–5 years	—	—
Social security contribution rates	Total: 16 percent of gross wage. For work injury and occupational disease insurance, 2 percent. For old-age, disability, and survivor pensions, 14.5 percent (employer, 9 percent; worker, 5.5 percent)	8.75 percent of basic wage, paid by employee	8.75 percent of basic wage, paid by employee
Accrual rate	2.50 percent	4.17 percent	4.17 percent
Income measure	Average of all salaries during last two years. Final pay (that is, pay at time *R*) is adjusted downward or upward to ensure that 1.2*Pay(R-5) < Pay(R) < 1.6*Pay(R-5)	Last month wage	Last month wage
Ceiling on covered wage	No	No	No
Maximum replacement rate or maximum pension	75 percent of income measure	No	No
Pension indexation	Discretionary	Discretionary	Discretionary
Minimum pension	Equal to minimum wage	—	—
Economy-wide minimum wage	JD 960 a year in 2003		
Economy-wide average wage	JD 230 a month (2,760 a year)		

Sources: SSC; World Bank 2003c.
Notes: The SSC covers private sector workers and civil servants. Since 2002 the military pension system has been closed to new entrants, who are directed to SSC. The same has been applied to the civil service scheme since 1995.
— = Not available or not offered.

TABLE C.10

Characteristics of the Military Scheme, the Civil Service Scheme, and the Private Sector End-of-Service Indemnity Program in Lebanon

Characteristic	Military scheme	Civil service scheme	Private sector end-of-service indemnity program
Eligibility conditions			
Age	No age requirement	No age requirement	60 years for women and men
Vesting period	20 years. Individuals' years of contributions are multiplied by a factor ranging between 1.5 and 3, depending on the level of alert	20 years	20 years
Rules for early retirement	No	No	—
Rules for delayed retirement	A combination of lifetime pension and end-of-service compensation is provided to individuals with more than 40 years of service, with the end-of-service compensation being three times 85 percent of the last monthly salary for each year of service that exceeds 40 years	A combination of lifetime pension and end-of-service compensation is provided to individuals with more than 40 years of service, with the end-of-service compensation being three times 85 percent of the last monthly salary for each year of service that exceeds 40 years	—
Rules for abandoning the system	For less than 20 years of service, an end-of-service compensation is calculated based on 85 percent of the last monthly wage reference for each year of service for the first 10 years and two times 85 percent of last monthly wage per year of service after that	For less than 20 years of service, an end-of-service compensation is calculated based on 85 percent of the last monthly wage reference for each year of service for the first 10 years and two times 85 percent of the last monthly wage per year of service after that	Workers can withdraw their balance on leaving employment, but with increasing penalties the shorter the period of contribution
Social security contribution rates	6 percent paid by employee	6 percent paid by employee	8.5 percent of gross wage, paid by employer
Accrual rate	2.66 percent	2.13 percent	The lump-sum benefit is equal to the capital accumulated on the individual account with past employers; plus one month of salary for each year of contribution during the first 20 years of service spent with the last employer and 1.5 months after that
Income measure	Last month wage	Last month wage	—
Ceiling on covered wage	No	No	No
Maximum replacement rate or maximum pension	85 percent of final salary	85 percent of final salary	
Pension indexation	Ad hoc	Ad hoc	—
Minimum pension	No	No	—
Economy-wide minimum wage	LL 310,400		

(Continues on the following page.)

TABLE C.10 *(continued)*

Characteristic	Military scheme	Civil service scheme	Private sector end-of-service indemnity program
Economy-wide average wage	LL 930,000 (contributory wage). The preliminary number without the latest update is LL 1,142,417 for the civil service and LL 721,771 for the military. Both figures exclude allowances. Contributors, LL 307,800 for end-of-service (2000); LL 39,700 for civil servants (2001); LL 59,700 for the military (2001)		

Sources: NSSF and Ministry of Finance. See also World Bank 2005a.
Notes: NSSF provides the end-of-service indemnity.
— = Not available or not offered.

TABLE C.11

Characteristics of the SSF in Libya

Characteristic	SSF (basic regime)
Eligibility conditions	
Age	65 years for men and 60 years for women (non-civil servants); 62 years for men and 60 years for women (civil servants)
Vesting period	None
Rules for early retirement	62 years for men and 60 years for women (non-civil servants); 20 years of contributions (civil servants). In none of the cases do penalties apply
Rules for delayed retirement	None
Rules for abandoning the system	Nothing; can continue to contribute when rejoining
Social security contribution rates	15 percent of gross wage for civil servants and wage earners (employer, 70 percent; worker, 25 percent; government, 5 percent) or for foreigners (employer, 75 percent; worker, 25 percent). The contribution rate covers pension, 10.5 percent; basic health care, 2.5 percent; work accidents, 1 percent; and a basic pension, 1 percent For the self-employed, the contribution rate is 16.5 percent of gross wage (employer, 95 percent; government, 5 percent); the extra 1.5 percentage point goes to cash transfers, which in the other cases are paid directly by the employer
Accrual rate	2.5 percent for the first 20 years or less; 2 percent for more than 20 years of service
Income measure	Average of last three years; no revalorization applies
Ceiling on covered wage	No
Maximum replacement rate or maximum pension	80 percent
Pension indexation	Ad hoc
Minimum pension	80 percent of the minimum wage
Economy-wide minimum wage	LD 85 a month
Economy-wide average wage	LD 233 a month

Source: SSF.
Note: — = Not available or not offered.

TABLE C.12

Characteristics of the CMR and the CNSS in Morocco

Characteristic	CMR		CNSS
	Civil servants	Military	
Eligibility conditions			
Age	60 years for men and women	45 or 50, depending on grade	60 years for women and men
Vesting period	None	None	15 years
Rules for early retirement	15 for women; 21 for men; the accrual rate is reduced by 0.5 percentage point	Same as for civil servants	55 years for women and men; no penalties apply, but the employer pays the pension between ages 55 and 60
Rules for delayed retirement	—	—	—
Rules for abandoning the system	Employee receives his or her contributions (not employer's) without interest	Same as for civil servants	Individuals can only receive benefits if they meet eligibility conditions
Social security contribution rates	14 percent of gross wage (employer, 7 percent; worker, 7 percent); for old-age pension, 14 percent; for other benefits, noncontributory. Contribution is increasing to 20 percent at a rate of two percentage points a year; other benefits are financed directly by the government	21 percent of gross wage (employer, 14 percent; worker, 7 percent) to finance old-age pension; other benefits are financed directly by the government	20.39 percent (employer 16.09 percent; worker, 4.29 percent). Old-age, disability, and survivor pensions, 11.89 percent; family allowance, 7.5 percent; short-term benefits , 1 percent
Accrual rate	2.5 percent	2.5 percent	3.3 percent first 15 years, 1 percent afterward (law indicates 50 percent of the income measure for the first 3,240 days, then 1 percent for each block of 216 days; simplification assumes that one year is 216 days of work)
Income measure	Last salary	Last salary	Last eight years (no revalorization applies)
Ceiling on covered wage	No	No	DH 6,000
Maximum replacement rate or maximum pension	Maximum pension is 100 percent of net wage	Maximum pension is 100 percent of net wage	70 percent of gross wage
Pension indexation	Ad hoc	Ad hoc	Ad hoc
Minimum pension	DH 500 a month	DH 500 a month	DH 500 a month
Economy-wide minimum wage	DH 2,009 a month		
Economy-wide average wage	DH 2,750 a month		

Source: CMR and CNSS.
Note: — = Not available or not offered.

TABLE C.13

Characteristics of the CMR and the RCAR in Morocco

Characteristic	RCAR (basic regime)
Eligibility conditions	
Age	60 years for women and men
Vesting period	21 years
Rules for early retirement	55 years for both women and men with 21 years of contributions. The pension is reduced by 4.8 percent for each year missing to reach the normal retirement age (60)
Rules for delayed retirement	If individual retires after age 60, the pension increases by 4.8 percent for each year above the age of 60
Rules for abandoning the system	Receives capital accumulated in the individual accounts
Social security contribution rates	18 percent of gross wage (employer, 12 percent; worker, 6 percent). Of these, individual accounts, 12 percent; family allowances, 0.65 percent; disability and survivor pensions, 1 percent; general fund covering future unfunded obligations of the scheme, 4.35 percent
Accrual rate	2 percent
Income measure	All remunerations (revalorized by the growth rate of the average covered wage)
Ceiling on covered wage	Four times the average salary (DH 11,000 in 2003)
Maximum replacement rate or maximum pension	90 percent
Pension indexation	Automatic indexation to consumer price index
Minimum pension	No
Economy-wide minimum wage	—
Economy-wide average wage	DH 2,750 a month

Source: RCAR.
Notes: RCAR covers contractual workers in the public sector.
— = Not available or not offered.

TABLE C.14

Characteristics of the CNRPS and CNSS in Tunisia

		CNSS			
Characteristic	CNRPS	RSNA	RSAA	RSA	RNS
Eligibility conditions					
Age	60 years	60 years	60 years	60 years	65 years
Vesting period	15 years	10 years	10 years	10 years	10 years
Rules for early retirement	At age 50 or 55, no penalty is applied	55 or 50 years; involves 2 percent reduction for each year short of normal retirement age	No	No	60 years with no penalty
Rules for delayed retirement	—	—	—	—	—
Rules for abandoning the system	Unknown	Unknown	Unknown	Unknown	Unknown
Social security contribution rates	15.7 percent of gross wage (employer, 8.95 percent, worker, 6.75 percent)	12.5 percent of gross wage (employer, 9.75 percent; worker, 2.75 percent)	7.5 percent of gross wage (employer, 5 percent; worker, 2.5 percent)	5.25 percent of gross wage (employer, 3.5 percent; worker, 1.75 percent)	7 percent of gross income for self-employed
Accrual rate	2 percent for the first 10 years; 3 percent for the next 10 years; 2 percent after that	4 percent for the first 10 years; 2 percent after that	4 percent for the first 10 years; 2 percent after that	4 percent for the first 10 years; 2 percent after that	4 percent for the first 10 years; 2 percent after that
Income measure	Highest of last wage or last two years average revalorized with the growth rate of covered wages	Average of last 10 years; past wages are revalorized by prices	Average of last three or five years; no revalorization of past wages	Average of last three or five years; no revalorization of past wages	Average of last three or five years; no revalorization of past wages
Ceiling on covered wage	No	No	No	No	No
Maximum replacement rate or maximum pension	90 percent	Maximum pension of 80 percent of earnings up to six times industrial minimum wage	80 percent	80 percent	80 percent
Pension indexation	Growth rate of covered wages	Industrial minimum wage	Agricultural minimum wage	Agricultural minimum wage	Industrial or agricultural minimum wage
Minimum pension	Two-thirds of industrial minimum wage	Two-thirds of industrial minimum wage	Two-thirds of industrial minimum wage	40 percent of agricultural minimum wage	30 percent of industrial minimum wage
Economy-wide minimum wage	Industrial minimum wage, DT 2,206 a year; agricultural minimum wage, 6.509 a day				
Economy-wide average wage	DT 5,138 a year				

Source: Centre de Recherche en Securité Sociale.

Notes: CNRPS covers civil servants, military, security forces, contractual workers, and local authorities. See Law 85-12; 1985. RSNA covers nonagricultural workers in the formal sector. RSAA covers agricultural workers in cooperatives. RSA covers agricultural wage earners employed at least 45 days a quarter by the same employer. RNS covers the self-employed. The industrial minimum wage, as of July 1, 2003, is DT 211.120 a month (48 hours a week) or DT 183.906 a month (40 hours a week). The agricultural minimum wage, as of June 30, 2003, is DT 6.509 a day.

— = Not available or not offered.

TABLE C.15

Characteristics of the West Bank Scheme, the Gaza Scheme, and the Security Forces Scheme in the West Bank and Gaza Prior to the Reform

Characteristic	West Bank scheme	Gaza scheme	Security forces scheme
Eligibility conditions			
Age	60 years	60 years	60 years
Vesting period	40 years	15 years	15 years
Rules for early retirement	At any age with 15 years of service, with approval; for more than 30 years of service, approval is automatic	At any age with 20 years of service with the following reductions for age: less than or equal to 45 years of age, 20 percent; 46–50 years, 15 percent; 51–55 years, 10 percent; 56–57 years, 5 percent. With involuntary resignation workers receive full benefits if they have 15 years of service	Minimum 15 years of contributions, varying by rank; early retirees do not receive a 70 percent add-on (from the general benefit formula, 70 percent*basic wage + 70 percent*80 percent*basic salary)
Rules for delayed retirement	Personal allowance (NIS 10+) plus family (wife and child) allowances	Personal allowance (NIS 300) plus family (wife and child) allowances	Modest social allowance for wife and sons
Rules for abandoning the system	—	With more than or equal to three years of service, workers receive a lump sum equaling 15 percent times annual final average salary times years of service	—
Social security contribution rates	Worker, 2 percent nominal contribution on wages; employer, 0 percent, but pays all benefits when due	22.5 percent (government, 12.5 percent; worker, 10 percent)	22.5 percent (employer, 12.5 percent; worker, 10 percent)
Accrual rate	2 percent	2.5 percent	For less than 15 years of service, 5.33 percent; for more than 15 years of service, higher accrual rate
Income measure	Basic salary (years before 1987), last basic salary + allowances (years after 1987)	Last wage	Basic wage
Ceiling on covered wage	No	No	No
Maximum replacement rate or maximum pension	70 percent	70 percent	No
Pension indexation	Ad hoc periodic adjustment equivalent to that given to active employees with same rank as when retired	Ad hoc periodic adjustment equivalent to that given to active employees with same rank as when retired	Ad hoc adjustments requiring approval of the president
Minimum pension	No	No	No
Economy-wide minimum wage	No		
Economy-wide average wage	NIS 17,924 a year (Palestinian territories)		

Sources: World Bank 2002c.

Notes: West Bank and Gaza schemes cover civil servants and local authorities. Newly hired civil servants after June 2001 participate in the Gaza scheme regardless of their location. The schemes for workers in Israel and Israeli settlements operate under the Histaadrut union agreements, according to which these workers have been contributing to occupational pension schemes in Israel, while others have contributed to the Solidarity Fund in Israel. Under Article III of the Gaza-Jericho Economic Accord between Israel and the Palestinian Authority, these funds should be transferred to the Palestinian Authority once certain conditions have been met, such as the creation of relevant "pension institutions."

— = Not available or not offered.

TABLE C.16

Characteristics of the GCSS, GASS, Police Pension Fund, and the Army Pension Fund in the Republic of Yemen

Characteristic	Private pension fund (GCSS)	Civil service pension fund (GASS)	Police pension fund	Army pension fund
Eligibility conditions				
Age	55 years for women; 60 for men	55 years for women; 60 for men	—	—
Vesting period	15 years for men; 10 years for women	15 years for men; 10 years for women	—	—
Rules for early retirement	At any age with 30 years (men) and 25 years (women) and no adjustments; 25 years of contributions in case of resignation. Men at age 50 with 25 years or at age 55 with 20 years; women at age 46 with 20 years. In none of these cases do reductions apply. Men and women can also retire at age 45 with 20 years of service, and the pension is reduced by 10 percent. Men can also retire at age 50 with 20 years of service, and the pension is reduced by 5 percent	At any age with 30 years (men) and 25 years (women) and no adjustments; 25 years of contributions in case of resignation. Men at age 50 with 25 years or at age 55 with 20 years; women at age 46 with 20 years. In none of these cases do reductions apply. Men and women can also retire at age 45 with 20 years of service, and the pension is reduced by 10 percent. Men can also retire at age 50 with 20 years of service, and the pension is reduced by 5 percent	Unknown	Unknown
Rules for delayed retirement	—	—	—	—
Rules for abandoning the system	Unknown	Unknown	—	—
Social security contribution rates	For pensions, employer contributes 6 percent times (total basic pay + total amount of allowances received + 6 percent of basic pay). Employee matches contributions; for disability, employer contributes 4 percent; for work injury, government contributes 1 percent	For pensions, employer contributes 6 percent times (total basic pay + total amount of allowances received + 6 percent of basic pay). Employee matches contributions; for disability, employer contributes 4 percent; for work injury, government contributes 1 percent	Unknown	Unknown
Accrual rate	2.5 percent	2.86 percent	12 percent of gross wage (employer, 6 percent; worker, 6 percent)	12 percent of gross wage (employer, 6 percent worker, 6 percent)

(Continues on the following page.)

TABLE C.16 *(continued)*

Characteristic	Private pension fund (GCSS)	Civil service pension fund (GASS)	Police pension fund	Army pension fund
Income measure	Average monthly wage for last two years (not to exceed 150 percent of the average of the last five years)	Last monthly salary	Unknown	Unknown
Ceiling on covered wage	No	No	—	—
Maximum replacement rate or maximum pension	100 percent	100 percent	100 percent	100 percent
Pension indexation	Ad hoc	Benefits are adjusted by 50 percent of the value of any salary increases granted to active civil servants	100 percent	100 percent
Minimum pension	No	Yrls 7,000 a month; there is also a minimum replacement rate of 50 percent	—	—
Economy-wide minimum wage	Yrls 8,750 a month			
Economy-wide average wage	Yrls 10,770 a month			

Sources: GCSS and GASS

Notes: Part-time workers, agricultural workers, domestics, seamen, and fishermen are excluded from the pension system.

— = Not available or not offered.

APPENDIX D

Tax Treatment of Pension Systems

The tax treatment of pension contributions and benefits has important implications for fiscal policy, individual decisions regarding savings and consumption, and equity. A generous tax system could encourage private saving, but it would do so at the cost of forgone tax revenue (reduction in public sector saving). Adverse redistribution may also result if high-income individuals benefit more from tax exemptions than low-income individuals. Three issues require attention: (a) What tax base should be used: income or consumption? (b) If the latter, should the taxation be front-loaded or back-loaded? (c) What role do subsidies (for example, preferential tax treatment) have in voluntary saving for retirement?

Most countries tax income under the personal income tax scheme (for a review of practices in the tax treatment of retirement savings, see Whitehouse 2001). Under such an approach, savings are undertaken out of taxed income, and interest income on these savings is taxed again. For mandated retirement income, however, most countries have a different type of treatment. In unfunded systems, contributions are typically tax exempt, while benefits are fully taxed. The same approach is used for funded schemes, where most of the interest earned is not taxed. For retirement income, the consumption-type tax approach is thus applied, which eliminates distortions on intertemporal consumption and saving decisions. This is the appropriate treatment of retirement income. However, not having taxes is not a good idea either. In some countries, retirement savings remain totally untaxed, leading to distortions in the other direction and questionable distributive outcomes, since essentially the higher-income groups profit from this treatment.

A consumption-type tax treatment can, in principle, be achieved by front-loading and back-loading taxation, while being neutral for the intertemporal budget constraint of government. Under the latter, contributions as well as interest earned remain untaxed, while benefits are taxed (hence an exempt-exempt-tax, EET, treatment). Under the former, contributions are taxed, while interest rates earned and benefits remain untaxed (hence a tax-exempt-exempt, TEE, treatment). In a model-type setting (including constant marginal tax rate), both treatments are equivalent. In a real-world setting, differences do emerge. From a political point of view, an EET treatment may be preferred, since a TEE approach may not be credible (because further taxation can be introduced in the future). For budgetary reasons, however, a TEE treatment may be preferred, because the government might not be able to finance the extended tax credit under the EET approach. When the tax system is progressive, TEE is likely to provide more tax revenues, but EET provides more incentives for individuals to participate. Also, if one stands by the notion that public investments have a lower marginal product than private investments, EET treatment has the advantage of freeing resources to be invested by the private sector. This will only hold if the government reduces expenditure to balance the budget effect while freeing resources to be used by the private sector. But it will not hold if the government issues debt to finance the budget problem. Hence, in a dynamic sense, EET treatment may provide, at least in theory and ceteris paribus, higher overall tax revenues than TEE treatment. Nonetheless, either EET or TEE is acceptable. The option a country chooses will depend on its politics and the outlook of its fiscal accounts. Any difference in the economic impacts of either option will be of a second order of magnitude.

While there is strong consensus about the tax treatment of mandated schemes (unfunded or funded) in the pension community, there is no consensus about the tax treatment of voluntary schemes. For some economists, preferential tax treatment (that is, consumption-type taxation) should also be applied, within limits, to voluntary schemes in order to encourage the take-up of these schemes and to allow governments to play a more active role in regulation and supervision. For other economists, such tax treatment does little to increase overall individual saving, and an increase in take-up reflects simply a substitution for other forms of saving. Even worse, the income effect of the preferential tax treatment may even reduce individual and government saving. Still, even though consumption-type taxation may not increase saving and may not deepen financial markets, it does change the composition of financial intermediation favoring long-term funds. This, in turn, reduces the refinancing risks of governments, banks, and enterprises and reduces the leverage of enterprises, making them more resilient to shocks.

A problem with consumption-type taxation under a progressive tax system is that the well-off benefit the most, since low-income workers with insufficient income to pay taxes do not benefit at all. Hence, an alternative approach is for the government to grant matching subsidies

TABLE D.1

Tax Treatment of Pensions in Select Middle East and North African Countries

Country or territory	Mandatory	Voluntary	Life insurance
Algeria	ETT	—	—
Bahrain[a]	EEE	EEE	EEE
Djibouti	EET	—	—
Egypt, Arab Rep. of	EEE	EEE	—
Jordan	EtE	EEE	TTT
Iran, Islamic Rep. of	TTE	—	—
Lebanon	EtE	T^2 TT	TtE, Ttt
Morocco	Ett	EEt	EtT, TtE, tEE, EEt
Tunisia	TtT	—	—
West Bank and Gaza	TET[b]	EET	—
Yemen, Republic of	E-T	—	—

Source: Authors' calculations based on several tax laws.
Notes: ETT means that contributions are exempted from income tax, while investment income of reserves and benefits are taxed. EEE means that contributions, investment income of reserves, and benefits are exempted from income tax. EET (exempted, exempted, taxed) means that contributions and investment income of reserves are exempted from income tax, while benefits are taxed. ETE means that contributions and benefits are exempted from income tax, while investment income is taxed TTE-tax, tax, exempted. TTT means that contributions, investment income, and benefits are subject to income tax. T^2 TT means that contributions are subject to income tax twice, while investment income and benefits are taxed once. TEE means that contributions are subject to income tax, while investment income of reserves and benefits are exempted. E-T means that there is no information on the tax treatment of investment income. Finally, t stands for a tax rate lower than the statutory tax rates, either because it is an implicit tax due to financial repression or because only part of the tax base is taxed.
— = Not available.
a. The country does not have income tax.
b. Proposed law adopts EET treatment.

to contributions to voluntary retirement plans. Moreover, using matching subsidies instead of tax preferences permits the design of a well-targeted, equitable, and transparent program. Such a program would be available to nontax payers, which could increase coverage rates by attracting the self-employed and informal sector workers to voluntary pension plans.

In the Middle East and North Africa region, there is large variation in the treatment of pension products (see table D.1). The tax treatment differs according to whether the pension plan is mandatory or voluntary and across providers—that is, pension funds or life insurance companies. Some countries in the gulf—for instance, Bahrain—do not have an income tax system.

Algeria, the Islamic Republic of Iran, and the West Bank and Gaza tax the mandatory pension plans twice. The same is true in Morocco, but at reduced rates. Tunisia taxes these plans three times, although investment income is taxed at a reduced rate. At the other extreme, Egypt provides a generous tax treatment to pension plans.

Some countries heavily tax voluntary pension plans. In particular, Lebanon taxes the contributions to the plans twice, while it taxes investment income and benefits once. In general, the tax system discourages voluntary long-term savings plans through life insurance. Some voluntary plans benefit from tax incentives without imposing limits on the level of contributions, while other plans impose limits.

Implicit taxation of investment income in the region results from restrictions on the investment of pension reserves, forcing these funds to purchase government or agency debt that is illiquid and bears below-market yields. In addition, in some cases public pension fund managers do not credit the full return into members' accounts.

The governments should adopt best tax practice for mandatory plans, either EET or TEE treatment. For voluntary plans, there should be a limit on the contributions to tax-preferred schemes. In addition, it would be advisable to consider implementing a pilot program based on matching contributions to voluntary plans, also with a limit. Finally, the governments should eliminate implicit taxation on investment income by liberalizing investment rules, while strengthening the governance, accountability, and investment policy of public pension funds.

Personal Income Tax Regulations in the Region

The following paragraphs summarize the personal income tax regulations in a sampling of Middle East and North African countries.

In *Algeria*, employees' social security contributions are deductible against the personal income tax. Pension benefits are taxable. The income tax schedule is as follows:

	Band lower limit (thousands of dinars)					
	0	*10,000*	*15,000*	*30,000*	*70,000*	*100,000*
Tax rate (percent)	0	5	10	15	20	25

In *Bahrain*, there is no personal income tax.

In *Djibouti*, pension contributions are deductible against the personal income tax. Pensions in payment are taxable. For incomes between DF 25,000 and DF 30,000 a year, the tax liability is DF 500. Thereafter, the schedule is as follows:

	Band lower limit (thousands of francs)			
	30	*50*	*150*	*600*
Tax rate (percent)	15	18	20	30

In *Egypt*, pensions are not subject to personal income tax. There is a general deduction of LL 2,000 a year for single taxpayers plus LL 2,000 a year additional allowance for earnings. The schedule applied after these allowances is as follows:

	Band lower limit (pounds)			
	0	*2,500*	*7,000*	*16,000*
Tax rate (percent)	20	27	35	40

In the *Islamic Republic of Iran*, there is a general income tax allowance of Rls 19.2 million. Income above this level is taxed at a rate of 10 percent. Social security contributions are not deductible for income tax purposes. Pensions in payment are not subject to tax.

In *Jordan*, employee social security contributions are deductible against the personal income tax. Pensions in payment are not subject to tax. There is no general allowance or basic relief, and the income tax schedule is as follows:

	Band lower limit (dinars)			
	0	*2,000*	*6,000*	*12,000*
Tax rate (percent)	5	10	20	25

In *Lebanon*, pensions in payment are subject to income tax. There is a general allowance of LL 7.5 million a year for a single person. The tax schedule, using 1999 numbers, is as follows:

	Band lower limit (millions of pounds)					
	0	*6*	*15*	*30*	*60*	*120*
Tax rate (percent)	2	4	7	11	15	20

In *Libya*, there is a general personal allowance in the income tax, which is LD 480 for a single person (higher for individuals who are married or have children). The rate schedule after this allowance is as follows:

	Band lower limit (dinars)					
	0	*1,800*	*3,000*	*4,800*	*6,600*	*8,400*
Tax rate (percent)	8	10	15	20	25	35

In *Morocco*, social security contributions are deductible against the personal income tax. There is a general relief against earned income, meaning that only 83 percent of wages is subject to the income tax. Similarly, only 60 percent of pension income is taxable. The personal income tax schedule is as follows:

	Band lower limit (dirhams)				
	0	*20,000*	*24,000*	*30,000*	*60,000*
Tax rate (percent)	0	13	21	25	44

In *Tunisia*, pension benefits are subject to tax, but there is an abatement of 25 percent. Social security contributions are deductible under the personal income tax. Furthermore, 10 percent of earnings are exempted from tax. The income tax schedule is as follows:

	Band lower limit (dinars)					
	0	*1,500*	*5,000*	*10,000*	*20,000*	*50,000*
Tax rate (percent)	0	15	20	25	30	35

In the *West Bank and Gaza*, employee contributions to the civil service scheme are deductible against the income tax. Although practice has varied in the past, pension benefits are not currently subject to income tax. The income tax schedule is as follows:

	Band lower limit (shekels)		
	0	*7,200*	*12,000*
Tax rate (percent)	0	8	16

In the *Republic of Yemen*, pension benefits are subject to tax. Social security contributions are deductible against the personal income tax. The income tax schedule is as follows:

	Band lower limit (rial)			
	0	*3,000*	*7,000*	*22,000*
Tax rate (percent)	0	10	15	20

APPENDIX E

Basic Formulas and Mathematical Results Used in the Analysis

Equivalence of the Standard Defined-Benefit Pension Formula and the Formula Used in a Points System

In a points system, the pension is calculated as follows:

$$B_R = \left(\sum_{t=1}^{R} \frac{\beta w_t}{p_t} \right) v_R, \tag{E.1}$$

where β is the contribution rate, w_t is the wage at time t, p_t is the purchase value of the point at time t, v_R is the liquidation value of the point at time R, and R is the time of retirement. Hence, the expression in parentheses gives the total number of points that an individual has accumulated between dates 1 and R. By multiplying the total number of points by the liquidation value of the point, we obtain the pension. Equation E.1 can be rewritten as:

$$\begin{aligned} B_R &= \sum_{t=1}^{R} \frac{\beta w_t v_0 (1+l)^R}{p_0 (1+r)^t} = \sum_{t=1}^{R} \frac{\beta w_t v_0 (1+l)^t (1+l)^{R-t}}{p_0 (1+r)^t} \\ &= \alpha \sum_{t=1}^{R} w_t \lambda_t (1+l)^{R-t}, \end{aligned} \tag{E.2}$$

where $\alpha = \beta v_0 / p_0$ and $\lambda_t = (1+l)^t/(1+r)^t$.

Equation E.2 is exactly the standard defined-benefit formula when all wages are included in the calculation of the pension. If $r = 1$, wages are indexed by $(1+l)^{R-t}$. Hence, a points system is like a standard defined-benefit system with an accrual rate equal to the contribution rate times the ratio of liquidation and the purchase value of the point. If both the purchase value and the liquidation value of the point are indexed by the same factor (that is, $1 = r$), then the points system is equivalent to a defined-benefit system like the RCAR in Morocco, where all salaries are included in the calculation of the pension and indexed by a factor of 1 (in the case of the RCAR, 1 is equal to the growth rate of the average wage).

Applying formula E.2 to the CIMR in Jordan, where $v_0 = 11.64$ and $p_0 = (1/0.1667)^*14.25$, we find that the accrual rate offered by the system today is equal to 0.82 percent ($\alpha = 0.0082$). This accrual rate is 40 percent of the accrual rate offered by the RCAR (2 percent), but the contribution rate is 33 percent of that of the RCAR.

Rates of Return in Earning-Related Schemes

In this section we investigate the equivalence between the virtual account formula and the standard defined-benefit formula and the implications for the expected internal rate of return on contributions.

Case of the Virtual Account Formula

We start by defining the formula to compute a pension in the notional defined-contribution system. It is given by:

$$p^{NDC} = \frac{\beta \sum_{t=1}^{R} w_t (1+g)^{R-t}}{\sum_{k=R}^{L} s_k (1+r)^{R-k}}, \tag{E.3}$$

where β is the contribution rate, g is the index for past salaries, r is the rate used to discount future pensions, s_k is the survival probability until time (that is, age) k, R is the retirement age, and L is the maximum age humans live (see figure E.1 for the survival probabilities used in Morocco). The denominator in equation E.3 is known as the G factor.

Figure E.1 Share of Cohort Surviving to Age in Morocco

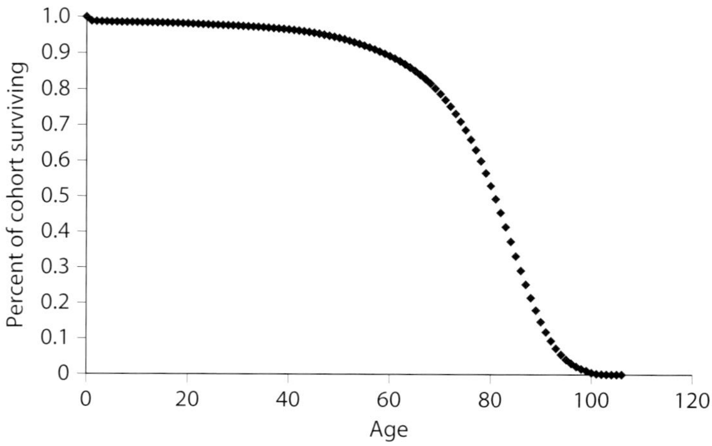

Source: Authors' calculations.

Let us call r^* the expected rate of return on contributions that an individual who enters the system at time 1 and retires at time R would receive from this system. This rate guarantees that the present value of contributions is equal to the present value of future pensions. Formally,

$$\beta \sum_{t=1}^{R} w_t (1 + r^*)^{-t} - \sum_{k=R}^{L} s_k p^{NDC} (1 + r^*)^{-k} = 0. \tag{E.4}$$

By substituting equation E.3 in equation E.4, we obtain:

$$\beta \sum_{t=1}^{R} w_t (1 + r^*)^{-t} - (1 + r)^{-R} \beta \sum_{t=1}^{R} w_t (1 + g)^{R-t} \times \frac{\sum_{k=R}^{L} s_k (1 + r^*)^{-k}}{\sum_{k=R}^{L} s_k (1 + r)^{-k}} = 0. \tag{E.5}$$

Or, after simplification, assuming that $r = r^*$, we obtain:

$$\sum_{t=1}^{R} w_t (1 + r^*)^{-t} - \sum_{t=1}^{R} w_t (1 + g)^{-t} = 0. \tag{E.6}$$

From equation E.6 it is easy to see that if an arbitrary number $r^* > 0$ is chosen, and if we set $g = r^*$ and $r = r^*$, then r^* verifies equation E.6, and therefore r^* is the expected implicit rate of return paid by the system. In other words, the policy maker can choose the rate of return that an individual gets in a virtual account by choosing the rate at which salaries are indexed and using this rate to discount future pensions (that is, to calculate the G factor).

The rate of return, r^*, is independent of the wage history, w_t, and the retirement age. This is a very important feature of the virtual account formula. If pensions are discounted by the same factor by which wages are indexed, then *all* individuals, regardless of their wage history, when they enroll, or when they retire, receive the same rate of return. Redistribution can still take place, but through more transparent mechanisms such as the introduction of a minimum pension.

Case of the Traditional Defined-Benefit Formula

It is easy to see that the traditional defined-benefit formula, *if* all the salaries are included in the calculation of the pension indexed by the rate g, can be expressed as a virtual account formula. Indeed, we can write:

$$p^{DB} = \alpha \cdot R \cdot \left(\frac{\sum_{t=1}^{R} w_t (1+g)^{R-t}}{R} \right) = \alpha \sum_{t=1}^{R} w_t (1+g)^{R-t} = \varepsilon \cdot p^{NDC}$$

(E.7)

$$= \varepsilon \frac{\beta \sum_{t=1}^{R} w_t (1+g)^{R-t}}{\sum_{k=R}^{L} s_k (1+r)^{R-k}},$$

where α is the accrual rate, the first expression in parentheses is the average of all past wages and $\varepsilon = \frac{\alpha \sum_{k=R}^{L} s_t (1+r)^{R-k}}{\beta}$. If $\alpha = \frac{\beta}{\sum_{k=R}^{L} s_t (1+r)^{R-k}}$, that is if α is equal to the contribution rate divided by the so-called G factor, then ε is equal to 1 and therefore the traditional defined-benefit formula gives *exactly* the virtual account formula (or notional defined-contribution formula).

However, if α is higher than the contribution rate divided by the G factor, the most frequent case across the world, then $\varepsilon > 1$. In this case, the rate of return, r, needs to verify the following:

$$\sum_{t=1}^{R} w_t (1+r)^{-t} - \varepsilon \sum_{t=1}^{R} w_t (1+g)^{-t} = 0. \quad \text{(E.8)}$$

Clearly, $r^* = r = g$ is not a solution to equation F.8. Indeed, with $\varepsilon > 1$, we would have:

$$\sum_{t=1}^{R} w_t (1+r^*)^{-t} - \varepsilon \sum_{t=1}^{R} w_t (1+r^*)^{-t} < 0. \quad \text{(E.9)}$$

The new rate of return, r^{**}, would need to be higher than r^* for equation E.8 to hold. Indeed, by increasing r, each of the terms in equation E.8 becomes smaller, but the second term (which has ε) becomes smaller "faster." Thus the difference between the two terms, eventually, becomes equal to 0. This is intuitive: the higher the accrual rate α, the higher ε and therefore the higher the rate of return that the individual receives.

Let us assume that r^{**} is the solution to equation E.8. Then we have:

$$\sum_{t=1}^{R} w_t (1+r^{**})^{-t} - \varepsilon \sum_{t=1}^{R} w_t (1+r^{**})^{-t} = 0. \quad \text{(E.10)}$$

Since ε is greater than 1, a change in the wage history, w_t, the enrollment age, or the retirement age will have a greater effect on the second component of the equation, which is multiplied by ε. This implies that the solution to equation E.10 will have to change, as the two components of the equation are no longer equal. Hence, even if all wages are included in the calculation of the pension in a standard defined-benefit formula, as long as $\varepsilon > 1$, rates of return will be sensitive to changes in individual socioeconomic characteristics. Redistribution will be a pervasive feature of the system, but it will be difficult to understand "who is getting what."

The solution to equation E.9 will also change if the contribution rate changes. Indeed, an increase in the contribution rate implies an increase in ε. Thus another important implication: the smaller the contribution rate (or the higher the accrual rate), the higher ε and therefore the higher the variation in rates of return resulting from changes in the wage histories and enrollment-retirement strategies.

Formulas for Individuals Transferring from One Fund to Another

In a well-designed defined-benefit scheme, the transfer of one employee from fund A to fund B will operate in the following way: the total contributions to fund A up to date T of the transfer, indexed by its sustainable rate of return, g, are calculated:

$$C_A = \beta_A \sum_{t=1}^{T} w_t (1 + g_A)^{R-t}. \tag{E.11}$$

The sum C is then transferred to fund B, where the contribution rate, the sustainable rate of return, and the accrual rates can be different from those in A, but set according to equation E.7. In fund B, the transferred C continues to be indexed, but this time at the new rate. The individual continues to contribute, at the new contribution rate, until retirement at time R. The pension will then have two components: one resulting from the new contributions in fund B and a second resulting from the initial capital transferred from fund A. We have:

$$p_B = \alpha_B \cdot (R - T) \cdot \left(\frac{\sum\limits_{t=T}^{R} w_t (1 + g_B)^{R-t}}{R - T} \right) + \frac{\alpha_B}{\beta_B} C_A (1 + g_B)^{R-T}. \tag{E.12}$$

In equation E.12, the capital C is divided by the contribution, because C already represents contributions, whereas the accrual rate has to apply to a sum of wages.

Some Clarifications Regarding the Calculations of Implicit Rates of Return in this Study

Formally, the implicit rate of return is the discount rate that makes the present value of pension payments equal to the present value of contributions. A technical difficulty with the calculation of IRR is that pension funds often do not separate the contributions allocated to various types of benefits. For instance, separate contribution rates for old-age, disability, and survivor pensions seldom exist. Even when the separation is made, cross-subsidies between branches exist. In some cases, the same contribution rate also finances short-term benefits such as maternity leave. The approach taken here is to consider the total contribution to old-age, disability, and survivor pensions. In those few cases where the contribution rate also finances short-term benefits, which are small relative to long-term benefits, the contribution rate is prorated. For simplicity, however, the implicit rate of return is only computed from the perspective of individuals who retire without benefiting from disability benefits and considering only a survivor pension for the spouse (if the individual is married). The resulting rate of return is a lower bound for the average rate of return paid by the system, which includes the payment of disability benefits and the presence of survivors other than the spouse.

APPENDIX F

Demographic and Financial Data on Pension Funds

Country and pension fund	Total contributors (thousands) (1)	Total beneficiaries (thousands) (2)	Labor force (thousands) (3)	Coverage (4)	Total expenditures (millions)[a] (5)	Total pension expenditures (millions) (6)	Ratio of old-age pensions to total expenditures (7) (%)	Total pension expenditures (percent of GDP) (8)	Total contribution revenues (millions)[b] (9)	Revenues (percent of GDP) (10)	Reserves (percent of GDP) (11)	Total GDP (local currency, millions) (12)	GDP per capita PPP[c] (13)	GDP per capita[d] (14)
Algeria (2002)														
CNR	4,000	1,450	—	36.4	—	132,000	—	3.0	140,000	3.1	—	—	—	—
CASNOS	400	150	—	3.6	—	10,500	—	0.0	11,000	0.2	—	—	—	—
Total	4,400	1,600	11,000	40.0	—	142,500	—	3.2	151,000	3.4	—	4,455,300	6,248	2,073
Bahrain (2002)														
GOSI	59.0	7.6	—	18.5	29	28	63	0.9	35	1.1	28.5	—	—	—
PFC (military and civil service)	35.5	15.5	—	11.1	55	52	66	1.6	102	3.2	24.0	—	—	—
Total	94.5	23.1	319	29.7	85	80	64.8	2.5	137	4.3	52.5	3,177	16,900	13,934
Djibouti (2002)[e]														
OPS	28.3	4.7	—	24.3	3,165	1,887	81	1.8	2,561	2.4	5.7	—	—	—
CNR	3.9	3.0	—	3.3	1,613	1,529	73	1.5	994	0.9	—	—	—	—
CMR (2000)	2.4	1.4	—	1.2	675	675	100	0.8	404	0.4	—	—	—	—
Total	34.5	9.1	116	27.7	—	—	—	4.0	—	3.8	5.7	105,210	2,144	1,373
Egypt, Arab Rep. of (2001)[f]														
Government fund	4,437	1,752	—	22.9	4,737	4,195	58	1.2	6,145	1.7	—	—	—	—
Public-private sector fund	13,423	3,276	—	69.4	8,922	7,011	43	2.0	4,894	1.4	—	—	—	—
Public sector (Law 79/1976)	915	879	—	4.7	—	—	—	—	—	—	—	—	—	—
Private sector (Law 79/1976)	4,692	390	—	24.3	—	—	—	—	—	—	—	—	—	—
Self-employed (Law 108/1976)	1,876	325	—	9.7	—	—	—	—	—	—	—	—	—	—
Workers abroad (Law 50/1978)	18	5	—	0.1	—	—	—	—	—	—	—	—	—	—
Casual workers (Law 112/1980)	5,922	1,677	—	30.6	—	—	—	—	—	—	—	—	—	—
Sadat pensioners	—	375	—	—	—	—	—	—	—	—	—	—	—	—
Total	17,860	5,028	19,339	92.4	13,659	11,206	48	3.1	11,039	3.1	35.6	358,700	3,950	1,036
Iran, Islamic Rep. of (2000)[g]														
CSRO	1,573	482		8.8	3,079,000	3,048,000	75	0.5	3,608,000	0.6	3.3	—	—	
SSO	6,095	1,144		34.0	6,702,000	4,422,000	39	0.7	7,626,182	1.2	2.8	—	—	—
Total	7,668	1,626	17,908	42.8	9,781,000	7,470,000	51	1.2	11,234,182	1.7	6.1	645,855,000	7,145	2,061
Iraq (2004)[h]														
SEP (civil)	1,045	585	—	17.1	—	816,781	—	2.7	—	—	—	—	—	—
SFP (military)	—	473	—	—	—	577,522	—	1.9	—	—	—	—	—	
SSW	76	14	—	1.2	—	11,683	—	0.0	—	—	0.06	—	—	—
Total	1,121	1,073	6,100	18.4	—	1,405,986	—	4.6	—	—	—	30,660,000	1,500	547
Jordan (2001)														
SSC	382	58	—	23.6	—	67	—	1.07	151	2.4	25.0	—	—	—
CSS	69	43	—	4.3	—	82	—	1.31	26	0.4	0.0	—	—	—
Military	132	147	—	8.1	—	209	—	3.34	11	0.2	0.0	—	—	—
Total	583	248	1,619	36.0	—	358	—	5.72	188	3.0	25.0	6,260	4,320	1,858
Lebanon (2003)[i]														
Military	59	30.8	—	3.6	—	574,060	—	2.00	57,829	0.2	—	—	—	—
Civil servants	40	8.3	—	2.4	—	152,060	—	0.53	—	—	—	—	—	
NSSF	308	0.0	—	18.7	—	—	—	—	—	—	9.2	—	—	—
Total	406	39.1	1,646	24.7	—	726,120	—	2.5	57,829	0.2	9.2	28,643,000	5,073	4,224

(Continues on the following page.)

APPENDIX F *(continued)*

Country and pension fund	Total contributors (thousands) (1)	Total beneficiaries (thousands) (2)	Labor force (thousands) (3)	Coverage (4)	Total expenditures (millions)[a] (5)	Total pension expenditures (millions) (6)	Ratio of old-age pensions to total expenditures (7) (%)	Total pension expenditures (percent of GDP) (8)	Total contribution revenues (millions)[b] (9)	Revenues (percent of GDP) (10)	Reserves (percent of GDP) (11)	Total GDP (local currency, millions) (12)	GDP per capita PPP[c] (13)	GDP per capita[d] (14)
Libya (2003)[j]														
SSF	1,401	236	—	87.3	722	655	—	2.2	511	1.69	—	—	—	—
Total	1,401	236	1,604	87.3	722	655	—	2.2	511	1.69	8.3	30,300	6,300	4,245
Morocco (2002)[k]														
CNSS	1,270	259	—	10.9	6.102	3,658	46	0.9	6,810	1.7	3.2	—	—	—
CMR	843	381	—	7.2	5,084	5,040	50	1.3	7,343	1.8	2.8	—	—	—
RCAR	224	42	—	1.9	736	700	46	0.2	900	0.2	5.8	—	—	—
Total	2,337	682	11,684	20.0	11,922	9,398	48	2.4	15,053	3.8	11.8	397,782	4,012	1,477
Tunisia (2003)														
CNRPS	552	172	—	13.6	—	696	—	2.22	710	2.3	—	—	—	—
RSNA	1,055	248	—	26.0	—	561	—	1.79	558	1.8	—	—	—	—
RSAA	60	5.8	—	1.5	—	2.8	—	0.01	7.3	0.0	—	—	—	—
RSA	15	16.4	—	0.4	—	10.8	—	0.03	0.8	0.0	—	—	—	—
RNS	319	61.9	—	7.9	—	72	—	0.23	72	0.2	—	—	—	—
Total	2,000	504	4,050	49.4	—	1,342	—	4.29	1,348	4.3	—	31,287	7,083	2,454
West Bank and Gaza (2000)														
West Bank	24	5.2	—	3.4	62	61	98	0.32	12	0.1	—	—	—	—
Gaza Strip	39	6.4	—	5.6	86	85	40	0.45	175	0.9	4.4	—	—	—
Military	53	0	—	7.6	—	—	—	—	—	—	—	—	—	—
Total	116	11.6	700	16.6	148	147	64	0.78	187	1.0	4.4	18,905	727	1,026
Yemen, Republic of (1999)[l]														
PSPPA	407	40	—	7.6	—	4,060	—	0.35	5,100	0.4	2.6	—	—	—
Military	240	50	—	4.5	—	5,048	—	0.43	—	—	—	—	—	—
Security forces	—	4.5	—	—	—	503	—	0.04	—	—	—	—	—	
GCSS (2003)	64	1.9	—	1.0	612	307	—	0.02	3,098	0.2	1.0	—	—	
Total	711	96	5,371	13.1	—	—	—	0.84	—	0.6	3.6	1,162,900	889	565

Sources: Authors' calculations.

Notes: — = Not available.

a. Total expenditures include administrative costs.

b. Where data are available, revenues are adjusted to show actual cash collections and exclude contributions to health and unemployment programs.

c. 2003, current US$, purchasing power parity (PPP) adjusted. The figure for West Bank and Gaza refers to 2002.

d. 2003, current US$.

e. For Djibouti, in column 1, the figure for the OPS is from 2000. CNR includes police and parliamentarians. In column 5; unusually high administrative expenses were reported in 2002. Column 7 is based on 2000 data and ignores administrative expenditures in total expenses. In column 9, CMR revenues exclude government subsidy.

f. For Egypt, Law 112/1980 is a quasi-noncontributory scheme. For column 5, administrative expenditures for the government and public-private pension funds are assumed to be 5.0 and 3.9 percent, respectively, based on 1997 data. For column 9, subsidies from the Treasury are not presented.

g. For the Islamic Republic of Iran, CSRO contributions in column 9 are on an accrual basis. Column 11 includes government arrears.

h. For Iraq, column 12 is based on an International Monetary Fund estimate.

i. For Lebanon, end-of-service lump-sum payments for NSSF are not shown in columns 2, 5, and 6.

j. For Libya, the GDP estimate and the figures in column 12 are based on an International Monetary Fund estimate. Column 6 includes pensions, basic pensions, and military pensions.

k. For Morocco, CMR includes the military forces.

l. For the Republic of Yemen, column 1 is based on combined estimated employment in military and security services. Totals in columns 4, 8, 10, and 11 assume constant numbers for individual funds over the measurement period.

References

Agénor, Pierre-Richard, and Karim El Aynaoui. 2003. "Labor Market Policies and Unemployment in Morocco: A Quantitative Analysis." World Bank, Washington, DC.

Alba, Pedro, Sherine Al-Shawarby, and Farrukh Iqbal. 2004. "Fiscal and Public Debt Sustainability in Egypt." Working Paper 38, World Bank, Social and Economic Development Group, Middle East and North Africa Region, Washington, DC.

Bailliu, Jeanie, and Helmut Reisen. 2000. "Do Funded Pensions Contribute to Higher Aggregate Savings? A Cross-Country Analysis." In *Pensions, Savings, and Capital Flows: From Ageing to Emerging Markets*, ed. Helmut Reisen. Paris: OECD.

Barrientos, Armando, and others. 2003. "Non-contributory Pensions and Poverty Prevention: A Comparative Study of Brazil and South Africa." Final Report DFID Project R7897, Institute of Development and Policy Management and HelpAge International, London, September.

Bloom, David, David Canning, and Jaypee Sevilla. 2003. *The Demographic Dividend: A New Perspective on the Economic Consequences of Population Change*. Santa Monica, CA: RAND.

Boersch-Supan, Axel, Robert Palacios, and Patrizia Tumbarello. 1999. "Pension Systems in the Middle East and North Africa: A Window of Opportunity." Mimeo. World Bank, Washington, DC.

Bonnerjee, Aniruddha. 2002. "Pensions in Sub-Saharan Africa: The Urgent Need to Act." Regional Paper, World Bank, Washington, DC.

Bosworth, Barry, and Gary Burtless. 2003. "Pension Reform and Saving." Discussion Paper, Brookings Institution, Washington, DC.

Bosworth, Barry, Susan Collins, and Yu-Chin Chen. 1995. "Accounting for Differences in Economic Growth." Discussion Paper in International Economics 115, Brookings Institution, Washington, DC, October.

Carmichael, Jeffrey, and Robert Palacios. 2004. "A Framework for Public Pension Fund Management." Paper presented at the Second

Public Pension Fund Management Conference, World Bank, Washington, DC, May 5–7, 2003.

Clark, Gordon. 2004. "Pension Fund Governance: Expertise and Organizational Form." University of Oxford, U.K.

Colina, Jorge, R. Lucas, and Mariano Tomasi. 2002. "Problemas para expandir el grado de cobertura en el sistema reformado de pensiones argentino." Centro de Estudios para el Desarrollo Institucional (CEDI), Buenos Aires, Argentina.

Creane, Susan, Rishi Goyal, A. Mushfiq Mobarak, and Randa Sab. 2004. "Financial Sector Development in the Middle East and North Africa." Working Paper WP/04/201, International Monetary Fund, Washington, DC.

Dasgupta, Dipak, Jennifer Keller, and T. G. Srinivasan. 2002. "Reform and Elusive Growth in the Middle East: What Has Happened in the 1990s?" Working Paper 25, World Bank, Human Development Group and Social and Economic Development Group, Middle East and North Africa, Washington, DC.

Dhonte, Pierre, Rina Bhattacharya, and Tarik M. Yousef. 2000. "Demographic Transition in the Middle East: Implications for Growth, Employment, and Housing." Working Paper 41, International Monetary Fund, Middle East Department, Washington, DC.

Disney, Richard. 1999. "Notional Accounts as a Pension Reform Strategy: An Evaluation." Social Protection Discussion Paper 9928, World Bank, Washington, DC, December.

———. 2004. "Pension and Employment." *Economic Policy*, Britain, July, 267–311.

Disney, Richard, and Edward Whitehouse. 2001. "Cross-Country Comparisons of Pensioners' Incomes." Report No. 142, Department of Social Security, Leeds, England.

Egyptian Ministry of Social Insurance. 2003. "Summary of Recommendations to Reform the Egyptian Pension System." Unpublished manuscript. Ministry of Social Insurance, Cairo.

Gill, Indermit, Truman Packard, and Juan Yermo. 2003. "Keeping the Promise of Old-Age Income Security in Latin America: A Regional Study of Social Security Reforms." World Bank, Office of the Chief Economist, Latin America and Caribbean Region, Washington, DC.

Góra, Marek, and Edward Palmer. 2003. "Shifting Perspectives in Pension Reform." Paper presented at the World Bank and RFV Conference on Notional Defined-Contribution Pensions, Sandhamn, Sweden, September 28–30.

Holzmann, Robert. 1998. "Financing the Transition to Multi-Pillar." Social Protection Discussion Paper 9809, World Bank, Washington, DC, December.

Holzmann, Robert, Richard Hinz, and Bank Team. 2005. *Old-Age Income Support in the Twenty-First Century: An International Perspective on Pension Systems and Reforms*. Washington, DC: World Bank.

Holzmann, Robert, Robert Palacios, and Aza Zviniene. 2004. "Implicit Pension Debt: Issues, Measurement, and Scope in International Perspective." Social Protection Discussion Paper 0403, World Bank, Washington, DC, March.

Holzmann, Robert, and Edward Palmer, eds. 2005. *Pension Reform through NDCs: Issues and Prospects for Non-Financial Defined Contribution Schemes*. Washington, DC: World Bank.

IBRD (International Bank for Reconstruction and Development). 2002. "Yemen—Poverty Reduction Strategy Paper and Joint Assessment, Volume 1." IBRD, Washington, DC, July 10.

Iglesias, Augusto, and Robert Palacios. 2000. "Managing Public Pension Reserves. Part I: Evidence from International Experience." Social Protection Discussion Paper 0003, World Bank, Washington, DC.

ILO (International Labour Organisation). 2000. "Estimates and Projections of the Economically Active Population, 1950–2010." In *Sources and Methods*, vol. 10. Geneva: ILO.

———. 2003. Laborstat Database. Geneva: ILO.

IMF (International Monetary Fund). 2002. "Tunisia: Financial System Stability Assessment," IMF Country Report No. 02/119, IMF, Washington, DC.

———. 2003. "Moscow: Financial System Stability Assessment," IMF, Washington, DC.

———. 2004. "Algeria: Financial System Stability Assessment," IMF Country Report No. 04/138, IMF, Washington, DC.

———. 2004. *International Financial Statistics*. Washington, DC: IMF.

Impavido, Gregorio, Alberto R. Musalem, and Thierry Tressel. 2001. "Contractual Savings Institutions and Banks' Stability and Efficiency." Policy Research Working Paper 2751, World Bank, Financial Sector Development Department, Washington, DC.

———. 2002. "Contractual Savings and Firms' Financing Choices." In *World Bank Economists' Forum*, ed. Shantayanan Devarajan and F. Halsey Rogers. Washington, DC: World Bank.

———. 2003. "Contractual Savings and Impacts on Securities Markets." Policy Research Working Paper 2948, World Bank, Financial Sector Development Department, Washington, DC.

Instituto Brasileiro de Geografia e Estadística. 2000. *Demographic Census 2000*. Available at http://www.ibge.gov.br/english/estatistica/populacao/censo2000/default.shtm.

James, Estelle. 2001. *Coverage under Old-Age Security Programs and Protection for the Uninsured: What Are the Issues?* Washington, DC: Inter-American Development Bank and Brookings Institution Press.

James, Estelle, Alejandra Cox-Edwards, and Rebecca Wong. 2003. "The Gender Impact of Pension Reform: A Cross-Country Analysis." *Journal of Pension Economics and Finance* 2 (July): 181–209.

Kaufmann, Daniel, Aart Kraay, and Massimo Mastruzzi. 2003. *Governance Matters III: Governance Indicators for 1996–2002*. Washington, DC: World Bank Institute.

Keller, Jennifer, and Mustapha K. Nabli. 2002. "The Macroeconomics of Labor Market Outcomes in MENA over the 1990s: How Growth Has Failed to Keep Pace with a Burgeoning Labor Market." Working Paper 71, Egyptian Center for Economic Studies, Cairo, August.

Lindeman, David, David Robalino, and Michal Rutkowski. 2003. *Notional Defined-Contribution Schemes in Middle- and Low-Income Countries: Promises and Constraints*. Washington, DC: World Bank.

Lindeman, David, Michal Rutkowski, and Oleksiy Sluchynsky. 2001. "The Evolution of Pension Systems in Eastern Europe and Central Asia: Opportunities, Constraints, Dilemmas, and Emerging Practices." OECD Financial Market Trends 80, Organisation for Economic Co-operation and Development, Paris.

López-Murphy, Pablo, and Alberto R. Musalem. 2004. "Pension Funds and National Saving." Policy Research Working Paper 3410, World Bank, Washington, DC, August.

Mackenzie, G. A., Philip Gerson, Alfredo Clevas, and Peter Heller. 2001. "Pension Reform and the Fiscal Policy Stance." IMF Working Paper 01/214, IMF, Washington, DC.

Mitchell, Deborah. 1999. "Pensions 2000: Options for Pension Reform in Yemen." Policy paper prepared for the World Bank, Washington, DC. Available at Global Links.

Musalem, Alberto R., and Robert J. Palacios. 2003. "Public Pension Fund Management: Governance, Accountability, and Investment Policies." In *Proceedings of the Second Public Pension Fund Management Conference, May 2003*, ed. Alberto R. Musalem and Robert J. Palacios. Washington, DC: World Bank.

Musalem, Alberto R., and Thierry Tressel. 2003. "Institutional Savings and Financial Markets: The Role of Contractual Savings Institutions." Working Paper, World Bank and International Monetary Fund, Washington, DC.

Myners, Paul. 2001. "Institutional Investment in the United Kingdom: A Review." Her Majesty's Treasury, London, March. Available at http://www.hm-treasury.gov.uk/media/2F9/02/31.pdf.

Palacios, Robert. 2001. "Moving to Formal Arrangements for Old Age Income Security." Unpublished manuscript for ADBI Conference, Delhi.

———. 2003. "Pension Reform in Latin America: Design and Experiences." In *Pension Reforms: Results and Challenges*. Santiago: International Federation of Pension Funds Administrators.

Palacios, Robert, and Montserrat Pallarès-Miralles. 2000. "International Patterns of Pension Provision." World Bank, Washington, DC.

Pritchett, Lant. 1999. "Has Education Had a Growth Payoff in the MENA Region?" Middle East and North Africa Working Paper 18, World Bank, Human Development Group and Social and Economic Development Group, Washington, DC.

Robalino, David A., and Tatyana Bogomolova. Forthcoming. "Implicit Pension Debt in MENA: Fiscal and Equity Implications." Policy Research Working Paper Series, World Bank, Washington, DC.

Robalino, David A., and Mohammed Marouani. Forthcoming. "Assessing the Impacts of Social Insurance Policies in Labor Markets in a General Equilibrium Framework." Policy Research Working Paper Series, World Bank, Washington, DC.

Robalino, David A., and Anca N. Mataoanu. Forthcoming. "Severance Pay Programs in the Middle East and North Africa Region." Policy Research Working Paper Series, World Bank, Washington, DC.

Robalino, David A., Oleksiy Sluchynsky, and Tatyana Bogomolova. 2005. "Pensions in Iraq: Issues, General Guidelines for Reform, and Fiscal Implications." Policy Research Working Paper Series, World Bank, Washington, DC.

Sala-i-Martin, Xavier, and Elsa V. Artadi. 2002. "Economic Growth and Investment in the Arab World." In *Arab World Competitiveness Report 2002–2003*, ed. Klaus Schwab and Peter Cornelius. Oxford, U.K.: Oxford University Press.

Schwarz, Anita, and Aslı Demirgüç-Kunt. 1999. "Taking Stock of Pension Reforms around the World." Social Protection Discussion Paper 9917, World Bank, Washington, DC.

Shatalov, Sergei, Aristomene Varoudakis, and Jean Luc Steylaers. 2004. "Tunisia: Strategy for Public Debt Management." World Bank, Washington, DC.

St. Joseph University. 2004. "Economic and Trade Statistics, Unemployment." In *FY 2004 Country Commercial Guide for Lebanon*, ch. 10. Lebanon: U.S. and Foreign Commercial Service and U.S. Department of State.

Steinhilber, Silke. 2002. "The Gender Impact of Pension Reforms: Case Studies of the Czech Republic, Hungary, and Poland." Paper presented to an OECD conference, Warsaw, May.

Swedish Pension System. 2003. *Third Swedish National Pension Fund Annual Report 2002.* Stockholm: RFV, National Insurance Board.

U.S. Census Bureau. 2000. International Data Base. Washington, DC. Available at http://www.census.gov/ipc/www/idbnew.html.

U.S. Social Security Administration. 2004. "Social Security Programs throughout the World, 2002–2004." Washington, DC. Available at www.ssa.gov.us.

Valdés-Prieto, Salvador. 2004. "A Market Method to Endow NDC with Automatic Financial Sustainability." Unpublished manuscript. Catholic University of Chile, Santiago.

Whitehouse, Edward. 2001. "The Tax Treatment of Funded Pensions." Unpublished manuscript. Axia Economics, London.

———. 2004. "Analysis of Pension Entitlements across Countries: Summary of Volumes I, II, and III. OECD Countries, Latin America/Caribbean, Eastern Europe, and Central Asia." Axia Economics, London.

Willmore, Larry. 2001. "Universal Pensions in Low-Income Countries." Discussion Paper IPD-01-05, Social Science Research Network Pensions and Social Insurance Section, Initiative for Policy Dialogue.

———. 2003. "Universal Pensions in Low-Income Countries." Discussion Paper IPD-01-05, Social Science Research Network Pensions and Social Insurance Section, Initiative for Policy Dialogue. Available at http://ssrn.com/abstract=381180.

World Bank. 2001a. "Kingdom of Morocco. Poverty Update." 2 vols. Report 21506-MOR, World Bank, Washington, DC.

———. 2001b. "Republic of Djibouti: Pension System Reform Strategic Note." Report 22087-DJI, World Bank, Middle East and North Africa Region, Washington, DC.

———. 2002a. "Democratic and Popular Republic of Algeria. Public Expenditure Review of the Social Sector." Report 22591-AL, World Bank, Middle East and North Africa Region, Washington, DC.

———. 2002b. "Egypt: Poverty Reduction in Egypt; Diagnosis and Strategy." World Bank, Washington, DC.

———. 2002c. "West Bank and Gaza. Pensions in Palestine: Reform in a Context of Unrest." Report 25046-GZ, World Bank, Middle East and North Africa Region, Washington, DC.

———. 2003a. "Assessment of the Tunisian Pension System." World Bank, Middle East and North Africa Region, Washington, DC.

———. 2003b. "Bahrain: Country Economic Memorandum." World Bank, Washington, DC.

———. 2003c. "Hashemite Kingdom of Jordan. Pension Reform: Consolidating the Social Security Corporation as the National Pension System." Report 25948, World Bank, Social and Human Development Group, Middle East and North Africa, Washington, DC.

———. 2003d. "Islamic Republic of Iran. The Pension System in Iran: Challenges and Opportunities." Report 25174-IRN, World Bank, Social and Human Development Group, Middle East and North Africa Region. Washington, DC.

———. 2003e. "Jordan: Poverty Assessment." World Bank, Washington, DC.

———. 2003f. *World Development Indicators.* Washington, DC: World Bank.

———. 2004a. "Kingdom of Morocco. Pensions in Morocco: Toward an Integrated Reform Strategy." Report 28605-MOR, World Bank, Social and Human Development Group, Middle East and North Africa Region. Washington, DC.

———. 2004b. "Lebanon: Assessment Report." In *Public Debt Management and Government Securities Market Development, Insurance Control Commission for Lebanon.* Washington, DC: World Bank.

———. 2004c. "Morocco Country Brief." World Bank, Middle East and North Africa Region, Washington, DC, March.

———. 2004d. "Republic of Djibouti." Poverty Reduction Strategy Paper and Joint Staff Assessment Report 28922-DJI, World Bank, Washington, DC.

———. 2004e. "Unlocking the Employment Potential in the Middle East and North Africa: Toward a New Social Contract." World Bank, Washington, DC.

———. 2004f. *World Development Indicators.* Washington, DC: World Bank.

———. 2005a. "Lebanon: Towards an Integrated Pensions System: Reforming the End-of-Service Indemnity Service." World Bank, Washington, DC.

———. 2005b. "Libya: Country Economic Memorandum." World Bank, Washington, DC.

———. 2005c. "Pensions in Egypt: Policy Note on Options for Reform." Concept Note, World Bank, Washington, DC.

———. Forthcoming *a*. "Algeria: A Medium-Term Macroeconomic Strategy for Algeria; Sustaining Faster Growth with Economic and Social Stability." World Bank, Washington, DC.

———. Forthcoming *b*. "Iran: Poverty in Iran; Trends and Structure, 1986–1998." World Bank, Washington, DC.

World Bank and International Monetary Fund. 2000. "Iran: Financial Sector Assessment Program." World Bank, Washington, DC.

———. 2003. "Morocco: Financial Sector Assessment Program." World Bank, Washington, DC.

———. 2004. "Algeria: Financial Sector Assessment Program." World Bank, Washington, DC.

Index

Note: *b* indicates boxes, and *f* indicates figures